REVISED, EXPANDED, UPDATED EDITION

Teaching Gifted Kids in the Regular Classroom

Strategies and Techniques Every Teacher Can Use to Meet the Academic Needs of the Gifted and Talented

Susan Winebrenner

Foreword by Sylvia Rimm, Ph.D.
Edited by Pamela Espeland

free spirit
PUBLISHING®

The Library of Congress has cataloged the earlier revised edition as:

Winebrenner, Susan.
Teaching gifted kids in the regular classroom : strategies and techniques every teacher can use to meet the academic needs of the gifted and talented / Susan Winebrenner ; edited by Pamela Espeland.—Rev., expanded, and updated ed.
p. cm.
Includes bibliographical references (p.) and index.
ISBN 1-57542-089-9 (pbk.)
1. Gifted children—Education—United States.
I. Espeland, Pamela. II. Title.
LC3993.9 .W56 2001
371.95'2'0973—dc21 00-057832

Assistant editor: Jennifer Brannen
Cover design by Dao Nguyen
Index prepared by Randl Ockey

20 19 18 17 16 15 14
Printed in the United States of America

Free Spirit Publishing Inc.
217 Fifth Avenue North, Suite 200
Minneapolis, MN 55401-1299
(612) 338-2068
help4kids@freespirit.com
www.freespirit.com

DEDICATION

To my late husband, Neil Winebrenner, who always saw my potential before I did.

ACKNOWLEDGMENTS

Thanks to Joan Franklin Smutny, who made me believe I could write.

To Pat Butti, friend and guide, whose response to me whenever I questioned whether I could really write and do staff development work was, "Why not?"

To Judy Galbraith, President of Free Spirit Publishing, and Pamela Espeland, my intrepid editor. I feel so honored to be part of Free Spirit, and I'm grateful to you both for all you've done to make my books so user-friendly and accessible to educators.

To my parents, Sam and Lillian Schuckit, who inspired me to actualize my potential in whatever areas I targeted, and who taught me by their example that hard work really pays off.

To my wonderful grandchildren, who really do light up my life.

And finally, thanks to all the teachers and administrators who have attended my workshops over the years and have given me feedback that helped me produce this revision.

★ CONTENTS ★

★ List of Reproducible Pages ★

★ List of Figures ★

Foreword

by Sylvia B. Rimm, Ph.D.

Excellent teachers understand that gifted students require challenge in the classroom. However, incorporating planning and continuity within the teaching responsibilities of the classroom has never been easy. Susan Winebrenner has gathered together her own classroom experiences as well as those of many creative teachers to provide a blueprint for teachers who wish to involve, excite, and entice gifted students in a manner that encourages them to be learners. This book provides answers to teachers who recognize that their students have been unchallenged in the regular classroom, but aren't certain how to provide them with appropriately interesting and in-depth curriculum.

This book also provides the rationale for the need for special curriculum for gifted children. As a psychologist who specializes in gifted underachievement, I can assure you that when gifted children lack motivation, it is not genetic but taught. Underachievement is unconsciously taught to children at home and in the classroom by family, peers, and teachers. The competitive pressures that gifted children internalize to be "smartest," "perfect," and "most popular" can be converted to motivation to achieve, learn, and contribute if parents and schools set high but realistic goals for their gifted children.

If gifted children are not challenged by curriculum early in their school lives, they will equate smart with easy, and challenge and hard work will feel threatening to their self-esteem. They will either become perfectionistic and avoid challenge, or they will search for easy-way-out solutions, such as avoiding handing in assignments, procrastination, and disorganization for fear conscientious work may reveal that they are not as smart as they are assumed to be.

The yearning for learning is stifled for children who sit in classrooms surrounded by lessons they could easily teach the rest of the class. Instead, these gifted children become defensive, angry, passive, bored, and resentful. They blame their parents, teachers, peers, and siblings, but hardly ever will they understand what has gone wrong for them. It takes concerned teachers and parents who are willing to lead gifted children to the excitement of challenging learning. This book is an excellent vehicle for guiding gifted children on the road to lifelong learning and achievement.

Teaching Gifted Kids in the Regular Classroom is a perfect complement to my own clinical experiences described in my book, *Why Bright Kids Get Poor Grades and What You Can Do About It.* Challenging gifted children in the regular classroom is critical to both the prevention and reversal of underachievement among gifted children. In my latest book, *See Jane Win,* successful women describe their need for challenge as an adventure in learning that permitted them to be resilient enough to break through glass ceilings and rise from sticky floors. For gifted children to be achievers, they must experience the relationship between their efforts and results, and the classroom must provide those appropriate learning experiences.

I predict that your copy of *Teaching Gifted Kids in the Regular Classroom* will soon be dog-eared from use, and your gifted students will be much more likely to have a great year in your classroom.

Sylvia B. Rimm, Ph.D.

INTRODUCTION

Of all the students you are teaching in a given class, which group do you think will probably learn the least this year? It may surprise you to find that in a class that has a range of abilities (and which class doesn't?), it is the *most* able, rather than the least able, who will learn less new material than any other group.

How does this happen? Mostly it's because of something with which we are all too familiar: the scope-and-sequence monster. Each year, we are given a certain slice of a student's entire school curriculum to teach, and we feel intense pressure and responsibility to teach everything assigned to our grade or subject to all of our students. This problem is compounded by the expectations of state standards and the public's concern about test scores.

As part of school reform, most states have created state tests based on standards all students are expected to achieve. During the time when the class is preparing for these tests, the plight of gifted students is just as dramatic as that of students who struggle to learn the material. Each year, you probably have students who could take the state tests in September and score at or above the 95th percentile. These kids don't need to prepare for the tests. They need to be excused from doing work that is unnecessary for them to do. This book will help you identify those students and others who need similar attention and give them alternatives to re-learning what they already know.

TEACHING VS. LEARNING

Gifted kids and their parents become frustrated when educators confuse the meanings of the words "teach" and "learn." A teacher's responsibility is not to teach the content. A teacher's responsibility is to teach the *students,* and to make sure that all students learn new content every day. Gifted students already know much of what we are planning to teach, and they can learn new material in much less time than their age peers.

When gifted students discover during elementary school that they can get high praise for tasks or projects they complete with little or no effort, they may conclude that being smart means doing things easily. The longer they are allowed to believe this, the harder it is to rise to the challenge when they finally encounter one.

The students I worry about most are those who bring home perfect report cards starting in first grade. They sail from grade school through high school, concluding along the way that smart people must always give the impression that they don't have to work hard. Often, we send these students to fine colleges, where everyone in the freshman class was in the top five percent of their high-school graduating class. Suddenly the competition for A's is fierce and learning takes serious study skills, not to mention time and real effort. Where do we want these kids to be when they realize they aren't perfect students? Surely not alone in a freshman dorm far from home.

A fourth-grade teacher who attended one of my two-day workshops had an interesting experience you may relate to. After the first day of the workshop, she started thinking about how happy she had felt the day before, when all of her most capable readers got A's on the end-of-the-unit test. She now wondered whether their grades actually reflected what they had learned from her. Was it possible that these students knew the material before the unit began?

Since there were two weeks between each workshop day, she decided to find the answer to her question. The next day, with no advance warning, she gave these same students the end-of-the-unit test for the following unit. They were tested on the skills and the vocabulary, but not on the content of the stories, which, of course, they had not yet read. Again, they got all A's. This experience was one of the most startling of the teacher's career. She began to consider alternate methods of teaching her most capable readers.

When gifted students realize that they already know a lot of the subject matter the teacher will be teaching, they have little choice but to dutifully go through the assigned curriculum, waiting and hoping for the rare times when there will be something new or challenging for them to learn. This book will help you make those times happen more frequently for your gifted students.

THE MYSTERY OF THE GIFTED UNDERACHIEVER

About 22 years ago, when I first became interested in teaching gifted students, one thing that perplexed me was the existence of the so-called "gifted underachiever." I could not comprehend how children with so much intelligence could get into a situation in school in which they were not doing their work. These kids were easy to label—"lazy," "not working up to potential," "poor attitude," "unproductive"—but hard to understand.

When I took a course many years later from Dr. Sylvia Rimm on preventing underachievement, I realized that the problem belonged to me as a teacher. Dr. Rimm expressed this eloquently when she said:

> The surest path to high self-esteem is to be successful at something you perceived would be difficult. Each time we steal our students' struggle by insisting they do work that is too easy for them, we steal their opportunity to have an esteem-building experience. Unless kids are consistently engaged in challenging work, they will lose their motivation to work hard.

Do you know any kids who don't turn in a stitch of work, yet dominate class discussions and ace unit tests? Or kids who can do the performance assessment before they have done the activities related to learning that content? These situations may lead to what I call the "empty grade book syndrome."

I have rarely met gifted kids who won't do their work, but I have met scores who won't do the *teacher's* work. This is the basis of most power struggles between gifted kids, their parents, and their teachers. When gifted students are forced to do work related to content they have already mastered, they resist, and the power struggle is on. This book will help you give your students their own work to do—work that is challenging and meaningful to them.

THE MYTH OF ELITISM

Many teachers and parents believe there is no need to do anything special for gifted kids. "After all," they reason, "most gifted students get good grades. They do just fine without extra help or attention." Some do (and some don't), but that's not the point. To understand why, let's look at the bell curve on page 3.

When we teach a class of students, we usually plan content, pacing, amount, and activities based on what we know about typical students at that age. Let's call those kids the Twos because they are in the middle of a heterogeneous group. On the bell curve, they're the students of average IQ.

Increasingly, more and more students enter a grade level missing many of the basic understandings they were supposed to acquire in earlier grades. Those kids are to the left on the bell curve; let's call them the Ones. We also have some kids who seem to be ahead of their age peers in what they know and can do. Those kids are to the right on the bell curve; we'll call them the Threes.

Now ask yourself, "What do I do differently for students who are having trouble keeping up to the grade-level standards?" Your answer might include these ideas:

- You adjust the amount of work they have to do.
- You change the pacing and adjust the amount of time they have to work.

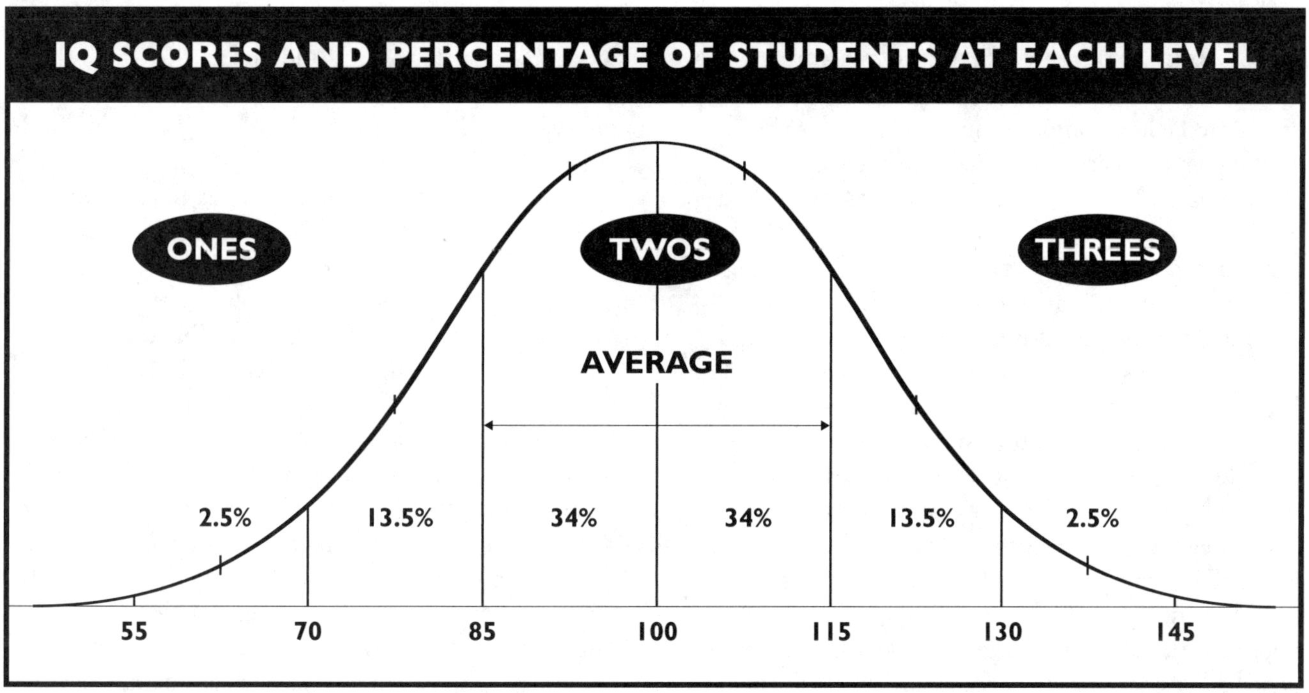

- You change the content in order to teach them what they are missing.
- You try to teach to their learning style strengths, and you adjust the ways they can express what they have learned.
- You try to find topics that interest them strongly, so you can entice them to learn some of the standards through their areas of interest.
- You change the peer interactions they have with their classmates, taking special care to pair them with students who can understand and help them.
- You seek out their parents and former teachers to get information that might empower you to help them learn more successfully.

Many of us make most or all of these adjustments daily for the benefit of the Ones in our classes. Do you feel guilty when you do these things? Do you fear that you will be accused of elitism because you're giving those students "special treatment"? Probably not.

Now visualize the bell curve folded in half, with the left side touching the right. Notice again that the Threes—those students we call gifted—are as far removed from average as the Ones. *By virtue of that fact alone, they are entitled to similar "special treatment."* Not because they are gifted, but because they are not average. The level, pacing, amount, and type of learning activities that benefit average learners are as inappropriate for them as they are for students who are working significantly below grade-level expectations.

It's been fashionable in American education to worry that providing accommodations for gifted students is elitist. We tell ourselves that America's public schools don't condone or practice elitism. I've worked with school districts in at least 40 states, and they all maintain an elitist system. Everywhere I go, there is a group of students who receive elitist treatment openly. They get to wear special clothing so even strangers can pick them out of a crowd in a hallway. Special teachers get special pay to help make these kids even more special. Sometimes these kids and their teachers get to take special field trips during academic learning time on transportation supplied by the district so they can travel far and wide to show how special they are. Any forms of recognition they get from these outings are prominently displayed in ways that make them highly visible to anyone in the school. And when other kids ask, "Can't we be part of this special group?" they are told they are not good enough to qualify.

Of course, you know I'm talking about athletics. You should also know that I was born and raised in Wisconsin. My Green Bay Packers were Vince Lombardi's Packers. My Milwaukee Braves won the World Series in the late 1950s. So rest assured that I'm not bashing athletics. I'm simply asking for equal consideration for academics.

GIFTED EDUCATION BENEFITS EVERYONE

Gifted education has significantly improved learning experiences for all students in heterogeneous classes. Every pedagogical method we've used with gifted kids over the years is now considered state-of-the-art for all kids. Project work, providing meaningful choices for students, self-directed learning, literature-based reading, problem-based curriculum—all were born in gifted education programs. Many of these components are now available as part of the regular learning program.

This doesn't mean that gifted kids' learning needs are being met in heterogeneous classrooms. It means that when we provide what gifted kids need, all other students are likely to benefit as well.

Why, then, are so few meaningful learning opportunities available for gifted students in heterogeneous classes? Perhaps because we worry that these opportunities will be considered elitist, or that other students and parents will think they're "not fair." Yet these worries don't prevent us from making sure the Ones on the bell curve get whatever they need to succeed as learners. Nor do they stop us from providing for kids whose differences are socioeconomic or culturally based.

Do you believe that all students you teach should learn something new on a regular basis? Let's define learning as "forward progress from what you know to what you don't yet know." When you put it in these terms, it's undeniable that of all the kids you teach in heterogeneous classes, those at most risk of learning the least today, tomorrow, and all year are the Threes.

Do you want all of your students to enjoy high self-esteem as part of their learning experience? Many gifted kids experience low self-esteem—partly because high intelligence is not always respected in school, and partly because they fear that one day people will see them working hard to learn and will perceive that they aren't really very smart after all.

Dr. Sylvia Rimm's work can help us understand how some gifted kids lose their motivation to learn. The figure below illustrates her theory of the conditions that create achievement or underachievement.*

One more important point about self-esteem: It is well-documented that many gifted kids are working significantly below their potential. At any time in a gifted child's school experience, she may have to decide whether to let the people in school know how intelligent she really is. When she perceives that being true to her intellectual abilities will lead to loss of peer approval, she may opt to act less capable.

I can't think of any situation more likely to diminish self-esteem than coming to school each

* Adapted from Gary Davis and Sylvia Rimm, *Education of the Gifted and Talented,* 4th ed. (Needham Heights, MA: Allyn and Bacon, 1998), p. 298. Used with permission of Sylvia Rimm.

CONDITIONS THAT CREATE ACHIEVEMENT OR UNDERACHIEVEMENT

QUADRANT 1 These are the high achievers. They perceive that when they work hard, they get good results. The curriculum is slightly beyond their grasp and requires significant effort to master. *All learners, whether below average, average, or above average, should be in this quadrant.*	**QUADRANT 2** These are the kids who get high grades with little or no effort. They have learned to resist challenging work. They fear that others will think they're not so smart if they have to work hard to get good results. *Many gifted kids are in this quadrant. They assume from experience that smart means easy.*
QUADRANT 3 These are the students who may work hard but rarely achieve success. They don't realize that if they used the appropriate learning strategies, their success in learning would noticeably improve. *Students in this quadrant may become discouraged and move into quadrant 4.*	**QUADRANT 4** These are the classic underachievers—students who have stopped putting forth any effort because nothing they do leads to any measurable success or satisfaction. *Our goal as educators is to prevent any student from moving into this quadrant.*

day and pretending to be someone different from who you are. Only in classrooms where individual differences in learning behaviors are recognized and accepted will gifted students' self-esteem truly flourish.

WHAT GIFTED STUDENTS NEED

To make forward progress from what they know to what they don't yet know, gifted students need *compacting* and *differentiation.* Compacting means condensing a semester or year's worth of learning into a shorter time period. Differentiation means providing gifted students with different tasks and activities than their age peers—tasks that lead to real learning for them.

There are five elements of differentiation: *content, process, product, environment,* and *assessment.*

1. Content. You are responsible for making sure that all kids learn the content they are expected to know. You are not responsible for teaching that content to all kids. Students who demonstrate that they already know some content, or who can learn required content in much less time than their age peers, are candidates for differentiation.

Content is differentiated through the use of more advanced, complex texts and resource materials, compacting, learning contracts, interdisciplinary learning, accelerated pacing, learning centers, and working with mentors. Content is sometimes changed to center around futuristic problems and challenges. The focus of differentiated content should be on understanding more than just the information. The focus should be on how a body of information is organized, the important questions and issues that are raised, and the way in which research in a particular field of study is carried out, sometimes referred to as depth and complexity. (For more on depth and complexity, see page 129.)

2. Process. This defines the methods students use to make sense of concepts, generalizations, and/or the required standards. It encompasses learning style considerations, creative and productive thinking and conceptualizing, focus on open-ended and problem-solving tasks, opportunities for meaningful research, and the skills to share what they have learned.

Gifted students should spend most of their learning time on tasks that are more complex and abstract than those their age peers could handle. They should gather information and data as though they were actually professionals in the field, assuming an attitude of inquiry rather than pursuing a goal of finding information. They should be expected to support their findings with evidence.

Process is differentiated through flexible grouping, using a learning styles or multiple intelligences approach, opportunities for learning at more complex levels, and sophisticated research. Flexible time limits are essential.

3. Product. This describes the ways in which students choose to illustrate and demonstrate their understanding of the content and process.

Many gifted students resist assignments that require a written product, since their brain usually moves so much faster than their hands can write or type. They are often more willing to produce an actual product—an exhibition, independent study, or performance. Gifted students should be guided to produce what Dr. Joseph Renzulli calls "real-life products for appropriate audiences." These go beyond the typical research paper or report to alternatives that develop individual students' talents and curiosities.

Product is differentiated by steering kids to exciting and unusual resources, and to people who can help locate those resources and demonstrate ways to use them.

4. Environment. This describes the actual physical setting where learning takes place, as well as the conditions under which a student is working.

Gifted students typically spend more time in independent study than their classmates, and they often work outside the classroom or school as part of their differentiated work. They thrive in a challenging atmosphere in which individual differences are valued and nurtured.

Learning environment is differentiated by changing the actual place where students work, altering the teacher's expectations, allowing flexible time limits, providing opportunities for in-depth research, and letting students work with mentors.

5. Assessment. This describes the method used to document mastery of curriculum. Gifted learners should experience consistent opportunities to demonstrate previous mastery before a particular unit of work is taught. They should also be encouraged to develop their own rubrics and other methods to assess their independent study projects.

Because of my own experience—first as a classroom teacher, now as a teacher trainer—I can identify with and completely understand the uncertainty and even terror you might be feeling as you contemplate finding out what your gifted students already know, giving them credit for it, and providing alternate activities. How will you gather the materials and resources you need? Won't differentiation take a lot of time and add more to your teaching load? Will you lose control of your classroom? This book will ease your doubts and fears—and make your efforts to teach gifted kids more successful and rewarding.

NOTE: Gifted students *do not* need extra credit work, nor do they need to become peer tutors. Extra credit work stifles motivation. Gifted kids wonder, "Why should I let the teacher know about my expertise if my 'prize' will be more work?" Gifted kids of any age have very adult-like preferences for learning opportunities. Would you like it if your principal asked you to work on more committees for "extra credit"?

In peer tutoring, highly capable students are expected to help less successful students. If gifted kids want to tutor other students, this should be limited to one class period per week. Or peer tutoring might be part of a schoolwide service project. Although many gifted kids appear to enjoy tutoring, it postpones their own opportunities to learn and work at their personal challenge levels.

ABOUT THIS BOOK

Teaching Gifted Kids in the Regular Classroom is written for teachers of all grades. Each chapter presents proven, practical, easy-to-use teaching/management strategies. Scenarios profile students* with whom the strategies have been used—either by me, or by a teacher I have trained—so you'll be able to notice similar characteristics, needs, and responses in your own students. The strategies are described in step-by-step detail. Frequently asked questions about the strategies are answered, and chapter summaries review the main points. Each chapter ends with a list of references and resources.

Several strategies make use of special forms, which are included here as reproducibles. Please feel free to photocopy these forms for use in your classroom. I often customize basic forms to meet the needs of specific students (my customized forms are shown as examples throughout the book), and I hope you'll do the same.** Instructions and tips for using the forms are given in the chapters.

Chapter 1 describes the learning and behavioral characteristics of gifted students. Special attention is given to populations that have been underserved in the past, including gifted children from multicultural and low socioeconomic populations and those considered "twice exceptional" (gifted and learning disabled or otherwise challenged).

The strategies in chapters 2 and 3 are designed to be used with content that is more skill-based and lends itself to pretesting, because it's likely that some of your students will already know much of what you plan to teach. These strategies will help you meet the needs of your gifted students in any skill work related to reading, math, language arts, handwriting, and vocabulary or any other subject area.

The strategies in Chapter 4 are designed to be used with subject areas that represent new learning for students, such as science, social studies, problem-based learning, and interdisciplinary and/or thematic units. Methods other than pretests are usually necessary for these types of curriculum. Chapter 5 covers appropriate reading and writing instruction for gifted students, and Chapter 6 explains how you can plan curriculum for all students at the same time and still create differentiated activities. Chapters 4 through 6 use many of the same principles and methods, so you may want to read and use these chapters together.

Chapter 7 shows you how to help gifted kids manage independent study. Chapter 8 describes issues that should be considered when grouping gifted students for instruction and learning. Strategies for making cooperative learning fair for gifted students, and methods for grouping gifted students in homerooms or self-contained classes, are presented in detail.

Chapter 9 discusses miscellaneous issues such as acceleration and grade-skipping, qualities needed by teachers of gifted kids, record-keeping for differentiation experiences, and how to deal

* Names and some details have been changed to protect students' privacy.

** All of the reproducible forms in this book, plus many additional extensions menus, are also on CD-ROM so you can easily print them out and customize them for your students.

with parents, administrators, and colleagues. Chapter 10 is for parents of gifted kids. Teachers should read it, too, so they can anticipate parents' questions and expectations.

Appendix A at the end of the book includes games, puzzles, and other challenges gifted kids love; I know, because I have used them in my own classes. Appendix B is a directory of additional resources including publishers of gifted education materials, magazines and journals, videos, organizations, and Web sites.

★

This book will help you meet the learning needs of the gifted kids in your classroom. As noted earlier, gifted education techniques benefit everyone, so you'll probably find that these strategies and techniques are good for many other students besides those who are formally identified as gifted.

However, teaching gifted kids in the regular classroom is certainly not meant to replace other gifted education opportunities available in your district, or to serve as a reason for eliminating such opportunities. Gifted kids are gifted 24 hours a day, not just during those times they spend in separate classes or on challenging projects or activities. When other elements of gifted programs are combined with differentiation in the regular classroom, gifted kids can experience consistent opportunities to enjoy learning and to be as challenged and productive as possible.

With that in mind, enjoy this book. It's written for you to use without much fuss. All methods have been field-tested with teachers like yourself who have found them to work very well. Many of these teachers have told me, "I wish I had known about these methods before now—I would have always used them." I hope you'll feel the same.

I promise you that the strategies presented here will work with your heterogeneous classes. I promise you that there will be no resentment on the part of the other students as they see the gifted students "doing their own thing." I promise you that you won't have to spend very much time preparing extra materials. Finally, I promise you the following results for your gifted students:

- They will be more motivated.
- They will be more productive—they will actually get their work done.
- They will have more positive feelings about school.
- Their parents will be very pleased with what's happening in your class.
- Their teacher (you) will be very pleased with their attitude and productivity, and with the professionally satisfying results your efforts produce.

Teaching gifted kids is really very simple. Just remember to never ask anything of them you wouldn't want someone to ask of you. Picture yourself at the last in-service you attended in which you knew your precious learning time was being wasted. Connect with your frustration, impatience, and hostility about being forced to sit there. And vow that as a teacher you will avoid imposing the "Jesse James syndrome" on any of your students.

When asked what it was like to be gifted in a regular classroom, a gifted student adapted some words from Richard Brautigan's poem, "The Memoirs of Jesse James," to create a metaphor for his school experiences:*

All the time I just sat there...waiting,
Waiting for something new to learn.
My teachers should have ridden with Jesse James
For all the learning time they have stolen from me!

To make sure your students never feel this way about you, just use the strategies presented in this book. Watch what happens as gifted students become more motivated to work, less sullen and hostile, and more likely to enjoy school and your teaching. Watch how other kids don't object when some of their classmates are engaged in alternate activities. Listen to what the parents of gifted students say as they thank you for making their children's school experience so enjoyable and rewarding. Notice the positive feelings you experience as you realize you are truly meeting the special learning needs of your gifted students.

Don't waste any time or energy feeling guilty about what you should have done differently in the past. If you had known what to do, you would have done it. This book will help you learn how to teach gifted kids well, starting now. So: No looking back. Time to move ahead. Let's get started.

Susan Winebrenner

* Adapted from "The Memoirs of Jesse James" from the book *Rommel Drives on Deep into Egypt* by Richard Brautigan. Copyright © 1970, copyright renewed by Ianthe Brautigan Swensen, 1998. All rights reserved. Used with permission of Ianthe Brautigan Swensen.

I

Characteristics of Gifted Students

Being gifted in America today is not necessarily a positive experience. Gifted students and their parents experience a lot of rejection from an educational system in which conformity is valued and most kids are expected to work along with the group without resistance or complaint. I have long wondered why we can spend considerable time and effort teaching students to appreciate diversity in ethnic and cultural terms, but we don't extend that mindset to differences in learning ability. I've never met a gifted kid who asked to be born that way. It just happens. We need to consider giftedness as simply another difference and make gifted kids as welcome in our classrooms as any other students.

There are already so many definitions of giftedness that I hesitate to offer another. However, in terms of classroom teaching, I define gifted students as *those who have ability in one or more learning areas that exceeds grade/age level expectations by two years or more.* By this definition, the regular curriculum can't possibly provide the challenge these students need to continually move forward in their learning.

In recent years, some fascinating new insights into giftedness have emerged from the work of Polish psychiatrist and psychologist Kazimierz Dabrowski (1902–1980). When Dabrowski studied a group of gifted children and youth, he found that they displayed what he called "overexcitabilities." They perceived all kinds of stimuli more intensely than others; they were super-sensitive to everything in their environment and felt the joys and sorrows of life more extremely than other children. (Today, overexcitability—OE—is considered a marker of giftedness, one of the many things to look for when identifying a gifted child.) Dabrowski believed that OE may lead to a series of "positive disintegrations," or developmental crises, during which the individual rejects the status quo and questions everything. When things go well, this process continues and the person emerges as an autonomous, authentic human being with carefully thought-out values and beliefs. When they don't, the person may get stuck in antisocial behavior, disharmony, and despair. Dabrowski's theories help us understand why living with and teaching gifted kids can be such an incredible challenge.

People often ask me for a "short list" of the characteristics gifted children have which make identification easier. I believe that any student who possesses most or all of the following five characteristics is probably gifted.

1. Learns new material faster, and at an earlier age, than age peers.

2. Remembers what has been learned forever, making review unnecessary.

3. Is able to deal with concepts that are too complex and abstract for age peers.

4. Has a passionate interest in one or more topics, and would spend all available time learning more about that topic if he or she could.

5. Does not need to watch the teacher to hear what is being said; can operate on multiple brain channels simultaneously and process more than one task at a time.

Other characteristics are described throughout this chapter. To be gifted, one does not have to possess all of these characteristics. However, when you observe students consistently exhibiting many of these behaviors, the possibility that they are gifted is very strong. Trust your own observations more than the "evidence" of mediocre standardized test scores or poor grades. Listen respectfully to parents whose descriptions of their children at home match some of the information presented here. Sometimes, gifted kids choose to not appear gifted at school while continuing to demonstrate gifted characteristics at home.

It's rare to find a child who is "gifted across the board." Most gifted kids are more likely to be gifted in one or two specific areas, and average or even below average in others. For example, many highly verbal youngsters appear deficient in bodily-kinesthetic abilities, especially in gym or physical education classes. I say "appear" because their physical abilities may be developmentally appropriate to their age but seem glaringly different from their intellectual abilities. Children who show evidence of giftedness in one or two areas are as eligible for compacting and differentiation opportunities as those who are gifted in many or all areas.

Before we get into the characteristics, I want to reassure you that you will probably never need all of this information. Chances are, you won't be asked to formally identify gifted students. In fact, as you'll learn in Chapter 2, gifted students often identify themselves by showing their readiness for compacting and differentiation. The characteristics are included here in case you want and need guidelines for recognizing gifted behaviors. You may choose to share this information with the parents of gifted students in your classroom.

LEARNING AND BEHAVIORAL CHARACTERISTICS

The gifted child:*

- Is extremely precocious, when compared to his age peers, in any area of learning and/or performance. Learns at a much earlier age than is typical and makes much more rapid progress in certain areas of learning.
- Exhibits asynchronous development. May be highly precocious in some areas while demonstrating age-appropriate or delayed behaviors in other areas. *Example:* Can read at an early age but can't tie his own shoes until age 5 or later. *Note:* Not all gifted kids learn to read before starting school; not all kids who do learn to read before starting school are gifted. One significant indication of giftedness might be the child who literally teaches himself to read, with little or no adult intervention or help.
- Has an advanced vocabulary and verbal ability for his chronological age.
- Has an outstanding memory. Possesses lots of information and can process it in sophisticated ways.
- Learns some things very easily with little help from others. May display a "rage to master" what he studies.
- Operates on higher levels of thinking than his age peers. Is comfortable with abstract and complex thinking tasks.
- Demonstrates ability to work with abstract ideas. Needs a minimum of concrete experiences for complete understanding.
- Perceives subtle cause-and-effect relationships.
- Sees patterns, relationships, and connections that others don't.
- Comes up with "better ways" for doing things. Suggests them to peers, teachers, and other adults—not always in positive, helpful ways.
- Prefers complex and challenging tasks to "basic" work. May change simple tasks or directions to more complex ones to keep himself interested.
- Transfers concepts and learning to new situations. Sees connections between apparently unconnected ideas and activities. Makes intuitive leaps toward understanding without necessarily being able to explain how he got there.
- Wants to share all he knows. Loves to know and give reasons for everything.
- Is curious about many things and asks endless questions. Each answer leads to another question.
- Is a keen and alert observer. Doesn't miss a thing.

* Throughout this book, I alternate use of gender pronouns "he" and "she," "him" and "her" when describing gifted kids to avoid the awkward "he or she" and "him/her" constructs. I usually alternate list-by-list or section-by-section. This is for ease of reading only and is never meant to imply that all characteristics in a given list or all statements in a given section refer only to gifted boys *or* gifted girls. They refer to both boys *and* girls.

- Is very intense. May be extremely emotional and excitable. Gets totally absorbed in activities and thoughts; may be reluctant to move from one subject area to another; may insist on mastering one thing before starting another. May experience periods of such fierce concentration that he is literally unaware of what is going on around him.
- Has many, and sometimes unusual, interests, hobbies, and collections. May have a passionate interest that has lasted for many years, such as dinosaurs.
- Is strongly motivated to do things that interest him in his own way. Loves working independently; may prefer to work alone. Enjoys making discoveries on his own and solving problems in his own way.
- Has a very high energy level. Seems to require very little sleep, but actually has a hard time calming down and going to sleep because he's so busy thinking, planning, problem-solving, and creating.
- Is sensitive to beauty and other people's feelings, emotions, and expectations.
- Has an advanced sense of justice, morality, and fairness. Is aware of and empathetic about global issues that most of his age peers aren't interested in; can conceptualize solutions to such problems when quite young.
- Has a sophisticated sense of humor.
- Likes to be in charge. May be a natural leader.

As with all good things, there are challenges associated with having outstanding talents. These challenges are often perceived as behavior, motivation, or attitude problems. The gifted child whose learning needs are not met in school might:

- Resist doing the work, or work in a sloppy, careless manner.
- Get frustrated with the pace of the class and what he perceives as inactivity or lack of noticeable progress.
- Rebel against routine and predictability.
- Ask embarrassing questions; demand good reasons for why things are done a certain way.
- Resist taking direction or orders.
- Daydream.
- Monopolize class discussions.
- Become bossy with his peers and teachers.
- Become intolerant of imperfection in himself and in others.
- Become super-sensitive to any form of criticism; cry easily.
- Refuse to conform.
- Resist cooperative learning.
- Act out or disturb others.
- Become the "class clown."
- Become impatient when he's not called on to recite or respond; blurt out answers without raising his hand.

When you notice these problems, don't panic! Before trying to "fix the child," fix the curriculum by following the suggestions in this book. More often than not, compacting and differentiation can noticeably diminish negative behaviors.

STRATEGY: THE NAME CARD METHOD*

If there's one thing almost all gifted kids have in common—except those who have given up on school and retreated into full-time daydreaming—it's the tendency to blurt out answers and dominate class discussions. Even kids whose learning needs are being met by compacting and differentiation have a hard time controlling these impulses.

An alternative to hand-raising, the Name Card method is the best solution I've found. I simply can't teach without using it, as its benefits are numerous. In my experience, the Name Card method:

- Minimizes blurting and other attention-getting, discussion-controlling behaviors.
- Ensures nearly total participation in all discussions by all students; makes it impossible for anyone to "hide."
- Greatly improves listening behaviors. Students want to hear every word said by the teacher and by other students.
- Eliminates teaching behaviors which may communicate ethnic, cultural, socioeconomic, or gender bias.

* Adapted from "Think-Pair-Share, Thinktrix, Thinklinks, and Weird Facts" by Frank T. Lyman Jr., in *Enhancing Thinking through Cooperative Learning,* edited by Neil Davidson and Toni Worsham. Columbia, NY: Teachers College Press, 1992. Used with permission of Frank T. Lyman Jr.

Start by trying this method with one subject area or class period. Don't add other subjects or classes until you feel comfortable with the method and can see evidence of its positive outcomes.

1. Write each student's name on a 3" x 5" card. (Some teachers prefer using tongue depressors.)

2. Tell your students that when you use the cards, you will call on the person whose name is on the card you've taken from the stack, instead of calling on people who raise their hands. Explain that you'll ignore any hand-waving, noise-making, deep sighs, rolling eyes, and other behaviors they use to get your attention.

3. Group students in "discussion buddy" pairs. Explain that they will stay in their pairs for about two weeks, after which you'll match them with other partners. Make it clear that you'll choose the pairs, and also that you'll change them on a regular basis. (This way, no one ever feels bad about being chosen last.)

Each pair should consist of one stronger student and one weaker student. *Exception:* Students who are exceptionally capable in that subject or content area should be grouped with each other—especially the blurters. They will be less likely to blurt and more likely to participate when their partners are similar to them in learning ability and understand and appreciate their passion for knowing everything.

If you have a student no one wants to partner with, privately ask a particularly sensitive and helpful student if he or she will be that student's partner for two weeks. "Future teacher/social worker" types are usually glad to oblige.

4. Tell the students that you're going to ask them a question. They will have time to think about their response and talk it over with their discussion buddies. Then, if you call on them using the cards, they will have to give an answer.

Explain that they should answer loudly enough for the whole class to hear, since you won't be repeating anyone's answer. Tell them also that they should not repeat what others have said, and that no one can say, "I pass." Since they will have time to confer with their partners, it's highly likely they will have an answer when you call on them.

5. Ask an open-ended question. Give the students 10–15 seconds of think time to consider their responses. Tell them they can jot down their ideas if they wish.

6. Demonstrate the signal you will use to indicate when pair time is over. (You might say "Time's up" and/or clap your hands.) When you give the signal, they should stop talking to each other and redirect their attention to you.

7. Give the students 30–45 seconds of pair time to talk with their discussion buddies and come up with several more responses to the question. Tell them to use soft voices. As before, they can jot down their ideas.

You may be worrying that your kids will get off-task during pair time. If you consistently keep the allotted time to under a minute, I promise they will stay on task.

8. Using the name cards, call on students to share what they have discussed. When you call on a student, she may share any response she and her partner came up with, as long as no one else has already given that answer.

To enjoy all the benefits of the Name Card method, it's important to follow these guidelines when calling on kids:

- Don't look at the cards before asking a question. If you do, you'll try to match the question's level of difficulty with your perception of the student's ability. This sends a clear message of your expectations for that student, whether high or low. Since you have paired struggling students with supportive partners, it's okay to ask challenging questions of all students.
- Don't show the cards to the students. Every now and then, you may want to call on someone other than the person whose name card you pull—such as a student who's getting very impatient to participate.
- Once you call on a student, stay with her until you get a response. Don't ask the class to help her. Wait 10 seconds (no more), and if she hasn't responded by then, start to coach her. Provide a clue or hint, give her a choice between two alternatives, or allow her more time to consult with her partner while you call on other kids. Always be certain to return to the student for her response within 60 seconds, so she'll know you have confidence that she is a capable learner. *Important:* Don't call on someone other than the partner to help her. This is embarrassing and counterproductive to the goal of total participation.

- When you finish with a name card, put it somewhere inside the stack, never on the bottom. Shuffle the stack often. This way, kids won't stop paying attention once they've been called on, because they know they might be called on again at any time. Of course, some students will get more chances than others to respond, but that's okay, since all students actually answer every question anyway—with their partners.
- If you use tongue depressors instead of cards, use only one can. Never put the used ones in another can, because brains will shut down.

9. Using the name cards, call on several students to share before commenting or giving your input. Simply "receive" their responses in a noncommittal way. You might nod or say "Thank you" or "Okay."

When you show that you'll receive multiple responses to the same question, students don't stop thinking about the question even after someone else has answered it. They know their name card might be next and they'll have to come up with a reasonable response as well.

10. Before moving on to the next question, and for the benefit of students who enjoy sharing their deep wealth of knowledge, ask, "Does anyone have anything to add that hasn't already been said? Raise your hand if you do."

Make it very clear that they may only add to the discussion; they may not repeat what has already been said. If they do repeat, they forfeit their right to add anything more to the rest of this particular discussion. (This encourages students to listen carefully to the contributions of their classmates.) They can continue to participate, however, because their name card stays in the stack.

Kids who have tended to dominate discussions in the past are now in a very satisfying situation. They get to tell the answers to all of the questions to their partners, and they always have the opportunity to add to a discussion.

PERFECTIONISM

You may have noticed that many gifted kids are perfectionists. In the primary grades, they are easy to spot. They work ever so slowly to create a perfect product, constantly asking you, "Is this okay? Is this what you want me to do?" In the upper grades, perfectionism becomes harder to identify, since it may look more like procrastination. Gifted kids begin avoiding assignments, reasoning that, "Since I probably can't do this perfectly because I don't have the right materials or the teacher hasn't given us enough time, I may as well not bother doing it at all." This handy defense mechanism hides an underlying anxiety that if they *do* give the assignment their best shot, and it isn't good enough to earn the top grade, they might not be able to handle the consequences.

Parents and teachers unwittingly contribute to the need of these students to be perfect at all times. In their early years at home, these children notice how the adults in their life make a pleasant fuss when they exhibit precocious behaviors. They grow up with the mistaken perception that they are valued for what they can do rather than who they are. Well-meaning teachers add fuel to the fire when they call attention to a student's exceptional work, holding it up as a model for the other students.

Meanwhile, capable students who just didn't feel like doing their best on a particular assignment get it back for revision, with some comment like, "C'mon, Amy, you can do better than this! I'll give you another chance to earn an A." To these students, the message is clear: "Adults like me more when I'm the best—when my work is perfect and deserves an A." Since most adults have been known to goof off occasionally and do a less than perfect job on some project that doesn't interest them, perhaps those same adults should lighten up on their expectations for gifted kids. We need to teach kids how to struggle to learn, not how to keep completing tasks without true effort.

It's also possible that praising a child too much can contribute to perfectionism, especially if the praise is for the child's natural abilities or products that didn't require much effort. High praise can make a child believe that if you're smart, all learning should come easily.

Starting in kindergarten, it becomes the teacher's responsibility to communicate to students that learning is struggle, and that what one already knows represents memory, not learning. The way to communicate these important concepts is by consistently providing gifted students with challenging, possibly even frustrating work. Furthermore, these students need to learn that A's represent a long-term goal of mastery, and that lower grades are not a reflection of inadequacy, but an indication that mastery has not yet been achieved.

Teachers can support this risk-taking behavior by refraining from always expecting perfect work and grades from gifted students, and by encouraging them to try tasks that are truly difficult for them. Gifted students need to develop an appreciation for the values that accompany the struggle to learn. They need to replace their self-talk that says, "I must make it appear that the work is effortless so no one questions my intelligence" with the message that, "True intelligence is reflected in my willingness to stay with a frustrating and difficult task until mastery is achieved."

NOTE: As you begin to develop appropriately challenging activities for your gifted students, don't be surprised when their first reaction is, "No, thanks! I'd rather just do what the other kids are doing." They may take one look at an activity and conclude that it will require a tremendous amount of effort. Then they may assume that if their classmates and teachers see them working so hard, everyone else will believe what they themselves have long feared: they are not really gifted! Of course, they will resist such activities. Wouldn't you? Keep reading for strategies that will lower your gifted students' resistance and make them more receptive to real learning.

Perfectionist Characteristics

The perfectionist:

- Believes that what she can do is more important and valuable than who she is.
- Believes that her worth as a human being depends on being perfect.
- Sets impossible goals for herself.
- Has been praised consistently for her "greatness" and exceptional ability; fears she will lose the regard of others if she can't continue to demonstrate that exceptionality.
- May suffer from the "Impostor Syndrome"—the belief that she isn't really very capable and doesn't deserve her success.
- Resists challenging work for fear that her struggle will be seen by others.
- Works very slowly in the hope that her product will be perfect.
- Discovers a mistake in her work; erases until there is a hole in the paper, or crumples up the paper and throws it away.
- Limits her options and avoids taking risks.
- Procrastinates to the point at which work never gets done or even started. In this way, she ensures that no one can ever really judge her work, and she doesn't have to face the possibility that her best may not be good enough.
- May cry easily in frustration when her work at school doesn't seem to reach a state of being perfect. (This is often misjudged as immaturity or the result of too much pressure from home.)
- Asks for lots of extra time to complete her work.
- Asks for lots of help and reassurance from the teacher. ("Is this all right? Please repeat the directions.")
- Can't take criticism or suggestions for improvement without being defensive, angry, or tearful. Criticism proves that she isn't perfect, and suggestions imply that she isn't perfect. Imperfection is intolerable.
- Expects other people to be perfect—especially classmates, teammates, and teachers.
- Is never satisfied with her successes.

Ways to Help the Perfectionistic Child

Our most important job as teachers of gifted students is to help them understand that it's perfectly all right to struggle to learn, and the world will not think less of them because that struggle is apparent. You need to make sure that all of your students, including those who are gifted, are always working on tasks that require real effort. In order to do that, you must be willing to assess and give full credit for previous mastery each time an instructional unit begins. Once you discover that some students have already mastered what you are about to teach, their class time should be spent on alternate activities that help them stretch toward the belief that hard work is necessary and desirable for all students, even the most capable.

- Help perfectionists learn that success with long-term goals is merely an accumulation of successes with short-term goals. The Goal-Setting Log on page 16 is a very effective tool you can use to teach this concept. Once students form the habit of taking pride in their ability to set and reach a goal during today's work period, they can worry less about whether the final product, due two weeks later, will be perfect.

- Teach them how to use creative problem-solving (CPS). In CPS, sometimes the best or most useful ideas come later in the brainstorming process. This relieves kids of some of the pressure to get the "right answer" quickly.
- Avoid the phrase "Always do your very best." When you want to encourage your students to work their hardest, say "Put forth your best effort." This shifts the emphasis from the product to the learning process.

How to Use the Goal-Setting Log

The Goal-Setting Log is designed to be used by students who have trouble getting started with a task, who work too slowly, and who never seem to be able to finish long-term tasks. It's especially helpful for perfectionists who must learn that the key to accomplishing long-term goals is setting and reaching reasonable short-term goals one at a time. This tool teaches them to take satisfaction from that process. You'll find a reproducible Goal-Setting Log on page 16.

1. At the beginning of each work period, have the student enter the date in the left column. In the center column, he should write a brief description of the work he predicts he can accomplish during that work period.

2. Five minutes before the end of the work period, have the student complete the right column by recording how much work he has actually accomplished. If he accomplished less than he predicted, he should move down a line, record tomorrow's date (or the date of the next work period), and briefly describe the work he has left to do.

Always keep the logs in the classroom—in the students' folders, their compacting folders (see page 33), or a community folder if necessary. Have all students who use the logs sit in the same general area. Work with them as a group to set and review their goals.

For some students, old habits die hard, and they may have trouble letting go of their perfectionism. Guide them through this review:

If the goal has been met, ask:

- What was your goal?
- Did you accomplish your goal?
- Who is responsible for your success in reaching your goal? (It may take patience and prodding, but the student must respond, "I am responsible for my success in accomplishing my goal.")
- How does it feel to be successful? (Again, you may have to prompt the student to say, "It feels good to be successful.")
- How can you congratulate yourself or give yourself some recognition for a job well done? (Offer suggestions if necessary.)

If the goal has not been met, ask:

- What was your goal?
- Did you accomplish your goal?
- Who is responsible for the fact that you didn't reach your goal? (The student may blame some external source. Don't ask how it feels to not accomplish the goal. Instead, prompt until the student can say, "I am responsible for not reaching my goal.")
- What plan can you make for tomorrow to prevent the same problem from happening again? (Have the student write his plan on the back of his Goal-Setting Log.)

Never punish students who don't reach their goals. The best way to get kids on track is to help them learn to set realistic goals and feel satisfaction from reaching them. The inability to earn positive feedback (from themselves and from you) is all the punishment they need.

If you must grade students' work under this arrangement, I recommend the following:

- Give a C for reaching a goal that is well below the work you expect from the rest of the class.
- Give a B for when the goal gets into the grade-level range.
- Give an A only for exceptional work.

Have students work on *one* area or subject at a time until progress is apparent and success feels comfortable to them. If you add other areas or subjects too quickly, students may develop a "fear of success." (As in: "Adults always expect more of you if you show them what you can do. I guess I should stop working so hard.")

★ GOAL-SETTING LOG ★

Student's Name: ____

Date	Goal for This Work Period	Work Actually Accomplished

CREATIVE THINKERS

Creative thinkers often aren't identified as gifted because their behavior tends to annoy teachers, and their apparent "fooling around" often results in incomplete work. Many creative thinkers don't do well in school. They get poor grades, refuse or forget to hand in work on time, and constantly argue for things to be done differently. They are so challenging that we sometimes forget that the people who have made the most significant contributions to humankind throughout history generally exhibit many characteristics of creative thinkers. It's the nonconformists who are the problem-solvers, artists, dreamers, and inventors, thinking "outside the box" in ways that profoundly affect our lives.

The creative thinker:

- Displays original ideas and products. Is sometimes characterized as thinking up "wild and crazy ideas."
- Is fluent in idea generation and development. Notices endless possibilities for situations or ways objects may be used.
- Is able to elaborate on ideas. Adds details others don't think of.
- Demonstrates flexibility of ideas and points of view. Can see merit in looking at things and situations from numerous perspectives.
- Experiments with ideas and hunches.
- Has an outstanding sense of humor. Loves to play with words and ideas.
- Is impatient with routine and predictable tasks. Adds or changes directions given by the teacher to make assignments more interesting.
- Has a tremendous capacity for making unexpected connections.
- Challenges accepted assumptions.
- Says what he thinks without regard for consequences. Is capable of great independence and autonomy.
- Has a great imagination; daydreams often. Enjoys pretending; may have several imaginary playmates.
- Dresses or grooms in nonconformist ways.
- Can persist at one task to the total exclusion of others.
- Is a brilliant thinker, but absentminded about details or where his work might be found.
- Is passionately interested in a particular topic or field of endeavor.
- May be talented in the fine arts.
- May do much better on standardized tests than his class work leads you to expect.

Ways to Nurture Creative Thinking

- Encourage children to observe and explore their environment and universe from many perspectives.
- Encourage children's natural curiosity and accompanying need to ask zillions of questions. Remember that you're not expected to know all the answers. Help the children predict their own answers and/or locate resources where they might find the answers themselves.
- Provide numerous open-ended learning experiences—those without a single right answer, solution, or method of exploration.
- Provide many opportunities for children to engage in meaningful decision making.
- Provide regular opportunities for daydreaming or reflection. In the creative thinking process, this is called incubation—the time when great ideas synthesize and emerge.
- Group creatively gifted kids together with others like themselves on projects and other activities. This experience validates their sense of self-worth and gives them courage to continue in their talent and interest areas.
- Help creative children find outlets and audiences for their creative products. *Example:* Pair them with adult mentors who can help them explore their creative interests.

Creativity Inhibitors

Creative thinkers may be blocked and frustrated when:

- They perceive they must succeed at everything they do, and/or that every product must be perfect.
- They feel pressured to conform in order to be accepted. Some of this pressure may come from peers; some may come from parents, teachers, and the media.
- They lack opportunities to work alone.

- They are told to "stop daydreaming" and don't understand the importance of daydreaming in the creative process.
- They spend too much time with highly structured toys and games, not enough playing with ordinary objects in creative ways.
- Their creativity is met with misunderstanding, suspicion, or disdain from significant adults.
- Their creativity clashes with gender-related expectations.
- They are told that creativity is a waste of time when compared to more important endeavors.
- Their parents and teachers are authoritarian ("Do this because I say so").

STUDENTS WHO ARE TWICE-EXCEPTIONAL

Some gifted students exhibit behaviors that confuse their parents and teachers and frustrate the students themselves. They have exceptionally high ability in one or more areas of learning while simultaneously exhibiting significant weaknesses in others. Their strengths are often evident in the arts and in their ability to think and speak creatively. But when you ask them to write down their thoughts, they may claim they "can't write."

Scenario: Elizabeth

Elizabeth had a serious learning disability and didn't appear to be very gifted. But she also had an avid interest in geography, maps, and national parks. During the year she was in my sixth grade, I took a class period to introduce an upcoming review unit on map skills. At the end of the period, Elizabeth came up to me, and we had the following conversation.

> *Elizabeth:* "You know, Mrs. Winebrenner, I know a lot about maps."
> *Me:* "You do? How did that happen?"
> *Elizabeth:* "I don't know. I just love maps. I've always loved maps. Maps are just really interesting things to me."
> *Me:* "What do you do with this love of maps?"
> *Elizabeth:* "Well, when my family goes on a trip, I get to plan the trip on the map."
> *Me:* "No kidding! Where did you go last year?"
> *Elizabeth* (proudly): "Yellowstone National Park."
> *Me:* "And how did you get there?"

Then Elizabeth told me how she had gotten her family to Yellowstone—remembering all the highways, states, time zone changes, national monuments, and national and state parks!

> *Me:* "Pretty impressive. Where did you go the year before?"
> *Elizabeth* (happily): "Great Smoky Mountains."
> *Me:* "How did you get there?"

Once again, I heard the same breadth of details.

> *Me:* "Hmmm. I bet the prospect of spending several weeks reviewing basic map skills is not very appealing to you."
> *Elizabeth:* "I've thought about that."
> *Me:* "I'll tell you what. I'll bring in the end-of-the-unit test tomorrow, and if you pass it with the equivalent of an A, you won't have to do the map work we're doing. You'll be able to spend your social studies time on a different activity of your choice."
> *Elizabeth* (smiling): "Thanks!"

Next, I did something I've learned to do routinely when offering "special consideration" to gifted students: I offered the same opportunity to everyone in the class. Sixteen of my 27 students volunteered to take the pretest, which they did during the next day's social studies period. Students who opted not to take the test watched a video about the national parks.

I told the students beforehand that if they didn't get an A, their tests wouldn't count. Six students completed the test. Two passed with A's—Elizabeth and a student named James. (For more about James, see pages 41–43.)

When I discovered Elizabeth's superior competency in map concepts, I faced a dilemma. Should I allow her to experience compacting and differentiation in the map work? Or should I use her social studies time, while her classmates studied maps, to help shore up her woefully inadequate skills in sentence structure, handwriting, number facts, and most other areas of the sixth-grade curriculum?

The dilemma was solved when I asked myself two critical questions: "When compared to her classmates, is Elizabeth clearly advanced in this particular content?" Yes. "By virtue of her exceptional ability, is she as entitled to compacting and differentiation as any other student who demonstrated mastery on the pretest?" Clearly, yes again. Therefore, I chose to allow her to work on differentiated activities during social studies. (For more about Elizabeth, see page 41.)

The Meaning of Twice-Exceptional

Although there are several reasons why gifted students fail to achieve at a level compatible with their potential (see page 22), many students in this group are now recognized as "twice-exceptional." Their giftedness coexists with a learning challenge of some sort, most commonly a learning disability, behavioral problem, and/or Attention Deficit Disorder.

These kids have some noticeable academic learning strength, but it may never be recognized as giftedness. Their learning challenge depresses the exceptional learning ability down to the normal range for their age. Since most schools usually stop looking for exceptional educational abilities once a learning deficiency has been identified, their giftedness will probably go unidentified.

Anywhere from 10–30 percent of gifted kids may have some form of learning disability. A study of twice-exceptional students by Sally Reis, Terry Neu, and Joan McGuire led to these conclusions:*

1. Many high ability students who have learning disabilities are not recognized for their gifts and may have negative school experiences.
2. Traditional remediation techniques like special education classification, tutoring, and/or retention offer little challenges to high ability students with learning disabilities and may perpetuate a cycle of underachievement.
3. High ability students with learning disabilities need support to understand and effectively use their strengths.
4. Lack of understanding by school personnel, peers, and self may cause emotional and academic problems for students struggling to cope with learning disabilities and giftedness.
5. Parents are often the only ones to offer support to their high ability children who also have learning disabilities. They can increase their effectiveness by exploring all available options and advocating for their children from an early age.

Twice-exceptional children may demonstrate one or more of these learning challenges:

- On tests of ability, their scores may show significant discrepancies of 12 points or more between verbal and nonverbal subtests.
- They have large vocabularies which may be deficient in word meanings and the subtleties of language.
- They may be reading significantly below grade level but have a large storehouse of information on some topics.
- They have the ability to express themselves verbally but an apparent inability to write down any of their ideas.
- They may excel at abstract reasoning but seem unable to remember small details.
- They may seem bright and motivated outside of school but have difficulty with traditional school tasks.
- Their slow reaction speed may result in incomplete work and low test scores on timed tests.
- Their general lack of self-confidence may manifest itself as inflexibility, inability to take risks, super-sensitivity to any type of criticism, helplessness, socially inadequate behaviors, stubbornness, and other behaviors designed to distract others from their learning inadequacies.
- They may lack effective organization and study skills.
- Some of these children may have vision problems related to scotopic sensitivity that interfere with their reading ability. Colored overlays or lenses (try gray or yellow first) may help. For more information, contact the Irlen Clinic. See References and Resources at the end of this chapter.

* Reis, Sally M., Terry W. Neu, and Joan M. McGuire. "Talents in Two Places: Case Studies of High Ability Students with Learning Disabilities Who Have Achieved." Research Monograph 95114. Storrs, CT: NRC/GT, 1995.

Children with ADD/ADHD

When people look for children with ADD (Attention Deficit Disorder), they usually expect to see these four characteristics:

1. Hyperactivity (high energy).

2. Distractibility (inattention and difficulty with concentrating).

3. Impulsivity (which may be displayed as blurting or interrupting).

4. Disorganization (difficulty in finding materials and finishing tasks).

However, children who have ADD *without* hyperactivity may:

- Appear lethargic.
- Daydream a lot; seem like "absent-minded professors."
- Be easily distractible and unable to "pay attention"; have a short attention span.
- Have difficulty listening (attention wanders), following directions, and completing tasks or chores.
- Seem unaware of the risks or consequences of their actions.
- Lack social interaction skills; may be characterized as very quiet or shy.
- Pay little or no attention to details; make careless mistakes.
- Appear completely disorganized and forgetful; lose things; be unable to get homework, flyers, or notes to or from home and school.

And children who have ADD *with* hyperactivity (ADHD) may:

- Behave as if driven by a motor.
- Be fidgety and squirmy; have difficulty sitting still.
- Leave their seat without permission.
- Run, climb, and move about incessantly
- Blurt or talk excessively; be unable to wait for the teacher to call on them.
- Have trouble sharing; be unable to wait their turn.
- Intrude on other people's conversation and play.

CAUTION: These behaviors can often appear very similar to behaviors exhibited by gifted students who are not being challenged by the regular curriculum. If a child who possesses some characteristics of giftedness appears inattentive or frequently speaks out of turn, try compacting and differentiation *before* pursuing a diagnosis of ADD/ADHD. When ADD behaviors are present, accommodating the student's learning style strengths and teaching compensation techniques can often reduce the need to place the child on medication.

According to Dierdre V. Lovecky, Ph.D., director of the Gifted Resource Center of New England:*

> Misdiagnosis of AD/HD can occur in two directions. Highly energetic gifted children can be seen as AD/HD, and some gifted children who can concentrate for long periods of time on areas of interest may not be seen as AD/HD even when they are. Thus, knowledge about what is giftedness and what is AD/HD is vital in assessing AD/HD, and in ensuring that gifted children are not misdiagnosed.

Colleen Willard-Holt suggests these questions to ask in differentiating between giftedness and ADHD:**

- Could the behaviors be responses to inappropriate placement, insufficient challenge, or lack of intellectual peers?
- Is the child able to concentrate when interested in the activity?
- Have any curricular modifications been made in an attempt to change inappropriate behaviors?
- Has the child been interviewed? What are his/her feelings about the behaviors?
- Does the child feel out of control? Do the parents perceive the child as being out of control?
- Do the behaviors occur at certain times of the day, during certain activities, with certain teachers or in certain environments?

In May 2000, the American Academy of Pediatrics issued new guidelines for diagnosing ADHD in children ages 6–12. Treatment guidelines are in development. For more information, see References and Resources at the end of this chapter.

* Lovecky, Dierdre V., Ph.D. "Gifted Children with AD/HD." Providence, RI: Gifted Resource Center of New England, 1999.

** Willard-Holt, Colleen. "Dual Exceptionalities." ERIC EC Digest #E574, May 1999.

Children with Asperger's Syndrome

Asperger's Syndrome is present when a person has some features of autism but may not match the entire clinical description of that condition. Asperger's Syndrome is related to hyperlexia, a condition in which a child can read almost any word he encounters but doesn't understand many of the words he recognizes in print.

Children with Asperger's Syndrome tend to:

- Avoid direct eye contact with others.
- Have trouble forming relationships with peers.
- Lack empathy for others.
- Have monotonous speech patterns.
- Be unable to engage in small talk.
- Appear to lack enjoyment in certain situations.
- Exhibit repetitive motor mannerisms, such as tics or hand flapping, which may lead to a misdiagnosis of Tourette's Syndrome.
- Have an unusual but passionate interest in one topic.

Unlike people with autism, persons with Asperger's speak before age 5, experience increased interest in other people as they get older, and can become well-adapted within society.

Some gifted children who exhibit Asperger's characteristics may not be properly identified. Some children who are perceived as odd or eccentric may be victims of Asperger's Syndrome and may benefit from appropriate interventions. For more information, see References and Resources at the end of this chapter.

Ways to Help Twice-Exceptional Students Succeed in School

Twice-exceptional children cannot improve simply by "trying harder." They must be taught specific compensation strategies. They must know and appreciate the fact that they have normal or above-average intelligence. They and the adults in their lives need to understand that their brains are dealing with certain physiological factors that influence their ability to learn. For a better understanding of these issues, I strongly recommend that you watch Dr. Richard Lavoie's videos *How Difficult Can This Be?* and *Last One Picked, First One Picked On.* Or read *Faking It* by Christopher Lee. I also suggest that you read my book, *Teaching Kids with Learning Difficulties in the Regular Classroom.* For more information, see References and Resources at the end of this chapter.

Meanwhile, here are ways you can help the twice-exceptional kids in your classroom:

- Provide a nurturing environment in which individual differences are valued. Teach all kids to respect learning differences in all areas of learning.
- It's unrealistic to expect anyone to be equally capable in all learning areas. Strengths should be recognized and weaknesses compensated for. *Example:* Learning number facts through song and rhythm is much easier for some students with learning disabilities than rote memorization with flash cards.
- Before concluding that a gifted child is lazy or has an attitude problem, consider that poor performance may indicate a learning disability. Look for significant discrepancies in ability subtests, and for evidence of glaring strengths accompanied by equally glaring weaknesses.
- Provide materials that will help students understand their learning difficulties and learn ways to compensate. For suggestions, see References and Resources at the end of this chapter.
- Assess each student's learning style and create tasks that capitalize on their learning style strengths. *Examples:* Kids with learning difficulties often work better in low light, listening to soothing music on tape as they work. They prefer working in more relaxed positions and must be allowed to move about at regular intervals. Eating, chewing, and/or movement may also increase their concentration. Kids with ADHD are more likely to stay focused on a task if it's hands-on or related to a passionate interest. *Tip:* Ask parents to tell you about times at home when their children stay on task for long periods.
- Allow and encourage students to demonstrate their learning in learning-style compatible ways. Avoid traditional remediation techniques (special education classification, tutoring, retention). Instead, teach compensation strategies directly. Compensation enables one part of the brain to take over a function which another part of the brain is unable to do. Be aware that one's ability to compensate can be threatened by anxiety, fatigue, illness, or finding oneself in a totally new situation.

- For global, holistic learners, make sure they see and understand the "big picture" of a unit or story before asking them to learn about it in sections. Graphic organizers can help.
- If students have difficulty writing, give them other options. *Examples:* Instead of reading something and writing about it, they might dictate their learning into a tape recorder or use a computer.
- When students have significant reading problems, texts and other information should be read aloud to them. Recording for the Blind and Dyslexic provides audiotapes of most texts and literature books used in schools, from elementary through post-graduate and professional levels. See References and Resources at the end of this chapter.
- Provide clear, concise written directions, and don't give too many directions at one time. Use colors and shapes to help communicate what is expected. Ask students to describe what they think they are supposed to do before they begin any task.
- Teach organization skills directly to students who need them. Mastering these skills is as important as learning required content. Use the Goal-Setting Log (page 16) to teach students to set short-term, realistic goals, starting with things they can accomplish during the next 30 minutes. Coach them to take pride in these accomplishments. Emphasize that accumulating short-term goals eventually leads to accomplishing longer-term goals.
- Whenever possible, provide students with two sets of books and learning materials—one to use at school and one to take home.
- Recognize that twice-exceptional students, as well as all students with learning difficulties, need longer time periods for completing assignments and for testing. Some students do much better on tests if they can read the test items aloud (or if someone else reads them aloud).
- Whenever possible, design learning experiences for individual students around their passionate interests. Most standards can be taught in almost any context.
- Understand that gifted children with learning difficulties can experience and enjoy many of the same opportunities we offer to gifted students without disabilities. This includes interaction with complex and abstract thinking concepts and project work around areas of intense interest.

UNDERACHIEVERS

As noted earlier, some so-called gifted underachievers are really twice-exceptional. Let's talk briefly about those underachievers who don't have a learning disability or challenge...except the challenge of getting through another endless day at school.

Underachievement, a discrepancy between capability and achievement, can be caused or affected by a variety of factors including:

- Perfectionism.
- Work that is too easy or too difficult.
- The lack of opportunity to demonstrate what they know in their learning style strength.
- The perception that what they are learning does not have any meaningful, relevant, and/or useful real-life application.
- The lack of opportunity to learn about areas of passionate interest to them.
- Fears of being rejected for being different.
- The lack of dreams or goals, or the sense that their dreams or goals are unattainable.
- Family interaction patterns that may interfere with achievement.

The most common complaint about underachievers is, "They won't do their work." In my experience, the reality is that they won't do the teacher's work, but would be very happy to have the teacher provide opportunities for them to work on what is meaningful for them. Until this happens, everyone is caught in the "whose work is it anyway?" power struggle.

Throughout this book, you'll find strategies that will help you avoid and remedy the school-related factors that inhibit achievement while motivating your highly-capable students to demonstrate their advanced abilities in productive ways. When you want to understand the family dynamics that may contribute to underachievement, read Dr. Sylvia Rimm's book, *Why Bright Kids Get Poor Grades and What You Can Do About It*. See References and Resources at the end of this chapter.

STUDENTS FROM DIVERSE POPULATIONS

According to the latest federal definition of giftedness, "Outstanding talents are present in children and youth from all cultural groups, across all economic strata, and in all areas of human endeavor."* Yet many gifted children from ethnically and culturally diverse backgrounds, minority cultures, and economically disadvantaged families continue to fall through the cracks when children are identified for gifted programs and other learning opportunities. There are four main reasons why this happens:

1. Many standardized tests are culturally biased. They assume that all students have had similar life experiences, which many of the children in these groups might not have had. (One test question I saw asked children to imagine a garden party complete with chamber music and finger sandwiches.)

2. The tests use language and idioms with which many of these children might not be familiar.

3. Many of these children attend schools in which gifted education is not a priority. Gifted program opportunities may simply be unavailable.

4. Most teachers don't know how to notice and identify characteristics of giftedness in every student population.

Identifying Gifted Students from Diverse Populations

Despite what we know about standardized tests—they're imperfect, biased, and woefully inadequate at identifying gifted students from diverse populations—they are still used in many schools. It's possible that your school uses standardized tests to identify students for gifted programs and learning opportunities. At the very least, when administering any type of assessment to kids, it's imperative to first give them practice items or activities that will familiarize them with the format of the assessment and help them know what to expect.

There are other options available for identifying these students, and I encourage you to look into them. *Examples:*

- Project START (Support to Affirm Rising Talent) uses a multiple intelligences (MI) model to identify and promote talent in students from culturally diverse and low economic backgrounds in Charlotte-Mecklenburg, North Carolina. In their report on this program, Carolyn M. Callahan et al. concluded that "application of multiple intelligence theory leads to optimistic thinking about students and their nontraditional strengths." **
- Several schools around the country are using a tool called DISCOVER (Discovering Intellectual Strengths and Capabilities through Observation while allowing for Varied Ethnic Responses) created by C. June Maker and her colleagues. Children in kindergarten through second grade perform various problem-solving exercises while trained evaluators watch closely and record their findings. Although it's fairly expensive to train people to observe kids for gifted behaviors, this method accurately identifies students from minority populations.
- The Jefferson County Schools in Golden, Colorado, provide summer school programs for targeted minority students to build up their skills before formal assessment.
- The Mobile County Schools in Mobile, Alabama, are using the Entrada program to identify kids from underserved populations and help them move into gifted programs.
- In South Florida, a program called T.E.A.M. for Success (Teaching Enrichment Activities for Minorities) uses specific criteria to identify students from diverse populations and retain them in gifted programs. Retention is what separates this program from others of its kind, since it has historically been easier to identify gifted kids in minority populations than to keep them in programs for more than one year. The T.E.A.M. program is so successful that teachers of the gifted usually can't tell the difference between kids who entered gifted education via the program and those who entered through more traditional pathways.

For more information about these programs and other tools that can help your school identify gifted

* U.S. Department of Education, *National Excellence: A Case for Developing America's Talent,* Washington, DC: 1993.

** Callahan, Carolyn M., et al. "Project START: Using a Multiple Intelligences Model in Identifying and Promoting Talent in High-Risk Students." Research Monograph 95136. Storrs, CT: NRC/GT, 1995.

students from diverse populations, see References and Resources at the end of this chapter.

There are several nonverbal standardized tests that have successfully been used for this purpose, including the *Ravens Progressive Matrices* and the *Naglieri Non-Verbal Ability Tests.* (See References and Resources.) The results of these tests should be combined with teacher observations over time that look for evidence of particular strengths in any area of learning, especially in open-ended tasks that require creative, visual, and spatial thinking and the ability to solve real problems.

Texas uses an academic portfolio method which looks for evidence of the following:

- Unusual presentation of an idea that demonstrates in-depth understanding.
- Use of ordinary materials in unusual ways.
- Work advanced beyond age or grade-level expectations.
- Complex or intricate presentation of an idea.
- Support of research for the idea.
- Resourceful and/or clever use of materials.
- High interest and perseverance.
- Responses of unusual depth and understanding to art, music, dance, and sound-filled experiences.
- Interest in heroes within his own culture.

You can also watch for students who:

- Exhibit unusual fluency and/or advanced use of their native language.
- May develop fluency in English more quickly than others (if English isn't their native language).
- Can maintain their unique identity while functioning well in the American culture.
- Assume responsibilities maturely.
- Display leadership qualities.
- Absorb information quickly.
- Demonstrate a highly developed sense of humor.
- Have an intuitive grasp of situations; are highly able to adapt to changes.
- See cause-and-effect relationships.
- Show interest in how and why things work.
- Indicate intense interest in one or more topics.
- Display originality.
- Exhibit fluency in creative thinking activities.
- Make intuitive leaps in thinking and problem-solving.
- Exhibit many of the characteristics described on pages 10–11.

In *Teaching Young Gifted Children in the Regular Classroom,* Joan Franklin Smutny, Sally Yahnke Walker, and Elizabeth A. Meckstroth propose two basic guidelines when looking at children from diverse populations:

1. Use the broadest definition of giftedness to include diverse abilities.
2. Find and serve as many children with high *potential* as possible.

They suggest the following identification strategies:*

- Consider every possibility of exceptional skill when seeking to discover a child's outstanding abilities.
- Find a child's "best performance." Look for any sign of exceptional, even isolated, performance that could represent unidentified abilities. If you find one outstanding ability, such as memory for music, you can begin to invite a child's confidence by creating opportunities for her to use that talent. A single encouraging experience can often produce a ripple effect on the child's self-assurance and on the competence she begins to show in other directions.
- Consider "processing" behaviors, such as risk taking and the ability to hypothesize and improvise.
- Ask other teachers.
- Trust your hunches. If you suspect that a child has exceptional abilities, your hunch will probably be reliable.
- Make classroom observations, especially during multicultural-based activities.
- Interview the child to gain insight into her thinking, aspirations, home activities, and sense of self.
- Solicit the parents' views about the child's talents, abilities, and expressions of creative and critical thinking.

Three Ways to Help Students from Diverse Populations

1. Seek out information about how cultural values may impact a child's classroom behavior. *Example:* Many students from Latino cultures prefer working in a communal environment, rather than independently. They enjoy cooperative learning situations and subtle public recognition for their performance and

* Smutny, Joan Franklin, Sally Yahnke Walker, and Elizabeth A. Meckstroth. *Teaching Young Gifted Children in the Regular Classroom,* page 185. Minneapolis: Free Spirit Publishing, 1997. Used with permission of the publisher.

behavior. Many of these students are uncomfortable in competitive situations. Some have been taught at home never to maintain eye contact with an adult, since it is considered disrespectful to do so. Their families and ethnic communities are very important to them.

2. Whenever possible, send messages home in the child's native language. When visiting students' homes, take someone along who can either communicate directly with the family or provide translation assistance. Similar opportunities should be available when these students need counseling or social work services at school.

Joan Smutny et al. note that "language and cultural differences can keep parents away and can distance teachers from discovering children's exceptional abilities. One important and very effective way to bridge this gap is by working with your school or district to establish a 'cultural liaison,' a contact person for parents who are not comfortable speaking English."

3. Integrate curriculum from other cultures in literature, biography, and history activities. This shows students that the school values their uniqueness. It's much more effective than reserving cultural information and experiences for "multicultural fairs."

QUESTIONS AND ANSWERS

"Is it true that gifted kids are likely to have social problems?"

Gifted kids are often perceived as lacking in social skills. This is sometimes used as a reason to hold them back a year in school, so they have time to learn how to get along better with their peers. It's true that gifted children may seem socially inept when we observe them with their age peers. But put them together with their learning or passionate-interest peers—older kids, adults, or other children who share their gifts—and many function just fine. Please don't ever judge a gifted child's social skills based only on his interactions with his age peers. And please don't deprive him of appropriate learning opportunities in order to focus all of his school time on his social interaction skills.

Some gifted youngsters, especially those who are profoundly gifted, do need coaching in how to be more comfortable and functional in social situations at school and in the larger world. Role-playing can be helpful but should be done in private. What's most helpful—and most appreciated by gifted kids and their families—is providing regular opportunities for these children to be with each other in learning and social situations. Chapter 8 explores the topic of grouping gifted kids.

"In our school, children aren't formally identified as gifted until fourth grade. Given recent findings about how important it is to stimulate a child's brain at an early age, I wonder if this is too late."

It is more difficult to formally identify giftedness in young children. However, it's not impossible, and there are compelling reasons to make the attempt. Gifted kids who have experienced frustration and boredom in the primary years may "go underground" in the upper and middle school grades.

There are some formal instruments that are reliable and valid for this age group. *Examples:*

- The *Kingore Observation Inventory (KOI)* improves observational skills in teachers of kids from kindergarten to grade 3.
- The *Otis-Lennon School Abilities Test* assesses cognitive abilities of students in grades K–12.
- The *Peabody Picture Vocabulary Test–III* measures receptive English vocabulary in children as young as $2^1/_2$.
- The *Cognitive Abilities Test (CogAT)* assesses reasoning and problem-solving abilities of students in grades K–12.

For more information on identifying young gifted children and giving them the best education possible, I recommend that you read *Teaching Young Gifted Children in the Regular Classroom.* See References and Resources at the end of this chapter.

SUMMARY

Identifying gifted students has always been a tricky process. Historically, we have identified some kids as gifted who were simply high achievers, and we have failed to identify truly gifted students who were nonproductive in school. Some gifted students have not been identified because they have a learning disability that masks their gifted ability. Some have not been identified because their performance on standard identification instruments has been hampered by multicultural or socioeconomic issues.

This chapter has made you more aware of the various ways in which gifted ability can manifest itself and be identified. Subsequent chapters will demonstrate how your gifted students can actually identify themselves when you provide consistent opportunities for kids who need compacting and differentiation to demonstrate those needs and have them fulfilled in heterogeneous classrooms.

REFERENCES AND RESOURCES

This chapter is meant as an overview of gifted characteristics, not as the last word. When you want to know more about the topics touched on here, this References and Resources section will give you many options and much food for thought.

Giftedness

Clark, Barbara. *Growing Up Gifted: Developing the Talent and Potential of Children at Home and at School.* 5th ed. Paramus, NJ: Charles E. Merrill, 1997. The definitive textbook for parents and teachers; a comprehensive treatment of most aspects of educating and parenting gifted learners.
—— *Optimizing Learning: The Integrative Education Model in the Classroom.* Columbus, OH: Charles E. Merrill, 1986. Demonstrates how all students can learn more effectively.

Colangelo, Nicholas, and Gary A. Davis. *Handbook of Gifted Education.* 2nd ed. Needham Heights, MA: Allyn & Bacon, 1996.

Dabrowski, K. *Theory of Positive Disintegration.* MENSA Journal 327. Brooklyn, NY: Mensa Education and Research Foundation, 1989. See also:

- Hafenstein, N. L., and B. Tucker. "Psychological Intensities in Young Gifted Children." Denver, CO: Ricks Center for Gifted Children, 1995. Paper presented at the Esther Katz Rosen Symposium on the Psychological Development of Gifted Children (Lawrence, KS, September 8–9, 1995). This ongoing study is examining Dabrowski's ideas concerning psychic overexcitability in gifted children by describing the overexcitabilities exhibited by five young gifted children. The children, ages 3 and 4, attend a private school for gifted children and were selected to provide examples of the five different types of overexcitability postulated by Dabrowski.
- Piechowski, Michael. "Emotional Development and Emotional Giftedness." In *Handbook of Gifted Education,* 2nd ed. Includes a description of Dabrowski's theory.
- Bill Tillier's Web site (positivedisintegration.com). Includes an introduction to Dabrowski's psychological model, a glossary of terms and concepts, bibliographies, links, and more.

Kingore, Bertie. *Implementing Portfolios.* Austin, TX: Professional Associates, 1997. Using portfolios to identify gifted students and document learning progress for all students.
—— *The Kingore Observation Inventory (KOI).* Austin, TX: Professional Associates, 2000. An observational tool for identifying gifted kids in the primary grades.

Passow, Harry, ed. *Educating the Gifted and Talented.* Reading, PA: Addison Wesley Educational Publishers, 1999.

Schmitz, Connie, and Judy Galbraith. *Managing the Social and Emotional Needs of the Gifted.* Minneapolis: Free Spirit Publishing, 1985. Helpful information for classroom teachers who want to understand all aspects of gifted children.

Smutny, Joan Franklin, ed. *The Young Gifted Child: Potential and Promise: An Anthology.* Creskill, NJ: Hampton Press, 1998. Joan Smutny has collected a wealth of information from numerous sources in this comprehensive examination of the issues and practices surrounding the topic of young children who are gifted.

Smutny, Joan Franklin, Sally Walker, and Elizabeth A. Meckstroth. *Teaching Young Gifted Children in the Regular Classroom.* Minneapolis: Free Spirit Publishing, 1998. The companion to this book, for teaching gifted kids ages 4–9.

Torrance, Paul, and Dorothy Sisk. *Gifted and Talented Children in the Regular Classroom.* Buffalo, NY: Creative Education Foundation, 1998.

U.S. Department of Education, Office of Educational Research and Improvement. *National Excellence: A Case for Developing America's Talent.* Washington, DC: 1993. A conclusive, easy-to-understand report on gifted children's educational needs. Call (877) 4-ED-PUBS to request a copy, or read it on the Web (www.ed.gov/pubs/DevTalent/toc.html).

U-STARS by Mary Ruth Coleman. A Javits grant program to observe primary students doing science tasks and identify gifted behaviors. Contact the program's office at the University of North Carolina, Chapel Hill: (919) 966-2622.

Winner, Ellen. *Gifted Children: Myths and Realities.* New York: Basic Books, 1996. Examines commonly held beliefs about gifted children and advocates raising educational standards for all children.

Perfectionism

Adderholdt, Miriam, and Jan Goldberg. *Perfectionism: What's Bad About Being Too Good?* Rev. ed. Minneapolis: Free Spirit Publishing, 1999. Information on the causes and consequences of perfectionism and strategies for avoiding (or escaping) the perfectionism trap.

Creativity

de Bono, Edward. *Six Thinking Hats.* Boston: Little, Brown & Co., 1999. Teaches kids how to see any situation from several different perspectives. From the creator of *Lateral Thinking.*

Draze, Dianne. *Creative Problem Solving for Kids.* San Luis Obispo, CA: Dandy Lion, 1994.

Eberle, Bob, and Bob Stanish. *CPS for Kids: A Resource Book for Teaching Creative Problem-Solving to Children.* Waco, TX: Prufrock Press, 1996. Activities for students in grades 2–8.

Khatena, Joe. *Enhancing the Creativity of Gifted Children: A Guide for Parents and Teachers.* Cresskill, NJ: Hampton Press, 1999.

PRIDE, GIFT, GIFFI I, and GIFFI II by Sylvia Rimm. Available from Educational Assessment Service, Watertown, WI, (800) 795-7466 (www.sylviarimm.com).

Torrance Tests of Creative Thinking. Available from Scholastic Testing Service, Bensenville, IL, (800) 642-6787 (www.ststesting.com).

Twice-Exceptional and Underachievers

AEGUS (Association for Education of Gifted Underachieving Students). Contact president Lois Baldwin at the BOCES (Board of Cooperative Educational Services) office in New York.

American Academy of Pediatrics. "Diagnosis and Evaluation of the Child with Attention-Deficit/Hyperactivity Disorder." *Pediatrics* 105:5, 1158–1170, May 2000. Guidelines for children ages 6–12 based on recent research. Read it on the Web (http://aappolicy.aappublications.org/cgi/content/abstract/pediatrics;105/5/1158)

Armstrong, Thomas. *ADD/ADHD Alternatives in the Classroom.* Alexandria, VA: ASCD, 1999. Describes non-medical interventions for children with attention deficit disorders. Encourages educators to look beyond a deficit approach and teach to students' multiple intelligences and learning styles.
—— *Multiple Intelligences in the Classroom.* 2nd ed. Alexandria, VA: ASCD, 2000. Tools, resources, and ideas teachers can use to help all students achieve their full potential. Updated with information on the eighth intelligence (naturalist) and possible ninth (existential).

Baum, Susan, and John Dixon. *To Be Gifted and Learning Disabled.* Mansfield Center, CT: Creative Learning Press, 1991. Helps parents and teachers understand twice-exceptional students.

Birely, Marlene. *Crossover Children: A Sourcebook for Helping the Learning Disabled/Gifted Child.* Reston, VA: Council for Exceptional Children, 1995.

Coil, Carolyn. *Becoming an Achiever: A Student Guide.* Dayton, OH: Pieces of Learning, 1994. Covers goal-setting, time management, study skills, motivation, test-taking, and organizational skills.

Cummings, Rhoda, and Gary Fisher. *The School Survival Guide for Kids with LD (Learning Differences).* Minneapolis, Free Spirit Publishing, 1991. Specific tips and strategies for students with LD. For ages 8 and up.

Dixon, John. *The Spatial Child.* Springfield, IL: Charles C. Thomas, 1983. An excellent source for understanding right-brain, visual-spatial learners who often do not appear to be gifted, even though they are.

Edu-Kinesthetics, Inc., Ventura, CA, (888) 388-9898 (www.braingym.com). Publishes and distributes materials for kinesthetic learners. Their Brain Gym program has been used successfully by parents and teachers to significantly improve learning attitudes and achievement. It works on the assumption that people with learning difficulties have immature nerve networks in the brain which can be improved through certain forms of exercise. Teachers have found that if they precede each learning activity with 2–3 minutes of exercise, kids are more able to focus on the actual lesson.

Freed, Jeffrey. *Right-Brained Children in a Left-Brained World: Unlocking the Potential of Your ADD Child.* New York: Simon and Schuster, 1998. Helps parents and teachers understand and help right-brained learners. Lots of tips on how to help them develop more effective skills for learning content.

Gardner, Howard. *Intelligence Reframed: Multiple Intelligences for the 21st Century.* New York: Basic Books, 1999.

Guyer, Barbara, and Sally Shaywitz. *The Pretenders: Gifted People Who Have Difficulty Learning.* Homewood, IL: High Tide Press, 1997. How gifted people overcome learning difficulties.

Johns Hopkins University Center for Talented Youth Staff. *The Gifted Learning Disabled Student.* Rev. ed. Baltimore, MD: Johns Hopkins University, 1991. Contact the Center for Talented Youth, (410) 735-4100.

Jones, Carroll. *Social and Emotional Development of Exceptional Students: Handicapped and Gifted.* Springfield, IL: Charles C. Thomas, 1992.

Kay, Kiesa, ed. *Uniquely Gifted: Identifying and Meeting the Needs of Twice-Exceptional Students.* Gilsum, NH: Avocus Publishing, 2000. Chapters by 43 authors consider all types of situations in which gifted students also have significant learning difficulties. Read about it on the Web (www.uniquelygifted.org).

Lavoie, Richard. *How Difficult Can This Be? The F.A.T. City Workshop.* 70-minute video. Lavoie leads a group of parents, educators, psychologists, and children through a series of exercises that cause Frustration, Anxiety, and Tension, feelings familiar to children with learning disabilities. Available from PBS Video, (800) 531-4727 (www.shoppbs.org).
—— *Last One Picked...First One Picked On.* 62-minute video. Lavoie addresses the social problems that children with LD face and offers practical solutions. Available on Amazon.com.

Lazear, David. *Eight Ways of Teaching.* Arlingon Heights, IL: Skylight Publishing, 1999. Lazear's updated resource about multiple intelligences in the classroom.

Lee, Christopher, and Shirley Jackson. *Faking It: A Look into the Mind of a Creative Learner.* Portsmouth, NH: Heinemann, 1992. This book, written by a young man with serious learning difficulties, helps people without LD understand what it's like to experience it.

Levine, Mel. *Keeping a Head in School: A Student's Book about Learning Abilities and Learning Disorders.* Toronto: Educator's Publishing Service, 1990. Reader-friendly language, humor, and learning strategies for ages 9–12.

Lovecky, Dierdre V., Ph.D. "Gifted Children with AD/HD." Providence, RI: Gifted Resource Center of New England, 1999. Call (401) 421-3426 or read it on the Web (www.grcne.com/giftedADHD.html).

Reis, Sally M., Terry W. Neu, and Joan M. McGuire. "Talents in Two Places: Case Studies of High Ability Students with

Learning Disabilities Who Have Achieved." Research Monograph 95114. Storrs, CT: NRC/GT, 1995.

Rimm, Sylvia. *Why Bright Kids Get Poor Grades and What You Can Do About It.* New York: Crown Publishing, 1995. Describes how family interactions can create and maintain underachievement patterns in school. Touches somewhat on school-based issues.

Rourke, Byron P. *Nonverbal Learning Disabilities: The Syndrome and the Model.* New York: Guilford Press, 1996.

Supplee, Patricia L. *Reaching the Gifted Underachiever: Program Strategy and Design.* New York: Teachers College Press, 1990. Presents a successful, low-cost K–8 program designed and implemented specifically for gifted underachievers. Part I establishes a theoretical framework. Part II presents the program design, philosophy, rationale, and goals. Part III offers help in the day-to-day practice of teaching, providing curricula, materials, lesson plans, and instructional strategies. This book is out of print but worth looking for in libraries.

Thompson, Sue. *The Source for Nonverbal Learning Disorders.* East Moline, IL: Linguisystems, 1997. (800) 776-4332 (www.linguisystems.com).

Twice Exceptional Child Project. Elizabeth Nielsen and Dennis Higgins are directors of this program at the University of New Mexico in Albuquerque. A source for research and effective practices regarding twice-exceptional learners. Call (505) 277-6652.

Vail, Priscilla L. *Smart Kids with School Problems.* New York: New American Library, 1989. Describes gifted kids who also have learning difficulties.

Waldron, K.A. "Teaching Techniques for the Learning Disabled/Gifted Student." *Learning Disabilities Research and Practice* 6, 40–43, 1991.

West, Thomas. *In the Mind's Eye: Visual Thinkers, Gifted People with Dyslexia and Other Learning Difficulties, Computer Images, and the Ironies of Creativity.* Amherst: Prometheus Books, 1997. A thorough discussion of learning difficulties and an overview of neurological research.

Whitmore, Joanne. *Giftedness, Conflict and Underachievement.* Needham Heights, MA: Allyn & Bacon, 1983. A landmark book highlighting the case studies of several twice-exceptional students in the primary grades—all with high IQs who were misidentified only by their learning challenges. Demonstrates how much the school can do to reverse underachievement. Out of print but available in many college libraries.

Willard-Holt, Colleen. "Dual Exceptionalities." ERIC EC Digest #E574, May 1999 (www.eric.ed.gov). Discusses gifted persons with learning challenges in many areas, including physically, hearing, and visually challenged.

Winebrenner, Susan. *Teaching Kids with Learning Difficulties in the Regular Classroom.* Minneapolis, Free Spirit Publishing, 2006. Ways to help special education, "slow," and "remedial" students learn and achieve.

Diverse Populations

Borland, J.H., and L. Wright. "Identifying Young, Potentially Gifted, Economically Disadvantaged Students." *Gifted Child Quarterly* 38, 164–171, 1994.

Callahan, Carolyn M., et al. "Instruments Used in the Identification of Gifted and Talented Students." Research Monograph 95130. Storrs, CT: NRC/GT, 1995.

The Charlotte-Mecklenburg, North Carolina, schools have been working to develop identification and service methods for children from minority or low socioeconomic groups. Call (980) 343-3000.

Cline, Starr, and Dave Schwartz. *Diverse Populations of Gifted Children.* Upper Saddle River, NJ: Prentice-Hall, 1999.

CultureGrams, Provo, UT, (800) 521-0600 (www.culturgrams.com). Four-page briefings describe a nation's background, society, and highlight the people's daily living patterns, customs, courtesies, and lifestyles. Available for more than 200 countries around the world.

DISCOVER (Discovering Intellectual Strengths and Capabilities while Observing Varied Ethnic Responses) Projects. Trains teachers how to identify gifted children from culturally diverse populations, specifically Hispanic. Dr. C. June Maker designed the program. Contact the University of Arizona, (520) 622-8106.

Ford, Donna. "Desegregating Gifted Education: A Need Unmet." *Journal of Negro Education* 64, 52–61, 1995.
—— "The Recruitment and Retention of African American Students in Gifted Education Programs." Research Document RBDM 9406. Storrs, CT: NRC/GT, 1994. Also Collingdale: DIANE Publishing Company, 1994.
—— *Reversing Underachievement Among Gifted Black Students.* New York: Teacher's College Press, 1996.

Ford, Donna, and J. John Harris. *Multicultural Gifted Education.* New York: Teachers College Press, 1999. Guidelines for identifying and serving gifted students from multicultural populations.

Frasier, Mary, et al. "Core Attributes of Giftedness: A Foundation for Recognizing the Gifted Potential of Minority and Economically Disadvantaged Students." Research Monograph 95210. Storrs, CT: NRC/GT, 1995.
—— "A New Window for Looking at Gifted Children" (including minorities). Research Monograph 95222. Storrs, CT: NRC/GT, 1995.
—— "A Review of Assessment Issues in Gifted Education and Their Implications for Identifying Gifted Minority Students." Research Monograph 95204. Storrs, CT: NRC/GT, 1995.
—— "Toward a New Paradigm for Identifying Talent Potential." Research Monograph 94112. Storrs, CT: NRC/GT, 1994.

The Jefferson County Schools in Golden, Colorado, provide summer school programs for targeted minority students to build up their skills before formal assessment. Call (303) 982-6606.

Khatena, Joe. *Gifted: Challenge and Response in Education.* Itasca, IL: F.E. Peacock, 1992. Includes information on identifying culturally diverse gifted students.

Maker, C. June, and Shirley Schiever, eds. *Critical Issues in Gifted Education: Defensible Programs for Cultural and Ethnic Minorities.* Austin, TX: PRO-ED, 1989. Presents options about four multicultural groups: Hispanic, Native American, Asian American, and African American.

Maker, C. June. "Identification of Gifted Minority Students." *Gifted Child Quarterly* 40, 41–50, 1996.

Peterson, Jean Sunde. "Gifted—Through Whose Cultural Lens?" *Journal for the Education of the Gifted* 22:4, 354–383, 1999. Examines themes that emerged in the language of Latino, African American, Native American, immigrant Asian, and low-income Anglo individuals as they nominated individuals for a hypothetical gifted program.

Project STEP-UP (Systematic Training for Educational Programs for Underserved Pupils). A program to train teachers, administrators, and parents of high-potential minority economically disadvantaged students. Contact Dr. Dorothy Sisk, School of Education and Human Development, Lamar University, Beaumont, TX, (409) 880-8046.

Standardized Tests. Some standardized assessments that are culturally and economically bias-free are:

- *Culture Fair Test* by R. B. Cattell and A. K. S. Cattell. From the Institute for Personality and Ability Testing (IPAT), Champaign, IL, (800) 225-IPAT (www.ipat.com).
- *Naglieri Non-Verbal Ability Tests.* From Harcourt-Brace, (800) 211-8378.
- *Otis-Lennon School Abilities Test.* From the Assessment Resource Center, University of Missouri, Columbia, (800) 366-8232.
- *Peabody Picture Vocabulary Test–III.* Answers can be allowed in student's native language. From American Guidance Service, Circle Pines, MN, (800) 328-2560.
- *Ravens Progressive Matrices.* A group test of learning ability. From the Psychological Corporation (Harcourt-Brace), (800) 872-1726.

T.E.A.M. for Success (Teaching Enrichment Activities for Minorities). This program in Dade County, Florida, identifies gifted students from culturally diverse groups. It also teaches critical thinking to these kids, who have been dramatically successful in remaining in gifted programs once they were placed. Contact program administrators at (305) 995-1000.

Intelligence Testing and Identification

Contact the Psychology Department of any university. Ask for a trained psychologist or psychometrist to administer an individual IQ test. Ask specifically for *Stanford-Binet Intelligence Scale, Form L–M,* since it has no ceiling and extremely gifted youngsters can be properly identified. Although the norms are outdated, the no-ceiling feature is necessary.

Callahan, Carolyn M., et al. "Instruments Used in the Identification of Gifted and Talented Students." Research Monograph 95130. Storrs, CT: NRC/GT, 1995.
—— "Project START: Using a Multiple Intelligences Model in Identifying and Promoting Talent in High-Risk Students." Research Monograph 95136. Storrs, CT: NRC/GT, 1995.

Gifted Development Center, Denver, CO, (888) GIFTED1 (www.gifteddevelopment.com). Provides comprehensive testing, referrals to testers in other states, and referrals to counselors who have experience in working with gifted kids and their families.

Johnson, Nancy. *The Faces of Gifted.* Dayton, OH: Pieces of Learning, 1989.

Kingore, Bertie. *Implementing Portfolios.* Austin, TX: Professional Associates, 1997. Using portfolios to identify gifted students and document learning progress for all students.
—— *The Kingore Observation Inventory (KOI).* Austin, TX: Professional Associates, 2000. An observational tool for identifying gifted kids in the primary grades.
—— *Portfolios: Enriching and Assessing All Students: Identifying the Gifted Grades K–6.* Austin, TX: Professional Associates, 1993.

Riverside Publishing, Rolling Meadows, IL, (800) 323-9540 (www.riverpub.com). Publishers of the *Cognitive Abilities Test (CogAT)* and other assessment tools.

Slosson Educational Publications, Inc., East Aurora, NY, (888) SLOSSON (www.slosson.com). Sells intelligence and other diagnostic tests, including the *Slosson,* which can be administered by educators who are not trained psychologists.

Other Sources of Information

A.D.D. WareHouse, Plantation, FL, (800) 233-9273 (www.addwarehouse.com). Materials for teaching and parenting kids with learning challenges.

Center for Speech and Language Disorders, Elmhurst, IL, (630) 530-8551 (www.csld.org). Information on hyperlexia and Asperger's Syndrome.

Council for Exceptional Children, Arlington, VA, (888) CEC-SPED (www.cec.sped.org). A complete database for research and interventions for children with all kinds of special educational needs.

ERIC Clearinghouse on Disabilities and Gifted Education. See the archived list of ERIC Digests on the Web (www.eric.hoagiesgifted.org) including "Gifted but Learning Disabled" (E479), "Dual Exceptionalities" (E574), and "ADHD and Children Who Are Gifted" (E522).

Indiana Resource Center for Autism (IRCA), Bloomington, IN, (812) 855-6508 (www.isdd.indiana.edu/~irca). Publications include Stine Levy's "Identifying High Functioning Children with Autism."

The International Dyslexia Association, Baltimore, MD, (410) 296-0232 (www.interdys.org). Formerly the Orton Dyslexia Society.

Irlen Clinic for Perceptual and Learning Development, Long Beach, CA, (800) 554-7536. Ask for referrals to people in your area who can screen children for scotopic sensitivity.

LD OnLine (www.ldonline.org). Clearinghouse for information on children with learning difficulties.

National Research Center on the Gifted and Talented (NRC/GT), University of Connecticut, Storrs, CT, (860) 486-4826 (www.gifted.uconn.edu/nrcgt.html). Visit the Web site for research-based resources, links, and more.

PRO-ED, Inc., Austin, TX, (800) 897-3202 (www.proed inc.com). Materials for all categories of special education and gifted education.

Recording for the Blind and Dyslexic, Princeton, NJ, (866) 732-3585 (www.rfbd.org). The nation's educational library for people with print disabilities, with more than 500,000 titles. Many states have their own libraries. Contact the national office for information.

Supporting the Emotional Needs of the Gifted (SENG), Poughquag, NY, (845) 797-5054 (www.sengifted.org). Helps parents identify giftedness in their children; helps children understand and accept their unique talents. Provides a forum for parents and educators to communicate.

2

Gifted Students Identify Themselves

If you feel unsure about how to identify the gifted students in your class, rest assured that many teachers share your uncertainty. You may have had little or no training in gifted education, because in most states it has never been a required course in teacher education programs. Your administrators may know even less than you, since most of them have had no training either. No wonder you worry about doing the right thing. What if you identify the wrong students and they're not "truly gifted?" What if you fail to identify those kids who are gifted?

Relax! You don't have to formally identify anyone. All you have to do is set up learning opportunities that gifted students will appreciate, and a magical thing happens: The opportunities allow students to identify themselves—not necessarily as gifted, but as students who can benefit from working on activities that extend the regular curriculum. Your other students won't resent the "privileges" some students are getting because all students will have the same opportunities to qualify for extension activities.* With these strategies, "equality" means equal opportunity for everyone to learn at his or her own level of personal challenge.

BANISHING THE "B" WORD

"Boring" is a word that has the power to create a very emotional response in us as teachers. When we hear kids and parents use it, our first response is probably to get defensive as we struggle to explain why all students must do the grade-level work before qualifying for extension activities.

If we personalize the frustration gifted students feel with the regular curriculum, we can better understand their plight. Suppose you sign up for an adult education course. You choose an advanced class that you hope will allow you to expand your skills in a particular area. At the first meeting, you discover that most of the other people in attendance aren't ready for the advanced section. The instructor announces that she will spend several sessions reviewing the basics.

Your precious time is limited. What will you do? Chances are you'll drop the course and seek a more suitable alternative. We adults are allowed to go elsewhere when it appears that our time will be wasted. Gifted students in our schools don't usually have that option. When they think they are starting a year (or a class) filled with new and exciting content, then discover it's going to begin with four to six weeks of intensive review of material they have already mastered, what they feel may be close to panic. Certainly chagrin; certainly an overwhelming sense of "Oh, no, here we go again!" The Jesse James syndrome (see page 7) is alive and well.

The concept of teaching all students at their own challenge level is one with which most teachers agree in principle. Yet in today's heterogeneous classrooms, large class sizes and increasing ranges of ability create significant stresses for teachers who must find ways to reach and teach all of their students. Sometimes, when we try to offer gifted kids

---

* In most schools, these are called "enrichment activities." "Extension activities" makes more sense to me because all students deserve an enriched and enriching curriculum, but only gifted students consistently need us to extend the regular course of study beyond the grade-level parameters.

opportunities for challenge, they refuse to take us up on it. Complacency sets in when gifted students get high grades and everyone (including the students themselves, their parents, and their teachers) sees this as evidence that real learning is taking place. Why should they work harder if they don't have to?

When we assume that the state standards, curriculum guides, or scope-and-sequence charts must be taught to all students, we are confusing the words "teach" and "learn." There is no state or national assessment that can measure how well you have taught. The only thing such assessments can measure is how much your students have learned.

There are probably students in your class right now who could have taken any end-of-the-year standardized test at the start of the year and scored at or above the 95th percentile. They simply don't need the same type of preparation as students who aren't yet ready for the test. When we insist that all students in a given class learn the total content together, we create a situation that most gifted students find very difficult to cope with. Many of them, because they're teacher-pleasers, will go through the motions, do the work, produce some very respectable products, and easily get A's. Others who are less compliant will do some of the work, but it will be sloppy, messy, and/or careless. (Maybe what they're trying to say is, "I know I've got to do this, but I can't stand wasting all this time!") Still others will give up, reject any more repetition, and refuse to do the work at all. It's just *too boring.*

COMPACTING THE CURRICULUM

The work that we plan for our students is really our work. It doesn't become their work until it represents true learning for them. We need to find a way to let students "buy back" the school time we planned for them to spend in one way so they can spend it another way.

Happily, this process already exists. Dr. Joseph Renzulli calls it "compacting." Think of other contexts in which you use this word, and you'll probably come up with images of trash and garbage! Compacting helps students deal with the part of the curriculum that represents "trash" to them because it's expendable. They can throw it away without missing it and without incurring any academic harm, because they already have enough of it to demonstrate mastery.

This chapter describes two key strategies for compacting skill work in reading, vocabulary, spelling, grammar, handwriting, number facts, math computation, and other subject areas. You might anticipate some negative effects from compacting, particularly from students who don't qualify for it. Read on and you'll see ways to avoid this problem. The positive effects are plentiful. Students who have been going through the motions become actively engaged in learning. Messy, careless students start paying attention to the quality of their work. Bored, unmotivated students wake up and want to learn. You, their teacher, delight in observing these changes, and parents are thrilled that you're offering their kids appropriate learning opportunities.

To compact the curriculum, we need to determine what competencies certain students have and give them full credit for what they already know. Then we need to decide how to let them use their "choice time" so it doesn't become a burden to them, their classmates, or to you. Please don't call this "free time," as this is likely to concern parents and administrators. It really isn't free, it's choice.

★ ★ ★ ★ ★ ★ ★

Five Steps to Successful Compacting

1. Identify the learning objectives or standards all students must learn.

2. Offer a pretest opportunity to volunteers who think they may have already mastered the content, OR plan an alternate path through the content for those students who can learn the required material in less time than their age peers.

3. Plan and offer curriculum extensions for kids who are successful with the compacting opportunities.

4. Eliminate all drill, practice, review, or preparation for state or standardized tests for students who have already mastered such things.

5. Keep accurate records of students' compacting activities.

★ ★ ★ ★ ★ ★ ★

How to Use the Compactor

Joseph Renzulli and Linda H. Smith created a record-keeping form called the Compactor to use with students for whom compacting is done. You'll find a reproducible Compactor on page 34 and samples of compactors created for actual students throughout this chapter and in Chapter 7.

1. Use a separate Compactor for each student. You may need to use a new one each month for a student who requires a great deal of compacting.

2. Record all modifications in curriculum.

- In the left column, record the student's areas of strength, one per box.
- In the center column, describe the methods used to document the student's mastery of a particular skill, competency, chapter, concept, or unit.
- In the right column, describe the alternate activities the student will be engaged in during "choice time," while the rest of the class is doing grade level work.

Some teachers make a copy of the required standards in a subject area, insert it in the left column, and check off and date each item as the student demonstrates mastery on pretests.*

Alternate activities are usually drawn from the same subject area from which the student bought back time. Sometimes, however, they may represent different subject areas, or they may be ongoing projects related to the student's passionate interests.

3. Keep a compacting folder for each student for whom you compact the curriculum. Include dated pretests and post-tests, learning contracts (see Chapter 3), any logs of student work, evaluation contracts (see Chapter 4), brief notes about parent or student conferences, and any other pertinent information.

IMPORTANT: Never use the time students buy back from strength areas to remediate learning weaknesses. Always allow students to capitalize on their strengths through activities that extend their exceptional abilities. Remediate their weaknesses only when the whole class is working on those areas of the curriculum.

* Thanks to Carolyn Coil for this excellent suggestion.

Compacting and Flexible Grouping

Perhaps you've been expected to teach students in heterogeneous classrooms as one large group, using direct teaching methods which keep the whole group moving along together as one unit. This style of teaching is almost certain to hold gifted students back from the pace and depth they need.

A practice called flexible grouping provides opportunities for compacting without grouping the entire class in ability-based groups. To group flexibly means to group students together by interest, achievement level, activity preference, or special needs. This type of grouping is not in conflict with the philosophy of heterogeneous grouping. As a matter of fact, even when gifted students are grouped with each other, there is quite a range of abilities, interests, strengths, and weaknesses.

After reading this chapter, you should be ready to start compacting for several students who will benefit from it. The strategies described here and in the rest of this book allow you to regroup students unit by unit who need faster pacing or more complex activities in any area of learning. *Example:* If you have a student who is outstanding in mathematics but average in reading and writing, you would compact for her in math but not in reading and writing. And, no matter how tempting this might be, you would *not* insist that she use her earned choice time to improve her performance in reading and writing. That's not what compacting is about.

A Few Words About Grades

As noted in the Introduction, there's real danger in allowing students to coast through elementary and middle school getting high grades with little or no effort. They infer from this that smart means easy, which can set the stage for later underachievement. It's imperative for gifted kids to experience valid opportunities to work hard to learn new concepts. I'm not suggesting that you make your gifted students fail. I'm suggesting that you help them discover the real joys of learning—those that come from accomplishing difficult things.

When you create challenging learning situations for gifted students, they will probably stop earning easy A's. This may upset them and their parents. You may need to re-educate some parents so they understand the importance of having their children experience frustration and struggle. Chapter 10 provides

THE COMPACTOR
Joseph Renzulli and Linda Smith

Student's Name: ______________________________

Areas of Strength	Documenting Mastery	Alternate Activities

information and reassurance for parents who may be alarmed that their children are no longer bringing home straight A's. See page 204.

If your gifted students and/or their parents are hopelessly addicted to high grades, offer a compromise: In those subject areas where students work on extension activities after demonstrating mastery of grade-level work, their actual recorded grades will only reflect the mastered grade-level material. If the student wants credit for the extension activities, he can earn it by staying on task, adhering to predefined working conditions, persisting with frustrating tasks, or sharing what he learned with the class. In this way, kids will perceive it is safe to try the more challenging activities.

STRATEGY: MOST DIFFICULT FIRST

Most teachers realize that some highly capable learners don't need the same amount of practice and work as their age peers. However, many teachers are afraid to learn the truth about these kids, believing that once they do, they'll have to scramble to find appropriate extension materials.

The Most Difficult First strategy is designed to help you overcome that fear. Try it and you'll discover that your gifted kids would much rather work on activities they choose than ones you choose for them. Once you feel confident that compacting won't create lots of extra work for you to do, you can move on to other strategies in this book that link extension work to the content being studied.

Scenario: Aaron

Aaron was a fourth-grade boy with "great potential" who, according to most of his teachers, had made a career out of "wasting time and not working up to his ability." He had been denied permission to attend the gifted education class because of his poor work habits in his regular classroom.

I offered to visit Aaron's class and demonstrate the Most Difficult First strategy. I suspected it might help Aaron be more productive in math class, and I hoped that would convince his teacher to let him attend the gifted program meetings.

First, I taught the day's math lesson to the class, allowing 20 minutes of practice time at the end so they could start their homework. Aaron was noticeably uninvolved—there was nothing on top of his desk, since he had stated he had no book or materials—but I ignored him. At the end of the instructional time, I wrote the assignment on the board. It looked like this:

> Pages 59–60, 3–5, 8–9, 11–15, 21–23
> ★ #5, #9, #14, #15, #22

Then I told the class:

> I have assigned these problems for your homework, because I think most of you will need that much practice to master the concepts we talked about today. However, I may be wrong, so I've starred the five most difficult problems. Anyone who wants to do the starred problems first, and who can do them neatly, legibly, and correctly—without getting more than one wrong—is done practicing. The problems must be completed and corrected before this math period is over. You've got 20 minutes.

Aaron had been in his characteristic "I-dare-you-to-make-me-work" slouch. As I finished my explanation, his head shot up, and we had the following conversation.

> *Aaron:* "Excuse me...what did you just say?"
> *Me:* "What do you think I said?"
> *Aaron:* "I think you said that if I get those five problems right, and you can read them, I don't have to do my homework!"
> *Me:* "That's correct."
> *Aaron:* "Uh, is my regular teacher going to do this tomorrow?"
> *Me:* "I'm not sure, but I'll bet it has something to do with whether or not it works today."
> *Aaron:* "Yeah, right." *(Pause.)* "Uh, what happens if I get two wrong?"
> *Me:* "Aaron, how much of the 20 minutes' practice time is left?"
> *Aaron:* "Oh, yeah. Right. Okay, I'll give it a try."

Aaron suddenly "found" his math book, a pencil, and some paper in his desk. He got right to work and finished the designated problems accurately and neatly. His teacher had the evidence she needed that he understood the concepts, which made her more willing to let him participate in the

THE COMPACTOR Joseph Renzulli and Linda Smith		
Student's Name: Aaron		
Areas of Strength	**Documenting Mastery**	**Alternate Activities**
Math computation	Most Difficult First	Attendance in CHALLENGE program

gifted program. And Aaron had the joyful feeling that somehow he'd gotten away with something.

How to Use Most Difficult First

1. When giving your class an assignment of skill or practice work, start by determining which items represent the most difficult section of the entire task. These might appear sequentially near the end of the assignment or in various sections of the assignment. Five examples are a reasonable number, but you may choose a few more or less, depending on what seems appropriate.

2. Write the assignment on the board, star the Most Difficult First examples, then give this explanation to the class:

> The regular assignment should give just the right amount of practice for most of you to master the concepts we learned today. As a matter of fact, I expect most of you will need this much practice.
>
> However, some of you may have learned this material before and don't need as much practice. Instead of doing the regular assignment, you may choose to do just the five starred problems, which I consider to be the most difficult problems in the assignment.
>
> When you finish, come to me and I'll check your work. The first person who gets four or five correct will become the checker for the rest of the period, if that person wants the job. If not, I'll wait for someone else to become eligible.
>
> Once I announce who the checker is, anyone else who completes the five most difficult problems should stay at your desk, put your thumb up as a signal, and wait for the checker to get to you. If your work is neat and legible and has no more than one wrong, the checker will collect your paper to give to me.
>
> After the checker has collected your paper, you may use whatever time is left for anything you choose, as long as you follow the Three Magic Rules:*
>
> 1. Don't bother anyone else while you're working.
>
> 2. Don't call attention to yourself or the fact that you're doing something different—it's no big deal.
>
> 3. Work on the extension activity you've chosen.
>
> Anyone who can't follow these rules won't be eligible tomorrow for this opportunity.
>
> During practice time, I'll be helping students who are doing the regular assignment. If you think you'll need help, you should start at the beginning of the assignment, since you obviously need more practice.

3. As you walk around the classroom, giving assistance to students who need it, let those who are working on the Most Difficult First problems come to you. Once you identify the checker (the first stu-

* I call these the Three Magic Rules because they're all I've ever needed to manage a classroom in which some kids are doing something different from the other kids. They're simple, effective, and easy to remember.

dent to meet the criteria), he checks the papers of the remaining students working on the Most Difficult First problems, using his correct paper as the key. When he finds papers that meet the criteria, he collects them to give to you at the end of the period. *Tip:* Finding a checker usually takes less than 5 minutes. After that, you can devote your full attention to helping your struggling students.

4. When the checker delivers the papers to you at the end of the class period, simply put them in a stack to wait for tomorrow, when the papers come in for the rest of the class. Then, as you enter the grades, do a quick spot check for accuracy. If you find an error that wasn't caught yesterday, that student loses the option of trying the Most Difficult First problems for the next assignment. You might also ask your checkers to improve their accuracy.

5. If you use the beginning of the next period to check homework, the students who qualify may again have some choice time—as long as they follow the Three Magic Rules. As soon as you begin the new lesson, they should rejoin the rest of the class for instruction.

To make the most of this strategy, follow these guidelines:

- Limit practice time to 20 minutes or less.
- Don't allow students to correct their own papers. In my experience, gifted students are very competitive in this type of situation, and values get a little muddled. Students wondering how their buddies are faring may not be totally honest. That's why you should correct papers until you identify the checker, and the checker should correct papers after that.
- Don't allow students to correct any errors the checker discovers. Students who get more than one wrong are expected to complete the regular assignment, starting with the easier problems. In the first few days, some kids may come to you to protest, "I was working too fast. I made a careless mistake. I really know how to do it!" Your reaction is always the same: "Exactly right. Better luck tomorrow! Please begin the rest of the assignment." Once students realize that you're not going to become the court of last resort, they will stop bothering you, accept the checker's decision, and start doing more careful work.
- No student should be the checker more than once a week. Some students will want to be the checker all the time as a way to avoid doing the challenging extension activities.

As you can see, this strategy doesn't create any extra paperwork for you, nor do you spend any extra time entering grades. You can still do all of your bookkeeping at once and be available to help your struggling students.

NOTE: Most Difficult First is a very effective way to ask kids who return from pull-out programs to document their mastery, without requiring them to make up all the work they missed. You get the evidence you need that the kids are competent with the material, and they get the consideration they need that being in a pull-out class should not lead to more work for them.

QUESTIONS AND ANSWERS ABOUT MOST DIFFICULT FIRST

See also Questions and Answers About Compacting the Curriculum on pages 43–45.

"Why not require 100 percent accuracy to qualify for compacting?"

We can't convince gifted kids to take risks and try challenging new learning opportunities if we also communicate the expectation that they must perform perfectly. It's important for them to know that making mistakes is part of the learning process. When a student accurately solves four out of five most difficult math problems or correctly spells 90 percent of the spelling or vocabulary words, that's surely enough to indicate mastery.

"What will students do with the time they have left over after successfully completing the Most Difficult First problems?"

Remember, you're limiting practice time to 20 minutes or less. If the kids who are trying to qualify for Most Difficult First are concerned about neatness, legibility, and accuracy, the amount of choice time they have will usually be less than 10 minutes. Some teachers feel that it's perfectly acceptable for students to spend this time working on another subject, doing nothing, or even daydreaming, as long as they don't bother anyone else and don't call attention to themselves.

When we adults finish our work early, we appreciate having some time to spend just as we choose. The same is true for our students. There must be occasions in your classroom when kids can do whatever they like for short periods, even if you use this opportunity as a "carrot" to motivate students to finish their compacted work.

However, we also want to demonstrate that the world is full of exciting things to learn. Therefore, at the start of each unit, consider collecting materials that represent extension activities for the concepts taught in the chapter or the subject area in general. Create an informal Extensions Center in your classroom, using part of a shelf, an empty desk or table, or a learning center format. Students who successfully complete Most Difficult First problems can spend the remaining practice time there. (The Extensions Center will also be used by students working on learning contracts. See Chapter 3.)

You'll want to spend some time with kids as they work on extension activities. Be sure to keep records of their work in their compacting folders.

IMPORTANT: All extension activities should be self-correcting. You already have evidence that students know the content, so it isn't necessary for you to correct and grade their extension work. Make answer keys available so they can check it themselves.

"Shouldn't I be concerned if some students just 'vegetate' and waste their choice time?"

When you create a lesson plan, you're "budgeting" the time it will take for average students to master the material. When some kids demonstrate that they don't need all the time you've budgeted, any remaining time should become their own, to spend on choice activities.

The real purpose of Most Difficult First is to help you see that gifted students can use choice time without you having to hand them replacement activities. Knowing this, you can start trusting that it's okay to relinquish the need to control every minute of the time they spend in school, and you can move on to using some of the other strategies described in this book.

Gifted kids love the idea of "buying back time" (Dr. Joseph Renzulli's words); it's like being able to spend their allowance on whatever they want. And they're not the only ones who enjoy this. Try to set up situations every now and then when the whole class can buy back time for choice activities of their own.

"I rarely teach skills in isolation. How can I apply the Most Difficult First strategy in these cases?"

You might design an assessment instrument that gives students an opportunity to demonstrate mastery of concepts you're about to teach. Some students will still need differentiated activities that allow them to apply basic concepts to more complex activities. Here's where your kid-watching skills will come in handy. *Example:* When you see a child take a simple task in creating patterns and turn it into a complex pattern, this is evidence that she needs more challenging tasks.

Chapter 3 describes a Learning Contract strategy that might be more appropriate in this situation than Most Difficult First. Every holistic math or reading program I've seen lends itself to pre-assessment, with a little creativity on your part.

Finally, you might compact in days for these kids, allowing them one or two days off each week from group work when they demonstrate less need for direct teacher instruction and ongoing high levels of mastery.

"Is it okay for Most Difficult First to be the only differentiation method available to gifted students in my classroom?"

No, because the students are still required to stay with the class during the entire lesson, and you may be spending many days teaching concepts they have already mastered. Most Difficult First is designed to be used first, so you can see that compacting doesn't create that much extra work for you, and that most gifted students can be trusted to fill their choice time with activities that are meaningful to them.

Use this option for two weeks, then move on to other strategies described in this book. Or you might incorporate Most Difficult First into the Learning Contract strategy described in Chapter 3. Parents of gifted kids have a right to expect that their children will be challenged on a regular basis. Most Difficult First doesn't provide challenging activities as regularly as learning contracts do.

"Does Most Difficult First work as well for other areas of the curriculum as it does for math?"

Yes. Feel free to try it with grammar, language mechanics, reading vocabulary, handwriting, or other skill work which students may have previously mastered. It's also a good strategy to suggest to colleagues who want to try something for their gifted students, but are worried that this might create too much extra work for them. Most Difficult First will relieve this concern and free teachers to move on to other differentiation strategies.

STRATEGY: PRETESTS FOR VOLUNTEERS

Whenever you are teaching skills in any subject area, the assessment you plan to use at the *end* of the unit should be available for volunteers to take at the *beginning* of the unit. Give all students a few moments to look over the upcoming content. Then invite volunteers—students who think they can demonstrate they are already at a mastery level—to take the pretest.

I don't support the practice of having all kids take a pretest at the beginning of a unit. This is frustrating for students who aren't familiar with the content, and it can be totally disheartening for struggling students, who see their peers proceeding with some degree of competence at something that's totally new to them.

Scenario: Ardith

Ardith was a very talented speller who consistently earned high grades on her spelling tests, which made it clear that she didn't need the coming week's spelling lessons. I excused her from sitting through them and also from the post-test. Instead, I gave her the list of extension activities found on page 40.

This list is reproducible so you can use it with your students. *Tips:* In my experience, many students choose activity 1: "Working with a partner who also passed the pretest, find 10 unfamiliar words...." And many choose activity 2: "Keep track of words you misspell in your own writing." This is called functional spelling, since it helps students learn the words they need to function well in their writing. Some teachers use the Alternate Spelling Activities with all students. Kids who pass the pretest study the alternate words; kids who don't pass it study the regular words. All kids choose the way they will study their own list.

Activity 14 asks students to create Super Sentences. Learn about Super Sentences starting on page 111.

NOTE: Some teachers require really good spellers to pretest only once every six weeks during review units. Others skip the review units entirely, allowing all students in the class to choose their own personal spelling list that week. This enables the whole class to have a choice time in spelling on a regular basis.

THE COMPACTOR
Joseph Renzulli and Linda Smith

Student's Name: Ardith

Areas of Strength	Documenting Mastery	Alternate Activities
Spelling	Passed pretest with an A	Will choose from list of alternate spelling activities OR write ongoing stories, poems, etc.

★ ALTERNATE SPELLING ACTIVITIES ★

If you pass a spelling pretest with a score of 90% or higher, you are excused from the week's regular spelling activities and the final test. Choose from this list of alternate activities.

Using New Words

1. Working with a partner who also passed the pretest, find 10 unfamiliar words from glossaries of books in our room. (You choose 5 and your partner chooses 5.) Learn their meanings and spellings. When the rest of the class is taking the final spelling test, you'll test each other on your personal spelling list. Here's how:
   - **a.** Partner A dictates words 1–5 to Partner B, one at a time. Partner B gives a meaning for each word before writing it down.
   - **b.** Partner A dictates words 6–10 to Partner B, who writes them down (no meanings needed).
   - **c.** Partner B dictates words 1–5 to Partner A, who writes them down (no meanings).
   - **d.** Partner B dictates words 6–10 to Partner A, who gives a meaning for each word before writing it down.

   In other words, Partner A defines 5 of the words, Partner B defines the other 5, and both partners spell all 10. Words are counted wrong if either spelling or meaning are not correct.
2. Keep track of words you misspell in your own writing. When you have collected 5 words, learn them.

Keep a list of any words you don't master in activities 1 and 2. Learn them the next time you get to choose your own spelling list.

Using Regular or Alternate Words

3. Use all the words to create as few sentences as possible.
4. Create a crossword or an acrostic puzzle on graph paper. Include an answer key.
5. Learn the words in a foreign language. Use the words in sentences.
6. Group the words into categories you create. Regroup them into new categories.
7. Create greeting card messages or rebus pictures.
8. Create an original spelling game.
9. Create riddles with the words as answers.
10. Create limericks using the words.
11. Write an advertisement using as many of the words as you can.
12. Use all of the words in an original story.
13. Create alliterative sentences or tongue-twisters using the words.
14. Using a thesaurus, find synonyms for the words and create Super Sentences.
15. Use the words to create similes or metaphors.
16. Create newspaper headlines using the words.
17. Using an unabridged dictionary, locate and describe the history of each word (its etymology). Create flow charts to show how the meaning of each word has changed over time.
18. Create a code using numbers for each letter of the alphabet. Compute the numerical value of each word. List the words from the highest to lowest value.
19. Take pairs of unrelated spelling words and put them together to create new words. Invent definitions.
20. Create your own activity. Get your teacher's permission to use it.

Scenario: Elizabeth

Elizabeth was a twice-exceptional child with strong map skills, which she demonstrated by acing the end-of-unit test before the unit began (see pages 18–19). For the next six weeks, while the rest of the class learned basic map skills, she spent those 45 minutes a day working on a project that represented true learning for her. We discussed several options, and she chose to create an imaginary country. Because her learning disability prevented her from writing well, she made a papier-mâché model showing the population centers, natural resources, manufacturing centers, agricultural products, and other features.

During that time, how many students complained, "That's not fair! Elizabeth doesn't have to do the same work we're doing"? None, because everyone had been given the same opportunity to document mastery. However, students did ask, "Can we do what Elizabeth's doing? It looks like fun!" In response to their interest, and after Elizabeth had shared her project with the class in a verbal report, I used a similar activity for small groups as a culminating project for the map unit, and Elizabeth served as a "create-a-country consultant" to the groups. Her self-esteem soared as her image changed from a needy student with a learning disability to an expert others turned to for help and advice.

NOTE: This strategy suggests paper-and-pencil pretests, but I hope you'll feel free to use other types of assessment that are compatible with your teaching philosophy and style. *Examples:* Before beginning a map unit, you might ask students to locate features on actual maps. Or ask the class to tell you what they already know about maps, and observe for students who seem extremely knowledgeable. Any method that helps you identify students who need compacting is fine.

Scenario: James

The other student who aced the map unit pretest was James. He was one of the most gifted writers I had ever taught; at 11 years of age, he was already writing pieces typical of much older students. He knew he didn't need the map work, but he thought it was rude to second-guess the teacher, and he never would have dreamed of asking for any kind of special consideration.

James had been an excellent student in the first quarter of the year, and I was surprised when his parents suggested they might take him out of our school to send him to a special school for gifted children. When I asked them why, they replied that they were concerned that James was not being adequately challenged in my class. "As a matter of fact," his mother said, "his day really starts at about 3:45 P.M.

THE COMPACTOR
Joseph Renzulli and Linda Smith

Student's Name: *Elizabeth*

Areas of Strength	Documenting Mastery	Alternate Activities
Map unit	*Achieved an A on pretest*	*Will create a country from papier-mâché* *Will present report to class* *Will consult with other students to help them create their own countries*

THE COMPACTOR
Joseph Renzulli and Linda Smith

Student's Name: James

Areas of Strength	Documenting Mastery	Alternate Activities
Language arts, spelling, writing, grammar, mechanics	Pretest results of A on review tests	Will write his book when class is working on skills he has already mastered
Reading	Pretest results of A on review tests of skills and vocabulary	Will read to gather research for his book Will write his book Will join the class for two literature circles
Maps	Pretest results of A	Will write his book INSTEAD of doing extension activities in map-related work. Was given options and chose this.

It takes him 15 minutes to get home from school, and that's when he begins what he calls his 'real work.'"

"What is his 'real work'?" I asked.

"He's writing a book," she replied.

James was indeed writing a book. It was called "The Anatomy, Physiology, and Cetera of the Human Body by James T. Myers, Age 11." Since this happened before home computers were in common use, he was printing it in pencil in two columns to resemble a textbook, and illustrating it himself. Some of his pictures were very technical, similar to those found in anatomy textbooks. Others were cartoons where, for example, little men in green eye shades and sleeve protectors ran around shouting orders to each other to communicate the message of the DNA molecule. Each chapter described a different system of the human body, and James's incredible sense of humor was rampant throughout.

In James's mind, he came to school to do the work the teacher and the school required, whether or not he actually needed it. But his "real work"—that which represented true learning for him—didn't begin until he got home.

I asked his parents to give me a few weeks to try to solve the problem. During that time, I assessed James in all his areas of academic strength. He was ultimately able to buy back almost half of every school day. During that time, he went off to a corner he had named his "office" to work on his book.

The only times when James needed formal instruction in spelling, language arts, and writing were when I, as the editor of his manuscript, discovered some kind of consistent errors. He attended lessons only when other class members were learning about a concept he needed to master. For his spelling, he kept a list of the words he frequently misspelled in his manuscript, and when he accumulated 10 or so, he studied those (functional spelling).

By earning an A on the map unit pretest, James bought himself an additional three weeks of social studies time. Usually, the alternate activity is related to the curriculum area in which the student has bought back time. Although I showed James the same menu of alternatives I offered to Elizabeth, he opted to work on his book during the time the other students were learning about maps, and I opted to let him. He would have been eligible to buy some time in science and art, but they were both taught by other teachers, so they were not included in his compacting plan with me.

James's Compactor shows exactly where the time came from to work on his book in school.* Since he was obviously gifted in all of the language arts by virtue of his superior writing ability, he took pretests only of review units. His writing portfolio, which contained examples of his writing collected since the beginning of the year, clearly documented his outstanding writing ability and served as additional evidence of his mastery of grade level competencies. James was also able to buy time from our literature-based reading program because he was reading technical material to support the research on his book. Pretests were used to document his mastery of the skills and vocabulary.

How many students asked, "Why doesn't James have to do the work we're doing?" None, because I had described the criteria James had to meet before buying class time to write his book, and I had offered the same opportunity to anyone else who might request it. How many asked, "Why can't we write books, too?" Several, and his modeling led many to write chapter books themselves.

QUESTIONS AND ANSWERS ABOUT COMPACTING THE CURRICULUM

See also Questions and Answers About Most Difficult First on pages 37–39.

"If kids are allowed to get one out of five wrong on the pretest, what grade should I enter in my grade book? Four out of five is 80 percent, and that's a B in our school."

Count that score as 80 percent, then add 10–13 points as a bonus for demonstrating mastery. Or, if your school uses 93 percent as an A, and two wrong out of 20 spelling words represents 90 percent or a B, simply add a three-point bonus to make the A. The issue is mastery, not some arbitrary percentage score.

This may sound glib, but it's really very serious. The only way I know to entice gifted kids to work on more challenging material is to allow them to keep getting the highest grades possible with the grade-level work. If you don't offer compacting opportunities, high grades will happen anyway, but real learning might not.

If you want your gifted students to choose more challenging activities and to work on difficult problems for long periods of time, you must provide an environment where it's safe to risk being wrong. If you grade gifted students' extension activities and average those grades into their formal grades for that subject, they will resist challenging work, telling you that they would rather do "what all the other kids are doing."

If you use a computerized grading program, simply enter the A earned on the pretest in all required spaces for that unit. If your students are so addicted to grades that they won't work without them, allow them to earn an A for every day they follow the Three Magic Rules while working on their alternate activities.

"Where can I find the extension materials my students need, and how can I afford them?"

For suggestions, see pages 193–194. Don't worry; you won't need a large budget for extension materials.

"How should kids keep track of the extension work they do?"

Give each student a folder for storing work in progress. Give them copies of a student log (see pages 16 and 78) and explain how they should use it. Show the logs to parents at conferences, since they document that you've been differentiating the curriculum for their child.

"What if some students need my help to choose and do alternate activities?"

Gifted students who need help from the teacher are still gifted. They may lack the skills they need to work independently. Just because they qualify for alternate activities doesn't mean they automatically know how to manage their time well, use low voices, stay on task, use extension materials, ask for

* Used with permission of James T. Myers.

help when they get stuck, keep track of their work, put things away, and so on.

Meet with your students often to teach these skills—and to prove that they won't lose contact with you when they choose to work more independently. Some students have been known to avoid extension options because they fear losing contact with the teacher. Your plans should include spending regular time with students who work with alternate activities. See the Question Chip Technique on pages 54–55 for a classroom-management strategy.

Remind students often that the purpose of doing extension activities is to learn that it's okay to work on challenging material and still be considered smart.

"Won't students who never qualify for compacting have self-esteem problems or experience resentment?"

When you find yourself considering this question, you will have two choices: You can either deprive your exceptionally capable students of what they need, or you can learn what's causing the self-esteem and/or resentment problems and do something about them.

When you carefully explain that you expect most students will have to do the grade-level work in order to master a concept, students will realize that nothing is wrong with those who don't qualify for compacting. (Naturally, those who do qualify shouldn't brag about it or tease the others.)

Make sure that the activities available to qualifying students are also available at other times to all students. When class members perceive that only the most capable get to do the "fun stuff" on a regular basis, they are likely to resent it. All kids deserve an enriching curriculum—what author and educator Carol Tomlinson calls "respectful work." But only gifted students regularly need extensions beyond the regular curriculum.

As teachers, we meet with few objections when we make modifications that benefit struggling students. We need to offer the same consideration to students at the top end, whose learning needs are just as different. Justice Felix Frankfurter said it best when he observed, "There is nothing so unequal as the equal treatment of unequals." Equality in education has never meant that all students should be treated the same. Rather, it means that all students should enjoy equal opportunities to actualize their learning potential.

"Is it necessary to keep a Compactor for every student who works on differentiated activities during time bought from the regular curriculum?"

It's always a good idea to keep a brief record of changes you make from the regular curriculum for any student, gifted or otherwise, who needs differentiation. Accountability is a concern in education today, and if we choose to deviate from accepted practices, we should have records to document that we're following a specific plan and know what we're doing. Although I don't include compactors for all of the students described in this book, I did, in fact, keep careful records of what they were doing, and I advise you to do the same.

"Won't it harm the students not to do the regular work?"

The idea of compacting causes anxiety for some teachers. They feel that the curriculum publishers "must know what they're doing" and "there must be some important reason why the adopted program is teaching a certain concept at a certain time." If you're worried, for example, that some of your students won't learn a particular spelling rule because they're working on alternate activities, ask them to find words from other sources that demonstrate that rule. When the spelling book teaches compound words, have the students create their alternate lists with compound words. The students will still be learning the same concepts as the rest of the class. They'll just be doing it with words that are challenging to them. If you recall the difference between the concepts of teach and learn, you'll be able to look at this issue from a more relaxed perspective.

"What if some students sneak their spelling books home on Friday and cram for the test over the weekend? Won't they forget very quickly how to spell the words?"

Under present circumstances, when do students "sneak" their spelling books home to study? The answer is Thursday night or never! So let them sneak their spelling books home. How can it hurt your public relations if parents see their kids calling up their friends on the weekend and begging them to come over so they can study spelling?

You may observe that some kids do very well on spelling tests but seem unable to transfer good spelling to their written work. If this happens with the pretest method, we know it can happen anyway using a traditional format for spelling, so let's not blame the pretest method. Use functional spelling (having students keep track of and learn words they misspell in their own writing) to address this problem.

"What if a terrible speller accidentally passes the pretest?"

Congratulate him and let him pretend that he's a great speller for one week, as he works with other kids on the alternate activities he qualified for.

SUMMARY

For content where it's likely that some students have learned and mastered the material at an earlier time, compacting means:

1. finding the students' areas of strength,

2. pretesting to determine which of the concepts you're about to teach they already know,

3. giving them full credit for that content, and

4. allowing them to work on more challenging activities instead of the grade-level work.

Success on pretests provides the evidence you need that some students don't require as much practice as others. Compacting frees them to use that time for work that is more challenging to them.

Gifted students do *not* benefit from doing extra credit work. As soon as they figure out that their "prize" for showing what they know is more work, they might stop demonstrating what they can do. The only students who might benefit from extra credit work are those who actually need the credit, not those who are already getting high grades. Students with high ability should have frequent and consistent opportunities to demonstrate prior knowledge and use their school time for their "real work"—work that represents true learning and actual struggle for them.

Compacting is remarkably successful with students who have become behavior problems and who may be refusing to do their work. Many behavior problems of gifted students are caused by boredom and frustration. When we are in power struggles with such students and worry that they are not doing their work, we are actually insisting that they do *our* work. Use Most Difficult First and pretesting with your students and watch the amazing results.

REFERENCES AND RESOURCES

Reis, Sally, Deborah Burns, and Joseph Renzulli. *Curriculum Compacting: The Complete Guide to Modifying the Regular Curriculum for High Ability Students.* Mansfield Center, CT: Creative Learning Press, 1992. Ways to compact the regular curriculum are described by the educators who invented the process.

Starko, Alane. *It's About Time: Inservice Strategies for Curriculum Compacting.* Mansfield Center, CT: Creative Learning Press, 1986. The first book about compacting has some useful classroom management ideas.

Video staff development packages:

- *Challenging Gifted Learners in the Regular Classroom.* Alexandria, VA: ASCD, 1994. The accompanying manual is written by Carol Tomlinson.
- *Teaching Gifted Kids in the Regular Classroom* by Susan Winebrenner. Designed to support a school-based study group of educators who meet together to provide peer support as they learn and apply compacting and differentiation strategies. An 80-minute DVD demonstrates many of the compacting and differentiation strategies in actual classrooms. A *Discussion Leader's Guide,* written by Susan Winebrenner, assists the person who leads the group. Call (517) 592-8856.

3

Compacting and Differentiation for Skill Work

This chapter presents two strategies for compacting and differentiating instruction in any skill-based area of learning. Most of the examples given are for math skills, but the same techniques can be used with language arts skills, reading skills, and skill or vocabulary work from any other subject area. For specific examples in reading and writing, see Chapter 5.

STRATEGY: THE LEARNING CONTRACT

While trying out the Most Difficult First strategy described in Chapter 2, you might have noticed its shortcomings. Gifted students still have to sit through the teaching of concepts they may have already mastered. They are not allowed to demonstrate mastery until homework (practice) time begins. And some students may need more structure for the time they buy back.

The Learning Contract strategy has none of those shortcomings. It's the most effective strategy I've found for compacting and differentiating pretestable content and skills.

Chapter 4 describes a different strategy for compacting and differentiating in subjects where the material is new to students (so pretesting probably won't work) but gifted kids are likely to learn it much faster than their age peers. These subjects include science, social studies, problem-based learning in math and other areas, literature, and thematic units.

Scenario: Julie

Julie was a fifth grader who had been getting consistent A's in her daily math work and on her quizzes and tests. She appeared to remember most of what she had learned in previous grades, and she seemed to catch on quickly to new concepts. However, she began to develop some distracting behaviors during math class. She stared out the window, occasionally hummed softly, and was frequently found writing notes to friends. It became obvious that part of her problem was boredom with the pace and depth of the fifth-grade math curriculum.

When I explained the Learning Contract option to Julie, it was very appealing to her. She passed the pretest for Chapter 4 with an acceptable score, and I gave her the contract shown on page 48. Checkmarks indicated pages/concepts for which Julie did not demonstrate mastery on the pretest. On days when I taught those, Julie would join the class for direct instruction. No checkmarks indicated pages/concepts for which Julie demonstrated mastery on the pretest. On days when I taught those, Julie would do extension activities.

Julie started spending much more time on math each day, alternating between the regular content and extension activities. Her attitude and productivity in math improved dramatically, as did her behavior during math time.

Introducing the Learning Contract

In keeping with the practice of offering compacting opportunities to everyone in the class, you'll want to introduce and explain the Learning Contract to all of your students. Then they can decide for themselves whether to take advantage of the opportunity to demonstrate previous mastery—and they won't resent those kids who do.

★ LEARNING CONTRACT ★

For: Math Chapter 4

Student's Name: Julie

✓	Page/Concept	✓	Page/Concept	✓	Page/Concept
	60	✓	64	✓	68
✓	61		65		69
	62	✓	66 — Word Problems	✓	70 — Review (even only)
	63		67	✓	Post-test

Extension Options:

SPECIAL INSTRUCTIONS

Versa-Tiles

Write Story Problems

Cross Number Puzzles

Your Idea:

Working Conditions

1. Don't ask the teacher a question someone in your group can answer. Use your group's question chip carefully.
2. If you need help and the teacher is busy, ask someone else, keep trying, or go on to another activity until the teacher is available.
3. Work on math for the entire math period.
4. Don't bother anyone or call attention to yourself in any way.
5. Don't lose your contract.

Teacher's Signature: ______________________

Student's Signature: ______________________

Before starting a new chapter, tell your class:

> We're about to start working on Chapter X. I want everyone to take five minutes to look through the whole chapter. Notice how much of its content you already know.
>
> By the time you get to the end of the chapter, you may feel that much of the material is familiar to you. If you think you know at least 80 percent of the chapter, you may choose to take a pretest today to show me what you know.
>
> The score you get on the pretest will not be entered into my grade book, and it won't count toward your grade for the chapter. The only reason for the pretest is to find out how much you know about the chapter so I can tell if you're eligible for a Learning Contract.

After students have finished looking through the chapter, say:

Now I'm going to give a pretest to anyone who wants to take it. Those of you who score 80 percent or higher will be eligible for a Learning Contract for this chapter. This means you'll be able to work through the chapter more independently. You'll be invited to a meeting where you'll learn all the details about the contract.

Those of you who don't take the pretest, or who do take the pretest but don't score 80 percent or higher, will work through the chapter under my direction.

It's important to understand that I won't think any less of you if you don't take the pretest, or if you take the pretest but don't qualify for a Learning Contract.

CAUTION: Never do a quickie review before the pretest. You're not trying to identify kids who can learn quickly. You're trying to identify kids who already know what you're planning to teach.

You may be wondering, "While some students are taking the pretest, what will the others do?" I recommend letting them use this time to work on some of the same extension activities the contract kids will be working on. Or they might work on extensions related to concepts learned in earlier chapters. This simple technique effectively eliminates much of the potential resentment they might feel toward kids who get contracts. It also shows them that you believe all kids can benefit from extension activities now and then.

You may be thinking, "Kids dread tests. Won't they hate starting a new chapter or unit with a pretest?" In my experience, everyone looks forward to pretest day. Students who want to qualify for a Learning Contract get the chance to try. Those who probably wouldn't qualify get some teacher-directed time to work on extension activities. Gifted students are especially enthusiastic because going on contract means they'll have lots of opportunities to do activities at their own challenge level.

How to Use the Learning Contract

1. Collect extension materials for the chapter or unit you're about to begin, and set up an Extensions Center in your classroom. Use part of a shelf, an empty desk or table, or a learning center format.

If you don't have an Extensions Center, you'll need to think about where you want the contract students to work while you're teaching the rest of the class. Some teachers rearrange the seating chart for each chapter or unit they teach, keeping the students who aren't on contract in the part of the room where they do their direct teaching, and grouping those who are on contract toward the back of the room, where the extension materials are stored. In some schools, contract students spend some of their "extension days" in another room, under the direction of a resource person such as a media center specialist or a librarian.

2. Prepare a master Learning Contract for the chapter or unit. Use the reproducible form on page 50 or create your own.

The Learning Contract should have at least two sections. In the top section, list the content for the chapter or unit, either by page numbers or concepts to be mastered. The chapter tests in most teachers' editions indicate the page on which each concept is taught.

In the next section, list and describe the available extensions. *Tip:* To simplify contract management, offer one option for the first chapter of a unit, add a second option for the second chapter, and so on.

Be sure to include space for a "Your Idea" (student choice) option. Some teachers instruct their students to choose activities that reinforce the concepts covered in the chapter. Others allow students to choose any activity, as long as it relates to the subject being taught. All activities should be self-correcting.

At the bottom of the Learning Contract, you might list the working conditions you expect students to follow. Or create a Working Conditions chart to display in your classroom. That way, you won't have to include conditions on every contract and you can skip this section. As a third alternative, you can give each contract student a copy of the Working Conditions for Alternate Activities form on page 51.

3. Offer a pretest or other type of assessment. Use the same tool you plan to use for a post-test at the end of the chapter or unit. If the teaching materials you are using include both a chapter review and a chapter test, use whichever one is most comprehensive.

Text continues on page 52

★ LEARNING CONTRACT ★

For: ______________________________

Student's Name: ______________________________

✓	Page/Concept	✓	Page/Concept	✓	Page/Concept
___	___________	___	___________	___	___________
___	___________	___	___________	___	___________
___	___________	___	___________	___	___________
___	___________	___	___________	___	___________

Extension Options: ______________________________

SPECIAL INSTRUCTIONS

___________ ___ ___ ___ ___ ___ ___ ___ ___

___________ ___ ___ ___ ___ ___ ___ ___ ___

___________ ___ ___ ___ ___ ___ ___ ___ ___

Your Idea:

___________ ___ ___ ___ ___ ___ ___ ___ ___

Working Conditions

____

____

____

____

____

____

Teacher's Signature: ______________________________

Student's Signature: ______________________________

★ WORKING CONDITIONS FOR ALTERNATE ACTIVITIES ★

If you are working on alternate activities while others in the class are busy with teacher-directed activities, you are expected to follow these guidelines.

1. Stay on task at all times with the alternate activities you have chosen.
2. Don't talk to the teacher while he or she is teaching.
3. When you need help and the teacher is busy, ask someone else who is also working on the alternate activities.
4. If no one else can help you, keep trying the activity yourself until the teacher is available. Or move on to another activity until the teacher is free.
5. Use soft voices when talking to each other about the alternate activities.
6. Never brag about your opportunities to work on the alternate activities.
7. If you must go in and out of the room, do so as quietly as you can.
8. When you go to another location to work, stay on task there, and follow the directions of the adult in charge.
9. Don't bother anyone else.
10. Don't call attention to yourself.

I agree to these conditions. I understand that if I don't follow them, I may lose the opportunity to continue working on the alternate activities and may have to rejoin the class for teacher-directed instruction.

Teacher's Signature: ______________________________

Student's Signature: ______________________________

Text continues from page 49

If you want to add some items that aren't included in the tests the publisher provides, feel free—as long as you also include them in the post-test you use to assess the other students later. It's not fair to make the pretest more comprehensive than the post-test.

4. Correct the pretests. Don't allow students to correct their own pretests. Many gifted kids are afraid of losing face if anyone finds out they're not always perfect, so the temptation to "appear perfect" will be great. Also, don't use student checkers. Sometimes checkers are influenced by friendship issues. Plus you don't want other students to know how their classmates scored on the pretest.

5. Prepare contracts for students who score 80 percent or higher. You've already listed the page numbers or concepts for that chapter or unit on your master contract. For each student's contract, simply place a checkmark to the left of the page number or concept for which the student did not demonstrate mastery on the pretest. Those are the pages/concepts for which the student will join the rest of the class for direct instruction. See Julie's contract on page 48 for an example.

Tip: Before giving out the contracts, indicate in your grade book which pages/concepts you've checked for each student. One way to do this is by drawing a red box around the square that indicates a specific page/concept. As you begin each class, you'll be able to tell at a glance which students will be receiving direct instruction and which will be working on extension activities. For contract students, squares without red boxes indicate pages/concepts for which the student demonstrated mastery on the pretest.

If you use a computerized grading program and can't use the red-box method, keep copies of student contracts for yourself.

NOTE: If you use cooperative learning groups, create them now. Place contract students together in their own group or groups. Place all other students in heterogeneous groups in which kids who are capable in the subject are mixed with those who are average and below average. (For more on cooperative learning, see Chapter 8.)

6. Invite contract students to an informational meeting with you during class time. See At the Contract Meeting below.

7. Offer Most Difficult First (see pages 35–36) daily so gifted kids can still do compacted work even on days when they're being instructed with the larger group.

Remember that Most Difficult First is also an effective way to allow students returning from out-of-class experiences (such as pull-out programs) to document their mastery. If kids only have to make up five of the examples they missed, they won't feel so torn about leaving the home classroom in the first place.

At the Contract Meeting

1. Greet the students and explain that everyone there scored 80 percent or higher on the pretest. *Tip:* Since you're not recording the grades, don't tell students their exact scores. The perfectionists in the group will be upset to learn that they scored less than 100 percent.

2. Hand out the learning contracts. Draw students' attention to the first section—the one that lists the pages/concepts to be mastered. Explain that a checkmark indicates something they *have not* mastered. On those days, they will join the rest of the class for instruction. No checkmark indicates something they *have* mastered. On those days, they will work on extension activities.

3. Tell students that they are *not* to work on any of the checked pages/concepts independently. They must wait until the class learns that material under your direction.

This keeps students from racing each other to complete their contracts. As a side benefit, parents appreciate it. You're showing that you know their kids need some direct instruction, just like everyone else, and you're not abandoning them to work alone most of the time.

4. Explain how to use the Extensions Center. Demonstrate various activities and problem-solving techniques. Call students' attention to the last extension option on the Learning Contract, which invites them to create their own alternate activity. Instruct them to bring their ideas to you; they'll need your permission to proceed.

Demonstrate how to keep daily records of extension work. On the lines beside each activity listed on the contract, students write the date(s) when they work on that activity. Each line equals one day. When all the lines for a particular activity are used up, students should select another activity, unless they are involved in a long-term activity that requires more time.

Students will need a place to store their work-in-progress when they leave the center and on days when they join the rest of the class for direct instruction. One simple solution is to give each student a hanging file folder and provide a plastic crate that accommodates the folders. Unfinished work goes in the folders, and folders go in the crate.

5. Encourage students to work on different activities and help each other when help is needed. They don't all have to work on the same activity at the same time—in fact, it's better if they don't. Say that you want them to be there for each other—to support and motivate each other to work with challenging activities instead of always choosing the easiest ones. That's what learning is all about, and it's why we work so hard to produce differentiated learning options.

IMPORTANT: Don't direct students to do specific extension activities, and don't expect them to complete an entire activity during each period. If you do, students will be forced to choose easy activities, and your whole purpose for providing differentiated learning will be compromised. Your most important task with kids on contract is to encourage them to persevere even when they become frustrated.

6. Reassure the students that you'll be working with them on a daily basis, and that you expect them to need help with the extension activities from time to time. See the Question Chip Technique on pages 54–55 for a way to deliver on your promise without going crazy.

If gifted students perceive that students on contract rarely get the chance to work with you, they may stop taking the pretests. They have a right to your attention as they engage in challenging work.

7. Review the working conditions—whether you write them on the individual contracts, create a Working Conditions chart for your classroom, or hand out copies of the Working Conditions form on page 51. *Tip:* In my experience, the working conditions that work best are the ones listed on Julie's contract (page 48).

8. Tell students how their grade for the chapter or unit will be determined. (See How to Grade Contract Students below.) Make sure they understand that working on contract will not lower their grade.

9. Sign the learning contracts. This creates formal agreements with obligations and responsibilities for all.

I don't recommend having parents sign the contracts. These are between you and the students, not you and the parents. You want to avoid creating a situation in which parents become over-invested in having their children remain eligible for staying on contract. And, since most of the work will be done in school, there's really no need for the parents to sign.

You might send a letter home at the start of the chapter or unit, introducing and explaining the contract method. Then, at the end of the chapter or unit, send the contracts home, accompanied by any extension activities or student logs you'd like the parents to see. Coach students in how to tell their parents about what they've been doing on contract. Invite parents to look over the contracts and other materials, talk them over with their children, sign the contracts, and return just the contracts and logs to you. File them in the students' compacting folders.

10. Caution the students not to brag about being "on contract." Explain how their eligibility doesn't mean they are better than other students, only that they need a different type of learning plan.

How to Grade Contract Students

Some students may resist going on contract because they worry that their grades will suffer. Or, once they're on contract, they may think that choosing challenging activities will jeopardize their grades. You need to reassure them that going on contract and taking learning risks won't hurt them. Here's a way to grade contract students that's equitable and easy.

Each day you record the work done by the class, record the grades for the contract students. On days when contract students receive direct instruction with the rest of the class (the red-box days, if you use red boxes in your grade book), record the grades they actually earn. On days when contract students work on extension activities (the no-red-box days), record the A's they earned on the pretest. *Tip:* Don't record all of the A's in advance. When students are aware there are blank spaces in your grade book, it reminds them that anytime they can't follow the working conditions, you might invite them back to the direct instruction group.

At the end of the chapter or unit, simply average all of the recorded grades—some earned during direct instruction, some on the pretest.

IMPORTANT: If you decide to require a contract student to rejoin the direct instruction group, please be careful to avoid making that sound like a punishment. You wouldn't want those students who are always working in the direct instruction mode to feel there is anything unsatisfactory about that arrangement.

Especially for Primary Teachers

Many teachers in the primary grades believe that their gifted students don't yet have the necessary skills to work independently. In fact, there is ample evidence that these skills can be taught to gifted kids of all ages. Several primary teachers I have worked with have been successful in managing differentiation for their students.

Many young gifted kids start out each year with a desire not to miss anything the teacher is doing with the rest of the class. They may not be able to handle the paper Learning Contract. You can differentiate for them by preparing more difficult tasks ahead of time, keeping those kids with the class during the large group work, then grouping them together at a designated table to work on the more difficult tasks.

Reassure all the kids that it's okay with you that not all groups will be doing the same task. Once kids know that, it will be okay with them as well. When you tell the designated students to leave the large group to do their work, the work that awaits them is simply different from what the other kids are doing.

When your primary kids get ready for contracts, you could keep the papers together in a special folder and indicate daily which students should participate in direct instruction, and which will work on extension activities.

Use red boxes in your grade book to highlight the concepts for which each student needs direct instruction. Each day, when you write the instructions for a particular lesson on the board, list the names of contract kids who don't have to attend the direct instruction. Tell the class, "If your name is on the board today, you may work on extensions during the entire period. Start new work, or continue your work from yesterday, and I will come to see you about fifteen minutes after the start of the period." In this way, children can begin and work briefly until you can get to them.

Whatever method you use, call the differentiation group together for a few minutes before you teach the large-group lesson. Explain the task that awaits them, and coach them on how to go to the designated spot and start the work while you get the rest of the class going. Reassure them that you will visit their group often, so they know they won't lose contact with you.

The Question Chip Technique

Naturally, all this sounds a little overwhelming. You're wondering how you're supposed to get around to all of your students during a particular class or period, especially if different students are working on different tasks. Let me suggest a method that will help you offer these options without losing your mind!

First, consider that children's brains can only take so much direct instruction at a time before it must be processed or lost. Translating this into classroom practice means that you should never teach for more than 12 minutes at a time before giving students some time for guided practice. This allows you to be more available to the kids on contract, since you can spend some time with them while the other students are practicing the section or activity you just taught.

At the start of each period, give each group or pair of discussion buddies one Question Chip (poker chip). Tell everyone that it's important to respect the need of every group to have your undivided attention when you're with them. Explain that you've set up the groups so there's ample help available from groupmates. However, you're aware that a group might get stuck and need your help sometime during the period. You'll be able to take only one question from each group during each period.

Explain that if a group has a question for you, they should send one member of the group to ask the question. That person must bring the Question Chip, because when you answer the question, you will take the chip.

The most amazing thing will probably happen: Almost no one will come to ask questions. They want to keep their chip at all costs, so usually they work within their group until they find an answer.

If kids ask what they will get for their saved chips, you might suggest that the accumulation of a certain number of chips will lead to homework passes, head-of-the-line passes, or other equally desirable perks.

CUSTOMIZING THE LEARNING CONTRACT

Because the basic concept of the Learning Contract is so widely applicable, and because learning contracts are so easy to use, it's fairly simple to customize this strategy to meet the needs of individual students. Following are three scenarios about particular students and the contracts that were invented just for them. You may find some of these contracts useful for your purposes in their present form, or you may use them as starting points for customizing the contracts you use with your students.

Scenario: Dimitri

Once in a great while, you may encounter a student who is so precocious that he may be able to teach himself much of what he needs to learn. Such students may be given more independent working time than others. Keep in mind, however, that some teacher or mentor must be available to monitor their progress, keep checking to see they are making forward progress, and provide direct instruction when it's needed.

Dimitri passed the pretests for several math chapters with 95–100 percent accuracy. I had him do some math work that represented more complex concepts, and he completed that with zero errors. Clearly, here was a student who needed math instruction at a higher grade level.

I designed a special contract for Dimitri, shown below. This Contract for Accelerated Learning can be used to document mastery of 95 percent or higher on an entire chapter, in which case the student is not required to complete any pages in that chapter.

★ CONTRACT FOR ACCELERATED LEARNING ★

Student's Name: Dimitri

_____ Chapter One
_____ Chapter Two
_____ Chapter Three
_____ Chapter Four
_____ Chapter Five
_____ Chapter Six
_____ Chapter Seven
_____ Chapter Eight
_____ Chapter Nine

Chapter # and Concept	Extension	Acceleration

Teacher's Signature:_____________________ Student's Signature:_____________________

With students like Dimitri, pretests should continue until their instructional level is found. In some cases, these kids should be placed in higher grades for math and return to their own class for their other subjects. When this is done, it must become part of a written multi-year plan that involves the parents, administrators, and anyone else who would be affected by such acceleration.

For seriously advanced students, especially in math, it's not appropriate to have them spend an entire year on extension work only. Some acceleration is needed as well. See Chapter 9 for more information on when to accelerate kids or content, and for forms you can use to keep track of differentiated learning opportunities.

How to Use the Contract for Accelerated Learning

1. Give very precocious students the end-of-chapter tests for as many chapters as they can demonstrate mastery with a score of 95–100 percent. These tests may be taken out of sequence, since some students will have mastered concepts here and there throughout the text.

2. On the top part of the contract, record the dates when mastery was documented. Date all tests and keep them in the student's compacting folder.

3. On the bottom part of the contract, keep track of the activities or program changes you choose for the student. If acceleration is not an option in your school, describe the extension activities the student will be engaged in.

4. For students who demonstrate mastery of a great deal of grade level work, some acceleration of content is indicated. You might have the student attend the class in a higher grade and/or work on advanced materials in your classroom.

CAUTION: Accelerated students who stay in their own classroom for instruction should *never* use the actual materials used in a subsequent grade level, to avoid the very real possibility of repetition in the future. The only exception is if a separate class is formed for students accelerated in math, and a scope-and-sequence is developed that guarantees that these students will not repeat the use of texts, even if they fail to remain in the accelerated class.

Never make acceleration arrangements without informing the other interested parties, such as parents, other teachers, and administrators. Any acceleration of content requires careful planning beyond the current school year. For example, where will the accelerated student go next? Is the middle school or high school prepared to admit a youthful, precocious student? Questions like these must be addressed before you choose acceleration for a particular student.

Scenario: Elena

Elena's class was using a math text that stressed critical thinking and problem-solving. It didn't lend itself to the more traditional Learning Contract approach. Her teacher had been told to teach the entire class as one group, and she was having trouble keeping the gifted students interested while the rest of the class went over the same concept several times. Because Elena was a teacher-pleaser, she never complained. However, her parents were hinting that they didn't think their daughter was being adequately challenged.

Elena's teacher planned activities to extend the basic problem-solving experiences for highly capable math students. Then she created a special Contract with Problem-Solving Focus, shown on page 57. This contract made it easy to meet the differentiated learning needs of students like Elena.

Even when all students are working on similar problem-solving strategies, the problems themselves can be different, reflecting the degree of difficulty each student is capable of handling.

How to Use the Contract with Problem-Solving Focus

1. Find or design an assessment tool or pretest for each problem-solving strategy. Offer the pretest before you teach each strategy, or when you observe that certain students have mastered a particular strategy.

2. On the top part of the contract, record the dates when the student masters specific strategies.

3. Create extension options and list them on the contract. Explain how students should keep track of the extension activities they do. (See At the Contract Meeting, step #4, pages 52–53 .)

★ CONTRACT WITH PROBLEM-SOLVING FOCUS ★

Student's Name: Elena

___ Make tables or graphs	___ Estimate first, check later	___ Use objects; use manipulatives
___ Make pictures	___ Create an organized list	___ Use logical reading
___ Make diagrams	___ Work backwards	___ Simplify the problem
___ Find a pattern	___ Act it out	___ Write an equation

Extension Options

Create story problems for the class to do	___ ___ ___ ___ ___
Choose a method from the top of the contract; create 4–6 problems at different levels of difficulty	___ ___ ___ ___ ___
Study a math textbook from a higher grade level that is different from the adopted text; find and record problems that require specific problem-solving methods; name the methods	___ ___ ___ ___ ___
Select a problem that our school is experiencing; apply several of the methods listed above to solve it	___ ___ ___ ___ ___
Apply several of the methods to solve a personal problem	___ ___ ___ ___ ___
Create an activity related to problem-solving	___ ___ ___ ___ ___

Teacher's Signature:________________________ Student's Signature:________________________

CAUTION: Students' grades should come from the top part of the contract, which represents grade-level work. You may choose to give some credit for extension options, if the students insist, but this should *never* be "extra" credit in addition to completed regular work. It should be "instead of" credit to replace credit earned from easier activities related to concepts students have already mastered.

Scenario: Leandra

Leandra was reading several years ahead of her age peers. Her writing was sophisticated and colorful. Her teacher recognized that it was not necessary for Leandra to complete all of the skill-and-practice assignments at grade level, and she created the contract shown on page 58 so Leandra could spend more time doing what she truly loved: reading and writing.

You'll notice that this contract doesn't list any specific activities as extension options, since there's no such thing as "gifted grammar." Students may spend the time they buy back reading books they have chosen and/or writing and revising ongoing pieces. It's very important to realize that it isn't necessary to provide paper-and-pencil activities to replace those activities students have been excused from doing. Students should have much freedom of choice in how they spend time they buy back.

For more about compacting and differentiating for reading and writing, see Chapter 5.

★ CONTRACT FOR READING SKILLS/GRAMMAR/LANGUAGE MECHANICS ★

Student's Name: Leandra

___ 58 (plurals)	___ 62 (compound words)	✓ 65 (possessives)
✓ 59 (subject/verb agreement)	___ 63 (suffixes)	✓ 66 (possessives)
___ 60 (prefixes)	___ 64 (suffixes)	___ 67 (parts of speech)
___ 61 (prefixes)		

Alternate Activities

Record the way you spent your time while the rest of the class was working on concepts you have mastered. The only expectation is that you spend your time reading and/or writing.

Date	Activity

Teacher's Signature:________________ Student's Signature:________________

How to Use the Contract for Reading Skills/Grammar/ Language Mechanics

1. On the top part of the contract, list required skills or concepts, or textbook pages. Leandra's contract shows both.

2. To determine which concepts students have already mastered, allow them to take a pretest or to complete a product that demonstrates their competency.

3. Give contracts to students who achieve your predetermined criteria. Check only those skills they haven't yet learned, or pages that teach concepts they haven't yet mastered.

Students on contract must join the class for direct instruction only when you are teaching the skills, pages, or concepts you have checked on their contracts. On other days, they may read or write, keeping track of their activities on the spaces provided at the bottom of the contract.

USING CONTRACTS WITH STANDARDS OR PROBLEM-BASED MATH PROGRAMS

Many teachers have the idea that standards-based math programs or those that focus on problem-solving cannot lend themselves to the contract approach. I have discussed this issue with several math specialists around the country since the first edition of this book came out in 1992, and I believe that it's possible and practical to use learning contracts with these materials.

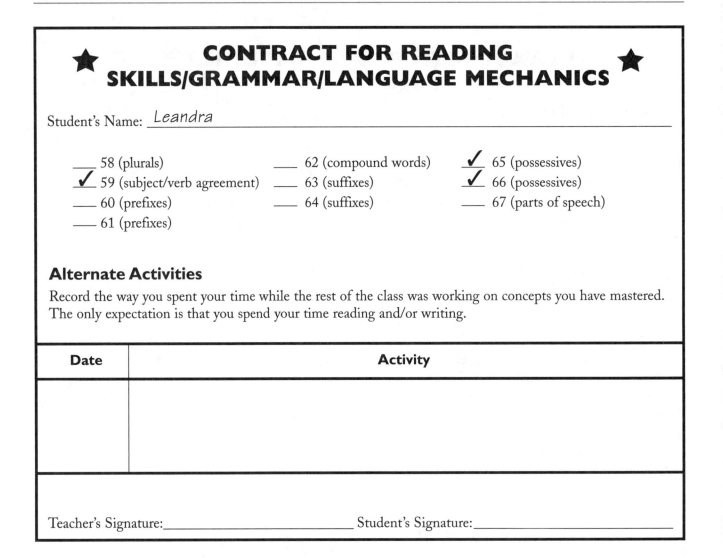

Teachers in the Forest Hills Public Schools in Grand Rapids, Michigan, have been using the contract system and extensions menus with the *Everyday Mathematics* curriculum with great success.* Volunteers take a pretest, and those who score 80 percent or higher receive a contract for that chapter. As contract students work on the extensions with each other, they spend time regularly with the classroom teacher, and sometimes with a learning consultant who works with the gifted and talented department. Students keep a Daily Log of Extension Work (see page 78) to document the work they do.

In other districts, teachers ask students to monitor and record the metacognitive processes they use in solving the problems. This information may be recorded on the back of the Daily Log.

Teachers always reserve the right to pull the contract students back into the regular instruction group if it becomes apparent that the students need more time with the regular concepts in the unit, and for special lessons they want all students to attend.

Cathy Bernhard, Math Specialist for the Beaverton Public Schools in Oregon, makes the following recommendations for using contracts with standards-based math programs.**

> "Kid-watching" as you begin teaching a unit will help you identify some students whose understanding of upcoming concepts is more advanced than most other students'. Invite them to participate in a formal assessment to document their ability to understand and communicate their mastery of concepts in a particular chapter, as well as their mathematical thinking ability.
>
> Group these students together and follow the same guidelines described for use of the Learning Contract. Since these math programs rely significantly on student interaction while learning, like-ability learners can still participate in this dialogue, but their topics will be about more advanced learning experiences. They will still be expected to describe their understanding of the process they use and to verify their solutions with other advanced students in their same group. Their removal from the mixed-abilities groups will not rob those groups of academic leadership. In fact, other students in those groups will emerge in leadership positions. Students on contract will join the other students for "special events" including group culminating activities.
>
> Contracts should reflect the state or district math problem-solving standards. For example, the Oregon standards include these four sections: Conceptual Understanding, Processes and Strategies including computation, Verification that students have checked work for accuracy, and Communication, showing the ability to understand and describe their mathematical thinking and what they have done in the process of problem solving. Since the advanced groups change for each chapter, based on the pre-assessment results, most kids who are eligible for contract some of the time will return to direct instruction for the chapters in which they cannot demonstrate previous mastery.
>
> If you'd like to use a method that does not require an actual contract, you might allow students gifted in math to skip the daily activities and the homework for several days each week, as long as they maintain a designated average in the quizzes, tests, and other assessment procedures. While they maintain their expertise, they work daily in class only on the extension activities. Some activities could be reserved for homework only, and students would keep a log of the time they spend on those activities instead of the regular homework tasks.
>
> Extension options for standards or problem-based programs could include:
>
> - Verifying problem solutions in several different ways.
> - Finding multiple solution methods for one problem.
> - Working with several number bases.
> - Projects connected to mathematical theories or methods.
> - Puzzles and games.
> - Conducting surveys and graphing results, including statistical analysis.
> - Patterning and algebraic relationships.
> - Working on more sophisticated homework tasks.
> - Designing more sophisticated homework tasks for other students.
> - Working with concepts from textbooks from higher grades, as long as they are not currently being used in those grades.

Other math specialists have suggested that the standards and problem-based math curriculum lends itself well to the Study Guide method described in Chapter 4. The Study Guide would describe the major concepts to be mastered, and an Extensions Menu would facilitate students' work on extension activities.

* Used with permission of Brenda K. Dieffenbach, Forest Hills Public Schools, Grand Rapids, Michigan.

** Used with permission of Cathy Bernhard, Math Specialist, Beaverton School District, Beaverton, Oregon.

STRATEGY: MATH ACHIEVEMENT TEAMS (MATS)*

This strategy is adapted from team learning approaches based on the ideas of author and educator Robert E. Slavin. I have adapted his method, called TAI (Team Accelerated Instruction), so that the most capable students are not held back by the learning needs of other students in heterogeneous groups. No contracts are used, but instruction is differentiated by teaching students the same concept on various levels of instruction, and by incorporating attention to different learning styles.

> **NOTE:** If assistance is available to you from special education teachers or teachers of gifted and talented students, ask them to co-teach with you whenever possible so you can spend more time with individual teams.

1. At the beginning of each chapter or unit, ask all students to demonstrate, by their performance on a placement test,** how much of the upcoming work they have already mastered. Choose an activity that is compatible with your preferred method of assessing student learning; anything from paper-and-pencil tests to performance tasks is fine. This should be the same assessment tool you'll use at the end of the unit.

Tell students they may stop their work on the placement test at their own personal frustration level. Reassure students that the results are confidential and will not be averaged into their grade for the unit. Scores will only be used to compute improvement points at the end of the unit. (See Calculating Improvement Points on pages 61–62.)

2. Based on the results of the placement test, record each student's name on one of four lists:

- The 1s: Students who have little or no knowledge of the standards that will be taught in a particular chapter.
- The 2s: Students who have some knowledge of the standards that will be taught.
- The 3s: Students who are already familiar with 80 percent or more of the upcoming content.
- The 4s: Students who have mastered almost all of the upcoming content.

Along with the students' names, record their placement test scores as baseline data for computing improvement points later in the MATS process.

For students who score above the 95th percentile on your placement test, continue testing them on subsequent units until you find the place where instruction should begin. (See Dimitri's scenario on pages 55–56.)

Another option is to group the 4s together for math, either within your class or a higher grade's class, and use material from a higher grade level. Of course, this creates another instructional group for you to deal with. Perhaps you could team up with another teacher at your grade level who's facing a similar challenge and trade off responsibility for this group. Each of you could teach them every other chapter or for an entire semester.

Remember that if you accelerate a child into a higher grade, a written multi-year plan must be designed and approved by all interested parties.

3. Create Math Achievement Teams for the chapter or unit. Each team should include representation from the 1s, 2s, and 3s. Teams should have the same number of members (or as close to the same as possible) so the improvement points system will work. The 4s—students who qualify for accelerated differentiation—are not included on the teams.

> **NOTE:** In some districts, the highest-achieving math students are placed in separate groups for instruction at accelerated levels. These groups should include *only* those students who have exceeded the grade-level expectations or standards, as documented through criterion-level testing. *Never* include students who have not demonstrated the expected competence, just for the sake of even distribution of students per teacher. This practice will ultimately lower the

* MATS is adapted from the ideas of Robert E. Slavin presented in *TAI Mathematics: Team Accelerated Instruction*, which is based upon work supported by the National Institute of Education under Grant Number NIE-G-80-0113, and by the Office of Special Education, United States Department of Education, under Grant Number G-00-80-1494. *TAI Mathematics* is published and copyrighted by Charlesbridge Publishing, 85 Main Street, Watertown, MA 02472.

** This is a placement test, not a pretest, because all students are required to take it.

instructional level of the accelerated class and will create negative attitudes about math in the minds of those students who have to struggle so hard to keep up in a program that is clearly too difficult for them. For more on this topic, see the Question and Answer on pages 197–198.

4. Start the chapter or unit with a global overview of the upcoming content. Have students discuss what they already know about the content. Use an attention-grabbing activity that helps kids understand how what they are about to learn is relevant and meaningful in real life.

5. Each day during math, meet separately with all of the 1s, all of the 2s, and all of the 3s. Give each group an assignment at an appropriate level. Explain that they will begin their work as soon as they return to their Math Achievement Teams.

Students at all levels will learn the same general concepts, but with strategies and at instructional levels that are likely to be effective with them. For example, you might give the 1s a lot of hands-on work with manipulatives and technology. Teach the 2s using your customary methods. The 3s should experience compacting and differentiation, spending some days on grade level content and others on accelerated content or extension activities. As a general guideline, between one-third and one-half of the work you give the 3s should be based on the regular curriculum content, and the rest should be extension activities.

Homework assignments for all students come from their group activities. Therefore, homework will be automatically differentiated, even though all students will be learning about the same general topic in a given unit or chapter.

6. Have students regroup in their Math Achievement Teams and work on the day's assignments. At any given time, at least 2 students on each team are working together, and there is always some assistance available for struggling students.

IMPORTANT: The 3s should not spend too much of their time helping others. They need to work on tasks at their own challenge level—specifically, extension activities. They should be allowed to work with 3s from other teams now and then, and even team up with the 4s for certain activities.

Do not grade the extension activities and average those grades into the students' overall grades for the chapter or unit. If you do, gifted kids may resist working on extensions, especially challenging extensions. Why should they risk getting a lower grade than they're used to? Instead, for each day they work on extensions, record the grade that represents their average for all the work in the unit. Based on their demonstrated performance in the chapter and on the placement test, give them the same level of credit they earned on the placement test for these concepts. Always remember that if you were not compacting and differentiating for these kids, the only work you would have to assess would be the grade-level work.

7. At regular intervals, offer the whole class a day to work on extension activities. When all students have opportunities to engage in learning tasks that are interesting, meaningful, and fun, there will be little or no resentment toward those students who spend lots of their time on extensions.

8. From time to time, have all students work on activities that provide practice in already mastered skills and concepts. Be sure these activities are highly interesting and motivational.

9. Give mini-assessments at regular intervals to make sure the groups are on track.

10. Give students a formal end-of-the-unit assessment—the same (or similar) assessment you gave at the start of the unit. Give it to all students on the same day.

11. Record the post-assessment grades and determine the improvement points. (See Calculating Improvement Points below.)

12. Start the entire process again for the next chapter. If necessary, reorganize the teams and instructional groups (1s, 2s, 3s, 4s) to make sure that the appropriate achievement levels are represented on each team.

Calculating Improvement Points

Any system that's compatible with your teaching practice is okay, as long as it doesn't hold back the advanced learners. When you put students of varying levels of ability on the same team and ask them to work together, you want to make sure that this helps weaker students without penalizing stronger students.

Improvement points are awarded on a sliding scale. Students who make the greatest learning gains during the course of the unit earn the most points. (The baseline for each student is the placement test score you recorded at the start of the unit.) This means that the 1s have the potential to contribute the most to the team's improvement points score—an incentive for group members to help struggling learners. In addition, students whose scores never go below 90 percent receive a point bonus equivalent to the highest bonus for any member of the team—an incentive for capable students to keep doing well.

Avoid setting up conditions that would make high-ability kids purposefully score low on the placement test to get the most improvement points for their team at post-test time. Kids who score A's on pretests and post-tests should earn the same number of improvement points as the highest scorer on the team.

Range of Growth	Improvement Points
1–5 points of improvement	5
6–10	10
11–15	15
16–20	20
21–25	25
More than 25	30

Each student earns her own improvement points. At the end of each chapter, total all team members' improvement points for a final team score. Celebrate.

What if some of the 4s feel frustrated because they aren't earning improvement points? Perhaps they can keep track of their individual progress through the accelerated content, and earn personal improvement points in that way. Perhaps they can earn improvement points in another subject area in which they are experiencing some difficulty. Be creative—or ask the kids themselves for suggestions on how to solve this problem.

Three Advantages of the MATS Strategy

1. There is no "busy work." All students always work at their personal challenge level in math, and struggling students always have the help of more capable students available to them.

2. The entire class works on similar concepts simultaneously, without the condition that some students have to slow their personal pace and wait for others to catch up. Any special activity you want to plan to extend the content for the whole class can be enjoyed by the whole class as a large-group activity, because it's related to the concepts everyone is learning.

3. Highly capable math students experience compacting and differentiation regularly in a way that gives them frequent access to the teacher and to direct instruction at their level. They don't work on their own too often, which relieves their parents. When gifted kids spend a lot of time working independently, parents perceive that their children are being neglected, and that teachers are focusing more on the needs of average and struggling students. MATS keeps parents from getting frustrated.

QUESTIONS AND ANSWERS

"What happens when students on contract forget to join the group for instruction on the days they're supposed to?"

Just because students are gifted doesn't mean they are well-organized or totally responsible. They need to be taught those skills.

If you use red boxes in your grade book, you'll be able to see at a glance which contract students should join you for direct instruction on any given day. When you announce which page the class will be working on that day, remind the contract students to check their contracts to see where they should be. For a few weeks, you may want to write their names on the board to help them form the habit of noticing when they should attend the class. When you notice that someone who should be with the group is absent, gently remind all of the contract students to check their contracts.

"What should I do if students on contract waste time or disturb the class on the days they are working on enrichment activities?"

Speak to the students once or twice, referring them to the working conditions on their contract (or classroom chart, or handout; see page 51). Meet with them to make sure they understand how to do the extension activities, and to find out if the activities are proving to be unrealistically difficult. Check to make sure you're spending enough time with them so they don't feel neglected.

Even after all of this support, there may be some kids who simply can't or won't do what is expected of them. You might have to advise certain students to rejoin the direct instruction group for the rest of the chapter—because they're wasting time and disturbing other kids, or because they can't learn the necessary organizational skills, they seem uncomfortable working more independently, or you feel they need more direct instruction. Be sure they understand that this is not a bad thing, and reassure them that they will have the chance to qualify for a contract for the next chapter.

Do not lower the grade earned on any pretest because of behavior problems. Record the actual earned grade, but reserve the right to have the student rejoin the direct instruction group at any time during the length of the contract.

You can avoid potential problems if you plan to meet with contract students several times during the first few days of the unit. This helps them feel in touch, gets them focused, and starts them off on the right track.

"Will correcting work for students on contract create a lot of paperwork for me?"

The work that contract students do with the class as a whole is corrected at the same time as everyone else's work, and their grades are entered into your grade book at the same time as you enter everyone else's grade. All extension activities should be open-ended (with no one correct answer) or self-correcting. Provide answer keys whenever possible. Parents of gifted kids might be willing to help you create the extension activities and the answer keys, since their own children will benefit from them.

To save even more on paperwork, you may find that it's not necessary to keep compactors for students on learning contracts. Keep their completed contracts in their compacting folders, along with all tests, as evidence of the alternate work they have done..

"Where can I find the extension materials my students need, and how can I afford them?"

None of the strategies in this book requires the purchase of costly materials. However, if you are trying to find some, see References and Resources at the end of this chapter. For more suggestions, see pages 193–194.

"How can I figure out the grades for students who do less work from the text than others?"

By averaging their grades, the same as for any other student. Students on contract have the same number of grades as all other students. The difference is that these students earn some of their grades from the pretest, and some from the actual work they do on days when they join the class for direct instruction.

"What can I do when students who could qualify for a contract choose not to take the pretest and indicate they would rather work with the class?"

Many gifted students equate being gifted with getting their work done quickly and easily. In their minds, someone who struggles must be less intelligent than someone who breezes through assignments. Make it clear that their alternative work will not be averaged in with the grade-level work, and that the grade they earn for this chapter or unit will be no lower than what they would have earned had they stayed with the class for direct instruction.

Sometimes this avoidance behavior reflects a bid for social acceptance. Sometimes it's a way of playing it safe. If they take a risk—if they choose to struggle—they might fail. And if they fail, they fear this will "prove" that they aren't really smart after all. If quite a few students resist taking the pretest, this probably means that they don't understand that this option is risk-free.

Consistently communicate your firm belief that it takes more intelligence to hang in there when the going gets tough than it does to excel at easy work. Emphasize daily the importance of cherishing individual differences, instead of putting pressure on your students to be exactly alike.

"Some students seem unwilling to work without close direction from me. How can I give them the time they need without taking time away from the other students?"

When gifted students ask a teacher for help with extension activities, the last thing they want to hear is, "You're pretty smart—you should be able to figure that out yourself!" The unspoken message is that bright people should never have to ask for help.

Gifted students need and want time with the teacher. When you've gone to so much trouble to provide your students with truly challenging activities, they will need and welcome your assistance. The Question Chip Technique (see pages 54–55) can help you create time to work with contract kids (and the 4s in the MATS method) on a regular basis.

"Shouldn't my gifted students spend some of their time tutoring students who are having trouble learning?"

All students in your class have the right to learn something new in your class every day, including your most capable students. There may be some benefits for all students when gifted students interact in a teaching capacity with those who need help, but consistently having gifted students teach struggling students robs gifted students of their own right to struggle and learn. Your capable students might conclude, "Everyone else comes to school to learn math. Not me; I come to teach it!" Or, "Once I've finished the material in the book, there must not be any other math material for me to learn, since the teacher never provides other types of activities for me."

It's possible that your highly capable (though not gifted) students will gain a better understanding of what they are learning by tutoring other kids on a sometimes basis. We know they will be more patient teachers than many gifted kids are. Gifted students can become very frustrated at always being asked to tutor, and the students they are tutoring may say they understand a concept long before they do, just to escape from an uncomfortable situation.

"We don't use a textbook in math, except as a reference. We usually spend the entire math class on problem-solving experiences. Do my gifted students still need a differentiated program?"

In the late 1990s, backlash rumblings began to appear against math programs that focus exclusively on problem-solving and critical thinking to the near exclusion of attention to basic skills and computation. (For those of you who have been in education as long as I have, this debate has been heard before; so what else is new?) In fact, the NCTM standards were revised in the spring of 2000 to reflect this concern. It should be clear to educators that any reasonable program in any subject area should represent a balance between skills, content, and standards. The degree to which you need to differentiate your math program for your most capable students depends on the degree to which they regularly experience expectations that make them stretch as far as possible toward achievement at their highest potential.

"Isn't there a lot of record-keeping in the MATS method?"

Not significantly more than in any other program. However, if you want help computing improvement points, keeping track of test data, and reforming groups, a parent volunteer or even a student from your class can do the job. As always when involving others, address the confidentiality issue directly.

"Won't kids who are always 1s feel badly in the MATS method? Likewise, won't kids who never get to be on contract feel badly in the Learning Contract method?

Since the teams and contract kids change for every chapter, and since the team kids' numbers are never made public, this should not be an issue. Awareness and creativity on your part will help, too. For example, you might rearrange the order of the chapters in your math book so the second or third chapter is on geometry. Kids who would be 1s in other types of content often excel in spatial/visual abilities, and academically gifted kids often falter. Watch everyone's confusion and appreciation as 1s, 2s, and 3s change places! The lesson to be learned? We all have strengths and weaknesses.

"How do I use the Learning Contract with highly structured programs such as Saxon?"

Here are four suggestions you can try:

1. Always offer Most Difficult First, selecting problems from each category.

2. Pretest by categories of content and arrange the contract so students know which categories they can skip.

3. Allow students who maintain an average of 90+ percent to skip every other day of direct instruction and work on extension activities instead.

4. Assign only odd- or even-numbered problems as daily practice.

SUMMARY

Are your gifted students being adequately challenged in math? Find out by observing their learning behavior. If they seem to be going through the motions but are unenthusiastic about the subject, they probably need to spend considerable learning time on extension activities. If they refuse to do the assigned work but get high grades on quizzes, tests, and other assessments, they need differentiation. However, if they are actively engaged in learning and appear to be struggling to learn for much of the time, the activities you are already using may be adequate and less differentiation may be needed.

This chapter presented two ways to manage differentiation for math and other skill-based areas: the Learning Contract and Math Achievement Teams (MATS). The main difference between these approaches and others you may have used in the past is that students who become eligible for differentiation aren't allowed to race through the grade-level assignments. Instead, they are required to wait until you instruct their group or the rest of the class on those topics. Students must also follow specific working conditions to remain eligible for differentiation.

Sometimes we teachers can force our students to do work they know they don't need, but they can make us wish we hadn't forced them. They respond with sloppy, careless, or messy work, turned in late or not at all. We fight back, sending notes home on a regular basis, but it's a losing battle. If you've been looking for a better way to motivate your students, try the methods described in this chapter. You'll need to do some preparation, but once a system is in place, it will practically run itself. Your reward will come as you watch your students perk up and willingly engage in challenging work.

REFERENCES AND RESOURCES

See also pages 197–198.

Books

Block, J. Richard, and Harold Yucker. *Can You Believe Your Eyes? Over 250 Illusions and Other Visual Oddities.* Philadelphia, PA: Brunner/Mazel, 1992.

Gardner, Martin. *More Perplexing Puzzles and Tantalizing Teasers.* Mineola, NY: Dover, 1988. One of many books of puzzles and brainteasers by this popular author.

Overholt, Jim. *Math Wise! Hands-On Activities and Investigations for Elementary Students.* West Nyack, NJ: Center for Applied Research, 1995.

Thompson, Frances M. *Hands-On Math! Ready-to-Use Games & Activities for Grades 4–8* and *Hands-On Algebra! Ready-to-Use Games & Activities for Grades 7–12.* West Nyack, NJ: Center for Applied Research, 1994 and 1998. Two books in a very popular series that teaches math in ways that appeal to kinesthetic learners and helps kids understand mathematical concepts.

Extension Activities

AIMS Education Foundation, Fresno, CA, (888) SEE-AIMS (www.aimsedu.org). Hands-on integrated math-science activities.

The Calculus Page (www.calculus.org). Links to problems, sample exams, classroom demonstrations, competitions, online tutorials, tools, and more. The managing editors are faculty members in the mathematics department at the University of California in Davis.

Creative Publications, Desoto, TX, (800) 648-2970 (www.wrightgroup.com). I can unequivocally recommend their general catalog as the best source of math extensions materials around.

ETA/Cuisenaire, Vernon Hills, IL, (800) 445-5985 (www.etacuisenaire.com). Source for Versa-Tiles, cuisenaire, and other hands-on materials for math, science, and reading/language arts.

Highline Advanced Math Program (http://home.avvanta.com/~math). Math enrichment for grades 5–7. Also has activities for Math Olympiad competitions.

Marcy Cook Math, Balboa Island, CA, (949) 375-1398 (www.marcycookmath.com). Materials that extend Standards and Problem-Based Learning.

Marilyn Burns Education Associates, Sausalito, CA, (800) 868-9092 (www.mathsolutions.com). Marilyn's goal is to eliminate math-phobic behaviors in all persons and to provide exciting math activities. Ask about her in-service courses, workshop sessions, and publications.

The Math Forum (www.mathforum.org). Located at the Drexel School of Education, this "online math education community center" features interactive projects, links, learning materials, and an online library. Example: MathMagic! (www.mathforum.org/mathmagic), developed by Texas math teacher Alan A. Hodson, engages student teams in online problem-solving dialogues.

Suntex International Inc., Easton, PA, (610) 253-5255 (www.math24.com). Publishers of the 24 Game and other products to use for math extension.

Distance Learning

Education Program for Gifted Youth (EPGY), Stanford University, (800) 372-3749 (www-epgy.stanford.edu). Offers advanced courses for students in elementary, middle, and high school in math, physics, English, and computer science.

Virtual High School (www.govhs.org). Offers 15 AP classes in art, science, language arts, and more.

Miscellaneous

Charlesbridge Publishing, Inc., Watertown, MA, (617) 926-0329 (www.charlesbridge.com). Information on the original Team Assisted Instruction (TAI) Mathematics program on which the Math Achievement Teams (MATS) strategy is based.

Everyday Mathematics. Everyday Learning Corporation, Desoto, TX, (800) 648-2970. A comprehensive K–6 math curriculum developed by the University of Chicago School Mathematics Project (UCSMP).

Forest Hills Public Schools, Grand Rapids, MI, (616) 493-8808. Contact the G.A.T.E.WAYS consultants for information on using contracts with problem-based programs such as *Everyday Mathematics.*

4

Compacting and Differentiation in Content Areas

The pretesting options described in chapters 2 and 3 are usable only if students have previously learned the curriculum. Other compacting methods are needed for situations in which the curriculum may be new, but gifted students can learn it much more quickly than their age peers.

Pretesting is not usually effective in these situations, except when there are students who clearly have learned the material before. They often surface at the beginning of a unit, when you survey your students to find out what they already know and discover that some know more than you're planning to teach! These students are candidates for pretesting, using the same assessment tool you plan to use at the end of the unit.

In non-pretestable subjects where the material is new for them, gifted students should be allowed to move through it at a faster pace than the rest of the class. These students are easy to spot. They are the ones who tend to ace quizzes and tests, sometimes dominate class discussions, but hand in little or none of the daily work or homework. They may also lack enthusiasm for going above and beyond the expectations of the regular classroom. They are trying to tell you that they can learn the material without doing the actual activities.

How can you let them work at a pace commensurate with their ability, while avoiding a power struggle over the work they may not need to do? The Study Guide method described in this chapter is one answer. It will help you to capitalize on your gifted students' exceptional learning ability by inviting them to move through the required content at a faster pace than their classmates, while sometimes becoming "resident experts" on related topics.* It is different from the options described in earlier chapters in that it is not immediately offered to all students and is not preceded by a pretest.

STRATEGY: THE STUDY GUIDE METHOD

The Study Guide method enables you to compact in literature, science, social studies, problem-based learning, and thematic, integrated units, reducing the amount of time gifted students must spend on designated content. You differentiate in these subjects by allowing gifted students to work on alternate activities and explore topics of their choosing in greater depth.

The idea of exempting some students from regularly assigned work may make you uncomfortable. You may worry that they will learn poor work habits, or that other students will resent what they perceive as "special privileges" for only a few. Remember that you never excuse students from the regular work until they have demonstrated that 1) they have already mastered the required concepts or 2) they can learn them in a much shorter time than their age peers. With the Study Guide method, you have documentation that students have learned the required material, and they are held accountable for demonstrating that mastery on your timetable. It's the alternate work they do that has a more flexible

* Chapter 7 discusses another type of resident expert—one who works on a Personal Interest Independent Study Project that may be related to the curriculum or to a topic in which the student has a passionate interest.

format. It's the faster pacing that makes them (and their parents) happy.

Scenario: Cleon

Cleon, a student in my fifth-grade class, was "gifted across the board." His ability was exceptional in every subject area, as well as in art and physical education. However, his actual classroom performance left a lot to be desired. I found it frustrating that he seemed to spend much of his class time daydreaming, and he seldom completed his homework assignments, but he always aced the tests! This happened even in social studies, where all of the material was supposed to be completely new.

Furthermore, Cleon behaved rudely during class discussions. He blurted out answers when he wasn't called on, and he seemed to delight in making remarks under his breath that were designed to amuse and distract the other students.

I slowly realized that Cleon's negative behavior was related to his superior learning ability. Rather than "disciplining" him, I decided to find a management system that would allow Cleon to learn social studies in a manner more commensurate with his ability. Naturally, I hoped that the added challenge would have a positive effect on his behavior.

When I discussed this situation with Cleon's parents, they wanted to take away his hockey lessons until he "shaped up in school." I asked them not to do that. Cleon was a champion player, and I don't believe there is anything positive to be gained by taking away a child's source of joy and satisfaction until his or her school work improves. Cleon's predictable reaction would be to become even more negative toward school. Since his performance on assessments indicated that he could learn the material without actually doing the regular work, I believe the solution should be found at school rather than at home.

At the time, our class was studying the Civil War. I explained the Study Guide method and asked Cleon if he might want to try it. Cleon was interested in trains, so he said he would like to draw the trains and locomotives of the Civil War period. However, simply drawing the trains would not have provided an adequate challenge to his superior learning ability. So we negotiated a project that allowed Cleon to draw his trains on a huge piece of tagboard on which he also located the major Civil War battlefields and manufacturing centers. His second task was to determine the extent to which the proximity of the manufacturing centers to the battlefields affected the outcome of the war. This forced Cleon to become more original with his thinking, and to synthesize information from many sources to create and defend a hypothesis—a legitimate activity for a gifted student.

Two Ways to Use the Study Guide

You may use the Study Guide alone or in combination with the Extensions Menu. The first option is the simplest. The guide itself is the differentiation tool; students use it to study another example of what the whole class is learning.

For example, if the unit is Tall Tales, and some students already know a lot about the characters you have selected for study, group those students together and invite them to use the Study Guide to learn about other Tall Tales characters from American or world literature. Likewise, if some students have already read a book you will be using for a class novel, the Study Guide can structure their reading of other books by the same author, or other books in the same genre. (For more about teaching reading to gifted students, see Chapter 5.)

The second option invites students to become resident experts on a topic related to what the whole class is learning. They choose a topic from the Extensions Menu (or come up with one of their own), pursue it in depth, and later report on what they learned to the class or other appropriate audience. This expands the unit and makes it more interesting and enjoyable for everyone.

In both cases, students are expected to master the same material as the rest of the class, and they are held accountable with regular assessments. But they can learn at a faster pace and spend the balance of their time on activities that are more challenging and rewarding for them.

The Study Guide with Extensions Menu is most useful for students in grades 3 and higher but may be modified for use with younger kids. Second graders (and even first graders) may be more comfortable using just the Study Guide to expand the content the class is studying.

A reproducible Study Guide and an Extensions Menu are shown on pages 71 and 72. The next section explains how to create your own guides and menus.

NOTES: If you're familiar with the first edition of this book, you may recall that I used a Civil War example here. Over the years, I realized that making study guides on more generic topics cuts down on preparation time and allows the Study Guide itself to serve as the differentiation tool. Examples:

Instead of this:	Use this:
Civil War	American Wars
Paul Bunyan	Tall Tales
Ancient Rome	Ancient Civilizations
Human Digestive System	Human Body Systems
Ramona the Pest	Beverly Cleary Books
Sarah, Plain and Tall	Life on a Frontier
Dinosaurs	Extinct Animals

Also in the first edition, I called the Extensions Menu the Tic-Tac-Toe Menu. However, I never meant to suggest that students should select topics in any particular order, or that they should be required to do more than one project for a unit of study, both of which Tic-Tac-Toe seemed to imply. Renaming this the Extensions Menu should clear up any misconceptions. If you're accustomed to calling your menus Tic-Tac-Toe and want to keep doing so, that's fine. Just be sure to give your students free choice of the topic(s) they want to pursue.

Preparing the Study Guide and Extensions Menu

1. Use the Topic Development Sheet on page 70 to plan the Study Guide and Extensions Menu for a generic unit. (See the Notes above for a short list of generic topics.)

In the left column, list no more than 10 key concepts you want all students to master by the end of the unit. You may choose to use the actual language of your state standards.

In the right column, list topics related to the unit theme but not included in the Key Concepts list. These may be topics you would want to include if you had unlimited time for this unit, or topics you think would appeal to kids with interests that extend beyond the unit parameters.

The related topics don't have to match the key concepts. In fact, this is a golden opportunity to bring in other topics that you may not have time to include in this unit but which some students may choose to study in depth if given the chance.

2. Create a Study Guide that includes only the key concepts. Gifted students will use the guide to learn the concepts at their own pace while you are teaching the unit directly to the rest of the class.

How will you know that the students are learning the material? You probably won't know until you get to the first checkpoint dates. I strongly recommend that the first checkpoint occur no more than 3 days after the students begin their work. In this way, it will be easy to notice if some students have made an inappropriate choice.

3. Create an Extensions Menu that includes 8 of the related topics. Leave the center space free for Student Choice. You'll find a reproducible Extensions Menu form on page 73.

Use a thinking model such as Bloom's Taxonomy (see Chapter 6) to describe activities that promote Application, Analysis, Evaluation, and Synthesis. Refer to the Taxonomy of Thinking chart (page 133) and use the trigger words for those 4 levels.

Notice that on the American Wars Extensions Menu (page 72), the key concepts are stretched to include patriotic music and creative alternatives to warfare.

IMPORTANT: Describe the topics, but not the specific ways students should present the information they find. They will choose how to do this, using a tool called the Product Choices Chart (see page 79).

Text continues on page 74

TOPIC DEVELOPMENT SHEET

Topic or unit to be learned: ______________________________

Key Concepts	Related Topics

★ AMERICAN WARS STUDY GUIDE ★

BE PREPARED TO:

1. Discuss the political, social, and economic causes of the war.

2. Explain the basis of the economy for both sides before the war began.

★ **CHECKPOINT:** _______________: **Assessment for 1–2** ★
DATE

3. Give the meanings of all designated vocabulary words.

4. Show on a map the disputed territory before the war began, at its midpoint, and at its end.

5. Recite from memory an important speech from this particular war period on a war-related topic. Be able to explain its background and significance.

★ **CHECKPOINT:** _______________: **Assessment for 1–5** ★
DATE

6. Describe typical battle conditions experienced by soldiers and commanders. Include information about commonly used battle tactics.

7. Narrate a first-person biographical sketch of a person connected to the war effort.

8. Write a newspaper account of a non-battlefield event related to the war.

9. Describe the peace plan—its location, components, and effects.

10. Summarize the implications of this war in today's time period. Hypothesize how history would have turned out differently if the other side had won. Make predictions for the decade following the war as well as for the present time.

★ **CHECKPOINT:** _______________: **Final Assessment for 1–10** ★
DATE

AMERICAN WARS EXTENSIONS MENU

Present a detailed biography of an important person during the time of this conflict. Include evidence of this person's influence during the war period.	Research the patriotic music used by both sides in the war. Point out similarities and differences. Describe how music influences patriotism in civilians and soldiers. Compare the patriotic music of this war to that of other wars.	Locate information about the medical practices used on the battlefield and in field hospitals during this war. Include biographical information about famous medical people of that time.
Discover how military people communicated with each other and with their commander–in-chief during this war. Focus on events in which poorly understood or poorly delivered communications influenced the outcome of a military effort.	**Student Choice**	Investigate battles in which creative or uncommonly used tactics were employed. OR design strategies that you think would have led to more victories and fewer casualties. Be sure to use only the technology available during that time period.
Choose 25 key words from this unit. Create a directory that lists each word, its meaning, and its effect on this war.	Investigate other types of wars: between families, clans, children in school, mythical creatures, etc. Share information about them and include a comparison of elements found in a traditional war between countries.	Create alternate ways for countries to solve their problems without resorting to warfare.

EXTENSIONS MENU

	Student Choice	

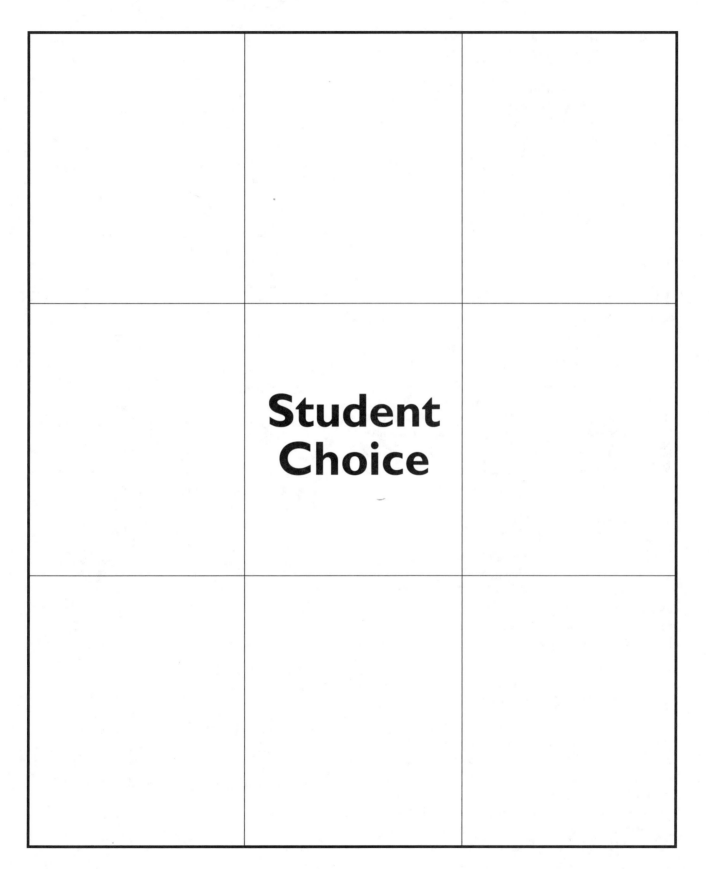

Text continues from page 69

TOOLS TO USE WITH THE STUDY GUIDE METHOD

Like any form of compacting and differentiation, the Study Guide method should be carefully documented. This helps you to know that your students are learning the required material, it holds students accountable for their learning, and it gives you a way to show parents and administrators that even though your gifted kids aren't doing the regular work, they're still learning what they're supposed to know. It also gives you proof in writing that you're providing numerous differentiation opportunities for each unit.

The Independent Study Agreement

The Independent Study Agreement is designed to guard against misunderstandings, disagreements, and claims such as, "You never told me I had to learn some content on my own!" All students who choose to use the Study Guide, with or without the Extensions Menu, must enter into an agreement with you that describes the conditions of their independent study, including both learning conditions and working conditions. If students fail to meet the conditions, the logical consequence is that they will have to return to the teacher-directed group for the remainder of the unit.

Reproducible agreements are found on pages 75 and 76. Feel free to change any of the conditions or add new ones of your own. Those I've included represent things I was afraid might go wrong with this method the first several times I used it. Once I had all of these issues on the table, I found it easier to sleep at night!

The Evaluation Contract

Once students choose a project from the Extensions Menu, they indicate their choice on the Evaluation Contract. The contract also lets them specify the grade they want to earn for their work, based on the kind of work they will do. A reproducible Evaluation Contract is found on page 77.

Because the contract describes learning on different levels of Bloom's Taxonomy, you'll want to make sure your students understand what this means. See the section on Bloom's Taxonomy in Chapter 6.

As noted in chapters 2 and 3, alternate work should not be graded when compacting pretestable content, since it's already apparent that the students have mastered the grade-level material. This is not the case in content areas where pretests aren't used. If you, the student, and the student's parents are comfortable with the actual grade for the content area units coming from only the checkpoint and final unit assessments, then no other grade is required. But by the time students are old enough to benefit from the Study Guide approach, they may have developed a resistance to doing any work that is not accompanied by a grade.

The grade earned by a resident expert should reflect the complexity and sophistication of content and thought processes rather than the appearance of the product. It should be based on substance rather than form. The Evaluation Contract includes a generic rubric which may be used for any project. I have found this rubric to be extremely valuable in helping students produce high-quality work on their projects. It virtually eliminates the frustration we face when students work on a project for a long time and produce somewhat shoddy work.

NOTE: Besides the Evaluation Contract, there are other ways to assure high-quality products from your students. Two that I especially recommend are John Samara's Product Guides and Bertie Kingore's Portfolio Assessment tools. See References and Resources at the end of this chapter.

The Daily Log of Extension Work

The Daily Log of Extension Work is useful as a portfolio record sheet and in conferences with parents and administrators. It also helps gifted underachievers who have trouble completing long-term projects. (For more on this topic, see pages 14–15.) A reproducible Daily Log is found on page 78.

Text continues on page 79

★ INDEPENDENT STUDY AGREEMENT FOR STUDY GUIDE ONLY ★

Read each condition as your teacher reads it aloud. Write your initials beside it to show that you understand it and agree to abide by it.

Learning Conditions

______ I will learn independently all the key concepts described on the Study Guide. I will not have to complete the actual assigned activities as long as I am doing work related to what the class is learning.

______ I will demonstrate competency with the assessments for the Study Guide content at the same time as the rest of the class.

______ I will participate in designated whole-class activities as the teacher indicates them—without arguing.

______ I will keep a Daily Log of my progress.

______ I will share what I have learned about my alternate topic with the class in an interesting way. My report will take 5–7 minutes and will include a visual aid. I will prepare a question about my report to ask the class before giving my report.

Working Conditions

______ I will be present in the classroom at the beginning and end of each class period.

______ I will not bother anyone or call attention to the fact that I am doing different work than others in the class.

______ I will work on my chosen topic for the entire class period on designated days.

______ I will carry this paper with me to any room in which I am working on my chosen topic, and I will return it to my classroom at the end of each session.

Student's Signature: ____

Teacher's Signature: ____

★ INDEPENDENT STUDY AGREEMENT FOR STUDY GUIDE WITH EXTENSIONS MENU ★

Read each condition as your teacher reads it aloud. Write your initials beside it to show that you understand it and agree to abide by it.

Learning Conditions

______ I will learn independently all the key concepts described on the Study Guide. I will not have to complete the actual assigned activities as long as I am working on an independent project.

______ I will demonstrate competency with the assessments for the Study Guide content at the same time as the rest of the class.

______ I will participate in designated whole-class activities as the teacher indicates them—without arguing.

______ I will keep a Daily Log of my progress.

______ I will work on an independent project and complete an Evaluation Contract to describe the grade I will choose to earn.

______ I will share a progress report about my independent project with the class or other audience by ____________ (date). My report will be 5–7 minutes long and will include a visual aid. I will prepare a question about my report to ask the class before giving my report.

Working Conditions

______ I will be present in the classroom at the beginning and end of each class period.

______ I will not bother anyone or call attention to the fact that I am doing different work than others in the class.

______ I will work on my project for the entire class period on designated days.

______ I will carry this paper with me to any room in which I am working on my project, and I will return it to my classroom at the end of each session.

Student's Signature:____

Teacher's Signature:____

★ EVALUATION CONTRACT ★

I am choosing a grade for my project based on these criteria.

For a grade of B:

1. I will use secondary sources. This means that I will locate what information I can from several existing sources.

2. I will prepare a traditional product. I will present it using a traditional reporting format.

3. I will be learning on the lower levels of Bloom's Taxonomy: Knowledge and Comprehension. This means that I will find information and be able to describe what I've learned.

For a grade of A:

1. I will use primary sources. This means that I will gather first-hand information myself through surveys, interviews, original documents, and similar methods.

2. I will produce an original type of product. I will present it to an appropriate audience using a unique format.

3. I will be learning on the higher levels of Bloom's Taxonomy: Application, Analysis, Evaluation, and/or Synthesis.

This is the project I will do: ____

____

____

____

This is the grade I intend to earn: ________

Student's Signature:____

Teacher's Signature:____

★ DAILY LOG OF EXTENSION WORK ★

Student's Name: ______________________________

Project Topic: ______________________________

Today's Date	What I Plan to Do During Today's Work Period	What I Actually Accomplished Today

Text continues from page 74

The Product Choices Chart

After students choose a topic from the Extensions Menu, they use the Product Choices Chart to choose a way to represent the information they find. The chart describes three types of products linked to three learning styles: auditory, visual, and tactile-kinesthetic.

- Auditory learners like typical school tasks that allow them to think logically, sequentially, and analytically. They like to read, write, make oral presentations, argue, and debate.
- Visual learners like to make posters, dioramas, collages, films and filmstrips, pictures on transparencies, videos, or other visual products.
- Tactile-kinesthetic learners prefer demonstrations, Reader's Theater, skits, plays, role-plays, or working with clay and other hands-on materials.

Don't be concerned if a student always chooses products from the same list. Your obligation is to demonstrate that students have mastered the content. How they show their mastery is secondary.

A reproducible Product Choices Chart is found on page 80.

GETTING STARTED

Identifying Students for the Study Guide Method

One way to help students decide if the Study Guide method is right for them is by describing the characteristics and abilities they need to be successful. It's best to do this during the unit before the one targeted for the Study Guide approach, but you can also do it at the start of a current unit.

Explain that students who are likely to do well with the Study Guide method are those who:

- Read well independently and enjoy reading.
- Find and bring to class information about curriculum topics from sources outside of class.
- Maintain a B average or higher on formal assessments during the unit.
- Show interest in becoming a resident expert on a topic related to the unit—someone who learns a lot about the topic and shares his or her expertise with the class.

Please notice that "Turn in all homework" is not listed here. The Study Guide method is designed for students who can demonstrate mastery on assessments without doing the actual daily work. They don't need to complete the same assignments as students for whom a more teacher-directed approach is desirable and necessary. Simply take a few moments to visualize several students who fit this description, and you may be identifying prime candidates for the Study Guide method.

You might also reassure the class that everyone could have a chance to become a resident expert at some time before the unit ends. This can happen as students complete assignments or projects ahead of others, or as a culminating activity for the entire class at the end of the unit. See page 85.

Hand out copies of your Study Guide to students who want to see them. Reassure students that the only concepts which will be formally assessed are those listed on the Study Guide. Students who want to learn at a faster pace might worry that they'll miss out on important concepts if they don't stay with the teacher-directed lessons every day.

NOTES: Recall that the Study Guide method is meant to be used with non-pretestable content. However, you may find some students who declare, after looking at the Study Guide, that they already know most of the required concepts. In that case, you may decide to let them take the end-of-the-unit assessment at that point. Make sure to use the same assessment you will later use with the rest of the class.

I don't recommend that you let students take the end-of-the-unit assessment any time they feel ready for it. Either they take it on Day One of the unit, or they use the Study Guide method for that unit. Otherwise, you'll get bogged down with more paperwork and record-keeping than you need.

Remember that it's counterproductive to provide a quickie review for students at the beginning of any unit. Some kids simply store this information overnight in their short-term memory, dump it out during the next day's assessment, then promptly forget everything they "learned."

★ PRODUCT CHOICES CHART ★

Auditory	Visual	Tactile-Kinesthetic
Audio recording	Advertisement	Acting things out
Autobiography	Art gallery	Activity plan for trip
Book	Brochure	Animated movie
Classifying	Coat of arms	Collection
Commentary	Collage	Composing music
Crossword puzzle	Coloring book	Dance
Debate or panel talk	Comic book or strip	Demonstration
Dialogue	Costume	Diorama
Documentary	Decoration	Dramatization
Editorial	Design	Exhibit
Essay	Diagram	Experiment
Experiment	Diorama	Field experience
Fact file	Drawing or painting	Flip book
Family tree	Filmstrip	Flip chart
Finding patterns	Flannel board	Game
Glossary	Flow chart	Game show
Interview	Graphic organizer	How-to book
Journal or diary	Greeting card	Invention
Learning Center task	Hidden pictures	Jigsaw puzzle
Letter to editor	HyperStudio or other multimedia presentation software	Learning center—hands-on tasks
Limerick or riddle	Illustrated manual	Manipulatives
Mystery	Illustrations	Mobile
Newspaper	Learning Center visuals	Model
Oral report	Magazine	Museum exhibit
Pattern and instructions	Map	Papier-mâché
Petition	Mural	Photograph
Position paper	Pamphlet with pictures or icons	Play or skit
Press conference	Photo album	Pop-up book
Reading	Photo essay	Project cube
Scavenger hunt	Picture dictionary	Puppet show
Simulation game	Political cartoon	Rap or rhyme
Song lyrics	Portfolio	Reader's Theater
Speech	Poster	Rhythmic pattern
Story or poem	Rebus story	Role-play
Survey	Scrapbook	Scale drawing
Teaching a lesson	Slide show	Sculpture
Trip itinerary	Transparency talk	Simulation game
Written report	Travelogue	Survey
	TV program	TV broadcast
	Video	
	Web site	

Introducing the Study Guide Method

Meet with interested students to explain the Study Guide method. Hand out copies of your Study Guide. Then start by saying something like this:

> Some of you could probably learn much of the content required for this unit simply by reading it on your own. If that's true for you, you're invited to move more independently through this unit in one of two ways.
>
> Although our class is concentrating on the Civil War, I've prepared a Study Guide about American wars in general, which you can use to learn the most important concepts in this unit.
>
> You can learn the concepts described on the Study Guide as they relate to the Civil War during school time or as homework. You can use your social studies time in school to learn about another war in which America was involved. The Study Guide will help you choose important aspects of the war to learn about.

Go through the study guide with the group, making sure that everyone understands the vocabulary and expectations. Inevitably, someone will ask, "Do we have to write down the answers?" Your response might be, "You can use whatever methods are necessary to make sure you learn the material. How you do it is up to you."

If you're using the Extensions Menu and/or Product Choices Chart, hand them out at this time. Introduce them to your students by saying something like this:

> There's a lot more to this unit than is included in our objectives. I have also prepared an Extensions Menu for this unit. You can use the Extensions Menu to become a resident expert on a topic related to the Civil War and report to the class on what you learn about that topic.
>
> Take a quick look at the options described there to see if you can find one that interests you. Then look at the Product Choices Chart. You can choose almost any product to link to any topic on the Extensions Menu. Of course, your topic must be related to the larger topic of American wars. The Student Choice section in the center of the menu allows you to use an original idea.
>
> You'll indicate your final choice on an Evaluation Contract, which I'll give you the next time we meet. You'll have two or three days to plan what you want to do, but you'll need to record each day of planning on a Daily Log of Extension Work, which I'll give you in a moment.
>
> You'll do the alternate work instead of the regular assigned daily activities, so you'll have work to do during social studies time that may be more challenging to you. You may work on your project in class, in the library, or in the Learning Materials Center, but you may not take it home until it has been completed and shared with the class.
>
> As long as you're prepared for the assessment at each checkpoint listed on the Study Guide, and as long as you follow the expectations listed on the Independent Study Agreement I'll give you the next time we meet, you'll be allowed to keep working on your project.

Hand out copies of the Daily Log of Extension Work (page 78) and tell students how to use it:

> At the start of any class period during which you're choosing and planning your project, fill in the left column with the date and the center column with a brief description of what you plan to accomplish during that time.
>
> Five minutes before the end of the period, complete the right column by recording information about the planning you actually accomplished.

Making It Official

A few days after the informational meeting described above, invite students who have decided to use the Study Guide method to a second meeting. Make sure that everyone has a Study Guide, Extensions Menu, Product Choices Chart, and Daily Log of Extension Work. Have extra copies available for students who need them.

1. Review the Study Guide, Extensions Menu, and Product Choices Chart. Help students select a product for the content they wish to learn about.

2. Hand out copies of the Independent Study Agreement (page 75 or page 76, depending on which one you decide to use). Go over it with the students and make sure they understand all of the conditions. You might say:

> This agreement explains my expectations for you while you are working independently. As you agree to each condition, please write your initials on the line to the left. Then sign your agreement, and I'll sign it, too.
>
> Keep your agreement with your Study Guide at all times, and always keep both at school. They should not go home until your project is completed.
>
> If you work on your project outside the classroom, bring your Study Guide and Independent Study Agreement with you.

When students take these documents along, the librarian or LMC person has concrete evidence that students are expected to behave appropriately and stay on task while they are away from the classroom.

A few conditions described in the agreement might need additional explanation. Share as much of this with your students as you think will be helpful.

• "I will participate in designated whole-class activities as the teacher indicates them—without arguing."

As a creative teacher, you involve your students in many other interesting and stimulating activities, some of which everyone should be present for. You need to reserve the option of calling in your Study Guide students for these "special events." They might include field trips, speakers, video or film events, simulations, or other activities all students will enjoy. Since it may be difficult to pinpoint at the beginning of a unit the exact dates on which such events will occur, reserve the right to announce that today (or tomorrow) will be a whole-class activity. When the special event ends, the Study Guide students are free to return to their projects.

• "I will share a progress report about my independent project with the class or other audience by ____________ (date)."

Resident experts (students working on Extensions Menu projects) are not required to complete an entire project by the end of the unit. That's why their reports are called "progress reports." In real life, researchers may spend a lifetime on one project.

The more often you bring the resident experts back for "special events," the less time they have to work on their project. Furthermore, gifted kids have a unique capacity for wanting to learn all there is to know about a topic of interest. If they think their learning will be limited by a timeline, they might not volunteer for the Study Guide option again.

Besides, you really don't want them to finish their project, since that would mean you have to help them find and plan another! The best thing that could happen is for a student to become so engrossed in a project that he wants to work on it for many weeks or even months—even into subsequent units. As long as the learning and working conditions are being met, there's no reason to insist that a student stop working on a project that clearly interests him.

Of course, it's also okay if resident experts want to switch topics at the end of the unit. Remember, they are being held totally accountable for the regular content. They will be given a new Study Guide for the next unit, for which they will also be held accountable for learning what the other students learn, during the same time frame. If this bothers you or the child's parents, you might consider asking students to complete one of every three projects they begin.

NOTE: The report does not have to be written. Writing slows down the mental processing for many gifted kids. The purpose of the report is to demonstrate that kids are learning alternate material. The format should be decided by the student, with your approval.

• "I will prepare a question about my report to ask the class before giving my report."

Resident experts should prepare a high-level question to ask the class. (See Build Blocks to Think on page 140.) This question should be recorded where everyone can see it before the progress report begins. An additional "mystery question" is allowed but not required.

This sets up ideal conditions for listeners. If you tell the class that the resident expert will be allowed to use the Name Card method (see pages 11–13) to call on them, listening will improve even more.

3. Tell students how their Study Guide work will be graded. Hand out copies of the Evaluation Contract (page 77) and say something like this:

> I'm assuming that this content is new for you. Therefore, there is no pretest. Since I don't have evidence of previous mastery, I can't grade you on content you haven't yet learned. You'll need to contract with me for the grade you intend to receive for doing the alternate work.
>
> I will record your assessment grades as you earn them. All other blank spots in the grade book will be filled in with whatever grade you contract for. The grade you choose will replace the grade you would have earned from doing the regular daily work with the rest of the class.
>
> As the Study Guide shows, you'll have to learn concepts 1 and 2 before the first checkpoint, when the whole class will have to demonstrate competence with those concepts. If you can demonstrate that you're knowledgeable about those concepts, you may keep working on your alternate topic or resident expert project until the next checkpoint.
>
> As long as you can keep demonstrating mastery of the designated concepts, and as long as you follow the working conditions described on your Independent Study Agreement, you may continue doing the alternate work.
>
> If it becomes clear that you're not keeping up with what you need to learn, or you can't meet the terms of the Independent Study Agreement, you'll be expected to rejoin the teacher-directed group and do the assigned activities from that day. You may finish your project at home or when the rest of the class works on projects in school.

NOTES: If students are required to rejoin the class while the unit is in progress, be careful not to make this seem like a punishment. It's simply a better learning option for kids for whom the Study Guide method isn't working.

If students rejoin the direct instruction group, they don't have to make up the work they missed, as long as they were following the working conditions in good faith. Since each assessment is cumulative—each includes all of the concepts previously assessed—the students will have to learn the material they missed and be ready to demonstrate mastery by the next checkpoint.

The Evaluation Contract has a space where students describe the project they plan to do. They can use words or draw a diagram. This is your chance to check the appropriateness of each project. A resident expert project should be:

- Broad enough to be relevant to the unit.
- Complex enough to hold the student's interest for an extended period of time.
- Sophisticated enough to provide a valid showcase for the student's talents.
- Manageable enough to be handled.
- Reflective of the student's ability to think in more abstract and complex ways than his or her age peers.

For an example, look back at Cleon's scenario on page 68.

4. Tell students that they will keep using the Daily Log of Extension Work, but in a slightly different way. Say:

> At the start of each class period during which you will work on your project, fill in the left column with the date and the center column with a brief description of what you plan to accomplish during that day's work period.
>
> Five minutes before the end of the work period, complete the right column by recording how much work you actually accomplished.
>
> If you discover that you accomplished less than you planned, drop down to the next line and write a note in the center column about the unfinished work. Don't write a date, because you may not know when you'll return to your project. But the next time you do, you'll know right where to start.

If your students are working at a location outside the classroom, ask the librarian or LMC person to help them remember to return to class 5 minutes before the end of the period, so they can complete their Daily Log and hear any announcements or discussion of plans for the following day.

NOTES: Never take a student off a project just because he isn't keeping good records. This is a skill many gifted kids have to learn; it doesn't automatically come with high intelligence. Offer frequent reminders as long as they're needed.

By giving kids permission to accomplish less than they planned, you're teaching them an important life survival skill: The world won't end if you don't finish everything today.

5. Have regular check-up meetings with your Study Guide students and resident experts. Provide technical assistance with their projects, and give them their fair share of your time and attention. Make sure that their logs are up-to-date and they're keeping up with the learning goals listed on the Study Guide.

It's important that gifted kids who work independently have access to their teacher on a regular, planned basis. You've worked hard to offer more challenging options so they can work at their own level. They need to know that it's perfectly all right to need assistance from you, even if they are smart kids.

There are several ways to make this happen. Some ideas are:

- When other students are working alone or in groups, spend some time with the kids using the Study Guide method.
- When you ask the class to read independently for 10–15 minutes, meet with your Study Guide kids. (Remember, they had to demonstrate that they were successful independent readers, so missing a little Sustained Silent Reading time can't possibly hurt them.)
- Invite kids on independent study to eat lunch with you in the classroom once a week.

You might also invite an interested parent to come into your classroom to help kids locate resources, to supervise time spent on the Internet, or to provide any other helpful services.

6. Insist that all students keep all documents related to the Study Guide method at school at all times. Provide special folders for that purpose, and keep the folders in a central location.

If students are having significant trouble completing tasks, show them how to use the Check-Off Sheet for Resident Expert Project (see page 163).

If parents wish to assist with the project at home, identify a separate part of the project as the "home project." Evaluate it separately from the school part of the project. Suggest that the student keep a separate Daily Log at home to document the differentiated homework.

★ ★ ★ ★ ★ ★ ★

The Study Guide Method Summarized

Opportunity: Students are excused from doing the daily work assigned to the class as long as they meet the learning and working conditions set forth in the Independent Study Agreement.

Study Guide: Preferably generic. No more than 10 key concepts all students are expected to master. Examples: Ancient Civilizations, Tall Tales, Human Body Systems, Personification in Stories.

Extensions Menu: Activities that extend the key concepts on the Study Guide, appeal to several learning styles, and require students to work at their personal challenge levels. Eight are defined and one is Student Choice.

Meetings: Two preliminary meetings with students—the first a general introduction to the Study Guide method, the second specifically for interested students. Regular check-up meetings with Study Guide students and resident experts.

Grades: Grades earned for independent study replace those students would have earned had they been required to do the regular work with the rest of the class.

Progress Reports: Resident experts share what they learned with the rest of the class in reports lasting 5–7 minutes.

Supporting Documents: The Evaluation Contract allows students to determine the grade they will get for their work. The Independent Study Agreement and Daily Log of Extension Work helps them maintain high standards and good progress. The contract, agreement, and log are kept at school at all times.

★ ★ ★ ★ ★ ★ ★

STRATEGY: ALLOWING ALL STUDENTS TO DO PROJECT WORK

Earlier in this chapter, I mentioned that there would be times when all students would have the opportunity to become resident experts.* There are at least two ways for this to happen.

1. Offer the same Extensions Menu to all students as a culminating activity at the end of the direct instruction time. Rather than working on projects independently, students might work with partners or small groups. They might be allowed to adapt the project idea so it takes less time to prepare.

2. Create a second Extensions Menu for students who aren't working with the Study Guide method. Make it available for use at designated times during the span of the unit. Allow students to use the Product Choices Chart (see page 80) to select products compatible with their learning styles.

Yet another way to involve the rest of the students as resident experts was developed by a seventh-grade science teacher, who was so pleased with the results that he decided to adapt the model for use with all of his students.

Using a unit on basic chemistry, the teacher began by giving his class a global overview of the chapter contents, reasoning that it would be very difficult for students to understand how to become an expert on a small piece of the unit if they didn't get the big picture first. Students then chose their topics, and the teacher allowed 2–3 days of in-class time for information gathering. Meanwhile, he brought in special materials from sources other than the textbook for the students to use as needed. He listed the topics on butcher paper while the students were doing their research, so everyone could see clearly which topics came before and after their own.

Instead of lecturing or doing a round-robin reading of the textbook material, the teacher launched the actual study of the unit by saying, "The first topic we will consider is the atom, and our resident expert, Janice, will tell us about it." Janice then came forward and shared what she had learned about atoms.

* If your teaching style is problem-based, all of your students are working on projects during the entire span of the unit. Be aware that gifted kids might still need access to more sophisticated projects within the same problem-based unit.

When she was finished, the teacher asked the rest of the class if anyone had anything to add. He invented an ingenious rule for this stage of the game: "Anyone who repeats something the expert already said won't be called on for the rest of the discussion." This is the kind of challenge gifted students enjoy, because 1) they must listen so they're sure not to add something that has already been said, and 2) they have more opportunities to contribute, since they always have something to add! This is all part of what it means to be gifted: learning and remembering so much, and taking such pleasure in letting the world know how much you know.

After giving the students a chance to speak, the teacher added any information he thought had been overlooked. Then he moved on to the next topic by asking, "Who is our resident expert on molecules?"

As subsequent resident experts described what they had learned, they were required to state, sometime during the first 30 seconds of their talk, how their topic was related to the previous topic. This encouraged students to listen to the other presentations and to think about connections as they learned the material.

Thanks to his inventiveness, this teacher made an important discovery: All of his students appeared to learn more with this method than with the traditional methods he had been using. They became more excited about the topics, and their motivation to learn was significantly higher. This is an excellent example of how strategies brought into the classroom to benefit gifted students can have serendipitous spillover effects with other students as well.

QUESTIONS AND ANSWERS

"What happens if the resident experts don't finish their projects?"

Ask yourself why you want them to finish their projects. Once they're through, you'll have to help them find and start another! Remind yourself that people who make their living in research sometimes spend a lifetime working on one project. Often, the only deadlines they have to meet are related to getting their grant applications in on time. So they hire logical-sequential thinkers with a penchant for meeting deadlines who are very successful at keeping the project on track.

Besides, your resident experts have to be ready for the checkpoint assessments, so they are meeting deadlines. If it weren't for the independent study option, that's all the content they would be learning. We need to lighten up about deadlines for independent study projects.

If you require your resident experts to participate in many whole-class activities and special events, this further limits the time they have available to work on their projects.

Some kids may not want to carry their current project into the next unit of work. Others will want to work on only one project for the semester or year. Always remember that the Study Guide holds students accountable for the required content. Make your decisions about their project preferences on an individual basis. I do think it's legitimate to hold students accountable for the progress reports as described on the Independent Study Agreement.

Keeping all this in mind, there may be times when you and a student decide it's in his best interests to return to the direct instruction group for the daily work. If you create resident expert opportunities for the entire class as a culminating activity, the student could finish his project at that time.

"What happens if students purposefully sabotage their results on an assessment because they really want to stop working on their project?"

During your initial meetings with the students, be sure they understand they should talk to you about any frustrations they encounter as they work through this method. During your check-up meetings as the unit progresses, ask students directly about their comfort level with the Study Guide method. If they are feeling overwhelmed, help them select smaller chunks to work on one at a time, rather than worrying about the entire project all at once. Show them how the Daily Log of Extension Work can help them break overwhelming tasks down into more manageable short term goals. If you want to make the goal-setting focus even more obvious, use the Goal-Setting Log (see page 15).

"How can I make sure that a student's parents don't get involved in trying to influence the content or quality of the resident expert project?"

Interested parents can assist their resident experts by helping them to locate information, or by taking them to museums and other sources of information. Or a certain portion of the project may be designated as the "home part." It is not included in the formal evaluation but may be included in the progress report. The student keeps a Daily Log at home to record his progress there. In this way, even his homework can be differentiated.

Remember that the project doesn't go home until it is completed. It is designed to be done in school so more capable students have meaningful work to do while the rest of the class is learning the basics with the teacher. The project represents the student's "real work" in school, and it must be available in school whenever it is needed. This includes work on any visual aid.

"How can I guarantee that students' independent work will be of high quality?"

The Evaluation Contract (page 77) is designed for that purpose. You can also use John Samara's Product Guides and Bertie Kingore's Portfolio Assessment tools. See References and Resources at the end of this chapter.

"Are identified gifted kids or kids who have been placed in a cluster automatically eligible for using the Study Guide method?"

No, they are not. Always remember that gifted kids who have been identified for a cluster in your classroom must demonstrate their eligibility for any compacting or differentiation option in the same way other students are asked to demonstrate it. Likewise, any student who has not been identified as gifted, but who can meet the criteria for eligibility for differentiation, should be allowed to participate in the compacting plan.

For more about cluster grouping, see Chapter 8.

"What if a resident expert is extremely uncomfortable presenting a progress report to his own class, or just refuses to do it?"

You might provide an alternate audience—another class, a community group interested in the topic, or even a private conference with you.

SUMMARY

This chapter described two ways to compact and differentiate the curriculum when the content is new to the student. The Study Guide without Extensions Menu allows gifted students to study other examples of the specific unit being learned by the class. The Study Guide with Extensions Menu invites students to become resident experts on topics related to the regular curriculum, learning new material from a more challenging perspective.

You have learned specific, classroom-tested ways to compact and differentiate instruction for students in subject areas that may not lend themselves to pretesting. Some teachers still provide pretesting opportunities in these subjects and use the Learning Contract approach described in Chapter 3 to manage the alternate activities for students who pass the pretest. Some teachers pretest and use the Independent Study Agreement to manage the students' alternate activities. The choice is yours.

REFERENCES AND RESOURCES

See also the References and Resources for Chapter 7.

General

Active Learning Systems, Epping, NH, (800) 644-5059. Developers of IIM (Independent Investigation Method), which helps children of all ages research and present information on any subject.

Black, Kaye. *Kidvid: Fun-Damentals of Video Instruction: Grades 4 Through 12.* Rev. ed. Tucson, AZ: Zephyr Press, 2000. Helps kids produce their own videos.

Challenging the Gifted in the Regular Classroom and *Differentiating Instruction for Mixed Ability Classrooms.* Two videos help teachers provide differentiated learning for gifted students. Available from ASCD, Alexandria, VA, (800) 933-ASCD (www.ascd.org).

Dunn, Rita, and Kenneth Dunn. *Teaching Elementary Students Through Their Individualized Learning Styles.* Boston: Allyn & Bacon, 1992.

Encyclopedia of Associations: National Organizations of the U. S. Farmington Hills, MI: Gale Group, updated often. A fabulous resource for free material for student researchers from national headquarters of thousands of companies in the United States. Look for it in a public or university library. Also from Gale: *Encyclopedia of Associations: International Organizations.*

Kingore, Bertie. *Implementing Portfolios.* Austin, TX: Professional Associates, 1997. Keeping track of students' projects and assessment tools for their work.

Product Guide Kits by John Samara. These excellent tools can eliminate the problem of gifted kids doing shoddy work on their projects. Each guide describes all of the parts that should be included in a type of product and describes the attributes for each part. Four kits are available: Level 1 (K–2), Level 2 (Grades 3–5), Level 3 (6–8), Level 4 (9–12). Each includes 16 product guides, 4 each in 4 different learning styles: kinesthetic, visual, oral, and written. Available from The Curriculum Project, Austin, TX, (800) 867-9067 (www.curriculumproject.com).

Timetables Books. These books help students see history and other disciplines from a chronological point of view. Each one serves as a rich menu for independent study topics. Unless otherwise indicated, all are published in New York by Simon & Schuster. Look for the latest edition of each.

- Bunch, Bryan, and Alexander Hellemans. *The Timetables of Technology: A Chronology of the Most Important People and Events in the History of Technology.*
- Cule, John. *The Timetables of Medicine: An Illustrated Chronological Chart of the History of Medicine.* New York: Black Dog & Leventhal Publishing.
- Grun, Bernard. *The Timetables of History: A Horizontal Linkage of People and Events.*
- Greenspan, Karen. *The Timetables of Women's History: A Chronology of the Most Important People and Events in Women's History.*
- Harley, Sharon. *The Timetables of African-American History: A Chronology of the Most Important People and Events in African-American History.*
- Hellemans, Alexander, and Bryan Bunch. *The Timetables of Science: A Chronology of the Most Important People and Events in the History of Science.*
- Romano, Frank J. *The Timetables of Communications.* Jewickley, PA: GATF Press.

Social Studies

Abby's Resource Page for Social Studies Teachers (home.windstream.net/abbysresources). Hundreds of links to social studies, history, and education Web sites.

American Memory: Historical Collections for the National Digital Library (memory.loc.gov). Multimedia collections of digitized documents, photographs, recorded sound, moving pictures, and text from the American collections of the Library of Congress bring primary sources into the classroom.

Education@nationalgeographic.com (www.nationalgeographic.com/education). Source for teaching world geography and national geography standards.

National Council for the Social Studies, Washington, DC, (301) 588-1800 (www.ncss.org). Lesson planning help for social studies teachers.

NewsCurrents Online (www.newscurrents.com). A weekly current events background and discussion program, available on the Web site 35 times a year by subscription. The same content is also available in nonelectronic form, including a filmstrip and teacher's discussion guide, from Knowledge Unlimited, Inc., Madison, WI, (800) 356-2303 (www.thekustore.com).

Debate

"A Pro/Con Issue" Series. From Enslow Publishers, Inc., Berkeley Heights, NJ, (800) 398-2504 (www.enslow.com).

"Opposing Viewpoints" Series. From Greenhaven Press, Farmington Hills, MI, (800) 877-4253 (www.galegroup.com/greenhaven).

Science

Discover Magazine Educator's Guides, (800) 829-9132 (www.discovermagazine.com). Hands-on activities, article summaries, and resources that correspond to topics in *Discovery* magazine.

Kinetic City (www.kineticcity.com). A crew of virtual kids take visitors on science-related adventures. Also contains information about experiments to do at home and school.

Mad Scientist Network (www.madsci.org). A science clearinghouse and "24-hour exploding laboratory" based at Washington University Medical School in St. Louis, Missouri.

Neuroscience for Kids (faculty.washington.edu/chudler/neurok.html). Experiments, activities, games, links, and more about the nervous system. Maintained by Dr. Eric Chudler at the University of Washington in Seattle.

Physics Applets (jersey.uoregon.edu). A virtual laboratory of interactive activities and experiments for use in physics, astronomy, and environmental science courses. Maintained by the University of Oregon Department of Physics.

Problem-Based Science Learning for K–8. Curriculum units created by the Center for Gifted Education at the College of William and Mary (cfge.wm.edu) include *Acid, Acid Everywhere, The Chesapeake Bay, Dust Bowl,* and *Electricity City.* Available from Kendall/Hunt Publishing Company, Dubuque, IA, (800) 228-0810 (www.kendallhunt.com).

Sandlot Science (www.sandlotscience.com). Science-related activities and projects, online exhibits, links to other classrooms, and more.

"Science Project Ideas" series. Books by Robert Gardner include *Science Project Ideas About Animal Behavior, Science Project Ideas About Rain,* and *Science Project Ideas About the Moon.* From Enslow Publishers, Inc., Berkeley Heights, NJ, (800) 398-2504 (www.enslow.com).

SpaceKids: Space Science for Kids (www.space.com/spacekids). This NASA site features many activities related to the study of astronomy and space, as well as a Teacher's Corner.

Students Can Learn on Their Own Home Page (users.erols.com/interlac). Information on independent learning and descriptions of recommended learning materials compiled by Robert Jackson, a former teacher, principal, and school superintendent. See especially "Science/Health/Social Studies/Environment" (users.erols.com/interlac/scienc.htm).

Catalogs

Delta Education, Nashua, NH, (800) 258-1302 (www.delta-education.com). Their Hands-On Science Catalog offers hundreds of products for K–8 science teaching.

Enslow Publishers, Inc., Berkeley Heights, NJ, (800) 398-2504 (www.enslow.com). Publishes many series in addition to the "A Pro/Con Issue" and "Science Project Ideas" already listed here. Examples: "Internet Library," "Great Science Fair Ideas."

Knowledge Unlimited, Inc., Madison, WI, (800) 356-2303 (www.thekustore.com). Learning materials for social studies, multicultural studies, global studies, science, and language arts.

Social Studies School Service, Culver City, CA, (800) 421-4246 (www.socialstudies.com). A mind-boggling collection of multimedia resources in social studies. Although designed for secondary students, some materials are suitable for younger gifted students.

5

EXTENDING READING AND WRITING INSTRUCTION

What kinds of reading and writing programs are you using? How well are they meeting the needs of kids who are gifted in those areas? How can you accommodate the passion for reading so many gifted students share? How can you provide appropriate challenge in all of the language arts for students who need it? This chapter answers these and other questions. It also describes many activities that gifted students truly enjoy.

CHARACTERISTICS OF GIFTED READERS

When trying to identify the gifted readers in your classroom (if you don't already know who they are), look for students who:

- Comprehend reading materials that are 2 or more years above grade level.
- Know, understand, and appreciate advanced vocabulary.
- Love to read and do so with great concentration and affection.
- Retain what they read.
- Make connections between various reading selections, and between reading selections and other content areas.
- Understand authors' styles and the use of various literary elements.
- Read earlier than other children their age. Some are spontaneous preschool readers; some start school having already mastered basic reading skills. Nearly all learn to read independently soon after classroom instruction begins.
- Read better than other children their age. Need less drill (if any) to master reading skills and techniques.
- Read more and longer than other children their age, especially during the peak reading years (grades 4–8).
- Interact with what they read in creative ways. Gifted readers don't simply read and absorb. They read and question; read and examine; read and think; read and argue; read and come up with new ideas.
- Have interests in reading that set them apart from other readers. Their preferences include science, history, biography, travel, poetry, and informational texts like atlases and encyclopedias.
- Read a greater variety of literature than other children their age. May branch out from realistic fiction to fantasy and historical fiction.

Scenario: Eric

Eric had failed fifth grade once, and he was now the tallest and biggest boy in his class. His former teachers described him as "lazy" because he never completed his homework in any subject. Some referred to his "poor attitude." Eric refused to read the stories from the required reader, never even opened his workbook, and had been overheard proclaiming, "I hate reading—it's dumb!" Over the years, he had spent many hours in the principal's office.

Eric's new teacher noticed that he always had a magazine about cars or trucks hidden in his desk. Furthermore, it was a magazine written for adults. Eric delighted in challenging his classmates to a contest of wits over the engine capacity and speed potential of the latest cars, and he always seemed to have that information at his fingertips. It was obvious to his teacher that he was actually reading and understanding the material in his magazines. Yet he was still failing all of his classes, including reading.

One weekend, Eric's teacher attended my seminar on the topic of teaching gifted students. While listening to me describe some characteristic behaviors of gifted kids, she realized that she had observed many of those behaviors in Eric. Upon returning to school, the teacher arranged to meet with other teachers and the school principal. She asked them to tell her which students came to mind as she read aloud a list of characteristic behaviors. Eric's name was mentioned over and over again. Could it be that his school problems were caused by boredom and frustration rather than laziness or a poor attitude?

The teacher decided to test her theory by offering Eric pretesting and compacting opportunities in several subjects, including reading skills and vocabulary. At first, Eric seemed unable to believe that a teacher would allow him to demonstrate mastery by doing less work than he had previously been asked to do. And when he learned that he could spend class reading time with his magazines, as well as novels and books about car racing and race drivers, his eyes nearly popped out of his head.

The results were just short of miraculous. Within days, Eric was back on the right learning track, completing his compacted work quickly and demonstrating a more positive attitude about school than anyone on staff had ever observed. His mother commented to the teacher about the remarkable changes she was seeing in her son. After about two weeks, the principal dropped by the class to see if Eric had been absent with some terrible illness. Since he was no longer being sent to the office to be disciplined, the principal assumed the worst!

Eric's story provides ample evidence that modifying the curriculum can allow us to see gifted kids who won't do the required work in a totally new light.

READING FOR GIFTED READERS

Most reading programs, whether traditional or literature-based, have failed to meet the learning needs of many gifted students. Most high-ability students have already mastered the vocabulary and skills they will be expected to "learn" this year. They need opportunities to demonstrate their competencies, and to replace work they don't need to do with meaningful reading experiences.

For all skill and vocabulary work, you should provide regular pretesting and compacting opportunities, using the methods described in chapters 2 and 3. You'll find a sample reading contract on page 95 of this chapter, and a sample writing contract on page 121. Contracts allow you to see which vocabulary words and specific reading and writing skills students have already mastered. Students who demonstrate mastery should be engaged in alternate activities at the same time as others in the class are doing the regular work. Ideas for alternate activities are presented throughout this chapter, as well as in Appendix A starting on page 219.

The reading program that is most appropriate for all students and essential for gifted students is one that allows them to read, discuss, analyze, and write about literature that challenges them, while being excused from practicing skills they have already mastered. The literature students read should:

- Include a variety of forms including prose, poetry, biography, and nonfiction.
- Be open to interpretation and various viewpoints.
- Contain rich, challenging, and varied language forms.
- Provide opportunities for readers to learn personal problem-solving behaviors.
- Be relevant to the reader's life and experience.

CAUTION: Be careful about having kids read books that offer challenging vocabulary and content but describe situations that are beyond their maturity and life experience.

In some districts, teachers are expected to use "whole-class" instruction, keeping all students on the same reading level. Although there may be a good reason to prevent students from using basal texts assigned to different grade levels, their access to literature at all levels of reading should never be restricted. Some staffs have decided to earmark a limited number of novels for each grade level, and they have asked their colleagues to refrain from using books not assigned to their grade. When the number of restricted novels is limited to six or so, this practice is perfectly reasonable, since there is clearly an abundance of materials remaining from which students may choose.

One of the most significant purposes of teaching reading is to generate a love of literature in children. Any classroom practices that accomplish that goal should be preferable to those that cause students to avoid reading and writing whenever they can. Talk to parents about their kids' attitudes toward reading at home, and observe the extent to which your students choose to read when they have opportunities to make choices in the classroom. Incorporating highly motivating strategies such as those presented in this chapter will help you to keep your gifted readers enthusiastic about reading.

The figure below shows, at a glance, how you might differentiate reading for your gifted students.* The Study Guide and Extensions Menu are explained in Chapter 4 and on page 97 of this chapter. The Reading Activities Menu is discussed on page 94. Information about the Great Friday Afternoon Event is found on page 123.

Reading for Gifted Primary Children

Not all gifted kids come to kindergarten reading, and not all kids who come to kindergarten reading are gifted. But show me a youngster who taught herself to read without any apparent support from adults, and I'll show you a child who is probably gifted, at least in reading.

* From a paper presented at the Association of Supervision and Curriculum Development (ASCD) Annual Conference, New Orleans, March 2000. Adapted and used with permission of the McMinnville Public Schools, McMinnville, Oregon.

DIFFERENTIATING READING

Whole-Group Instruction	Differentiation for Gifted Readers
All read the same book.	All read different books on the same theme.
Whole-class learning.	Study Guide with or without Extensions Menu.
Students read different books but do the same learning tasks.	Students read self-selected books and do different learning tasks.
Skill work by direct instruction.	Compacting and contracts for selective skill work and faster pacing.
Theme-based literature circles; teacher-directed learning.	Self-selected literature with Study Guide and Extensions or Reading Activities Menu.
Standards and regular curriculum are taught directly to students.	Students take direct instruction only on content they have not mastered.
Great Friday Afternoon Event.	Great Friday Afternoon Event.

For many decades, educators believed that most kids who were reading when they started school would "plateau out"—revert to the levels of more average readers—by third grade. Kids who did were cited as proof that Mom or Dad had taught them to read before they were truly ready. Recent studies have shown that advanced readers who were expected to do the regular reading program in kindergarten and first grade did become more average later...but advanced readers who were taught at their challenge level, regardless of their grade level, generally maintained their edge into the upper grades. Gifted readers need to be taught at their challenge level in reading, regardless of how soon (or late) they learn to read.

You can use the pretest and contract methods described here with your precocious primary readers. Start with the Study Guide alone, without the Extensions Menu, and add the alternate activities later, as your students become more able to use them. Please read (or reread) Especially for Primary Teachers on page 54 for suggestions on how to manage differentiation for students in the primary grades.

STRATEGY: THE CONTRACT FOR PERMISSION TO READ AHEAD

This simple strategy will save you many headaches as you differentiate for your gifted readers.

As you no doubt already know from experience, most gifted readers ask the same question at the beginning of any reading selection: "May I please read ahead?" Perhaps you think that if you tell them you don't want them to read ahead, they will honor your request. In fact, they will probably read ahead anyway.

Would you ever let anyone tell you how much time you should take to read a story or book, or how quickly or slowly you should read it? Especially one in which you're intensely interested? It's not surprising that these passionate readers will finish the whole story or book before dawn tomorrow. What can you do to manage this situation?

Group them together and ask each of them to sign a Contract for Permission to Read Ahead. Tell them it's okay to read ahead, but they need to understand how important it is to honor the terms of the contract. They shouldn't spoil the selection for others by giving away plot twists or endings. And when they hear other kids talking about a book or story and what might happen next, they should avoid joining in.

Page 93 is a sheet of two contracts you can copy, cut apart, and give to your students who want to read ahead. To keep them challenged and motivated in reading class while others are still reading the designated selection, use the strategies and activities in this chapter and in Appendix A.

STRATEGY: THE CONTRACT FOR READING SKILLS AND VOCABULARY

To differentiate skill work in reading programs, you can use the same general type of Learning Contract described in Chapter 3.

Make pretests available at the beginning of each new section of the curriculum to students who volunteer for them or seem to need them. Some students who you think should take the pretests may resist. Don't insist that they take them. Instead, let them observe what happens to kids who take advantage of the pretesting and compacting, and keep encouraging them to take subsequent pretests. Students who meet the expected criteria work with the class for direct instruction only when the class is learning concepts the gifted students have not already mastered. During other times, they are free to select activities from a menu of alternatives, keeping a Daily Log (page 78) to record those activities.

A reproducible Contract for Reading Skills and Vocabulary is found on page 95.

★ CONTRACT FOR PERMISSION TO READ AHEAD ★

Check each statement to show that you agree with it. Then sign the contract.

☐ I will not tell anyone anything about the story until everyone in the group has finished reading it.

☐ I will not participate in prediction activities.

Student's Signature:____

★ CONTRACT FOR PERMISSION TO READ AHEAD ★

Check each statement to show that you agree with it. Then sign the contract.

☐ I will not tell anyone anything about the story until everyone in the group has finished reading it.

☐ I will not participate in prediction activities.

Student's Signature:____

From *Teaching Gifted Kids in the Regular Classroom* by Susan Winebrenner, copyright © 2001. Free Spirit Publishing Inc., Minneapolis, MN; www.freespirit.com. This page may be photocopied for individual or classroom work only. For other uses, call 800-735-7323.

How to Use the Contract for Reading Skills and Vocabulary

1. Offer a pretest on vocabulary and skills for the upcoming reading unit. Students who achieve a score of 80 percent or higher are eligible for a contract.

2. Prepare contracts for eligible students.

- Fill in the top part with concept descriptions and/or page numbers from skill work sources. Check those that indicate concepts for which the student must join the class for instruction.
- Fill in the middle part of the contract with the vocabulary words the student has not yet mastered, as evidenced by the pretest. Designate activities students should do to learn their vocabulary words.
- At the bottom, list the working conditions you expect students to follow. Or create a Working Conditions chart to display in your classroom. That way, you won't have to include conditions on every contract and you can skip this section. As a third alternative, you can give each contract student a copy of the Working Conditions for Alternate Activities form on page 51.

3. Tell contract students that they may not work on any checked item until it is taught to the class as a whole, when they must join the other students for a teacher-directed lesson.

4. Explain that on days when they don't have to be with the rest of the class for reading, they can choose any activity that requires them to read and/or write. Have them record their extension activities on a Daily Log of Extension Work (see page 78).

> **IMPORTANT:** Don't expect contract students to start and complete a new project each time they work on extension activities. Instead, they can start a project, file it away as a work-in-progress at the end of the period, and return to it next time they are allowed to work on extension activities.

5. Call students' attention to the Working Conditions. Remind them that they must do their work without bothering anyone or calling attention to themselves. Make it clear that if they can't follow the conditions, they will rejoin the class for the rest of the unit.

STRATEGY: THE READING ACTIVITIES MENU

When you want to provide your more capable students with alternate activities that extend the regular reading unit, you might use a Reading Activities Menu. Students who buy back time in reading may choose from a list of options. The menu also allows for choice days, when students may create and do their own activities or continue with listed activities.

If you prefer, you may present alternate activities in an Extensions Menu format. See the American Wars Extensions Menu on page 72 and Preparing the Study Guide and Extensions Menu on page 69.

How to Use the Reading Activities Menu

1. Prepare a list of activities from which students may choose several they would like to do. Or use the reproducible menu on page 96, designed for use with any literature selection.

2. Tell students that they may choose an activity to work on during times you designate. They may continue working on their activity until it is completed; they don't have to start and finish an activity on the same day. They should record the dates they begin and end each activity on the Date(s) lines. *Example:* 10/5–10/7.

3. Invite students to come up with their own ideas for projects or activities. They should discuss their ideas with you before starting to work on them. After you give your permission for a specific project or activity, the student should record it on the menu in one of the blank spaces provided.

4. Have students record their work on a Daily Log of Extension Work (see page 78).

★ CONTRACT FOR READING SKILLS AND VOCABULARY ★

Student's Name: ____

✓	Page/Concept	✓	Page/Concept
____	______________________	____	______________________
____	______________________	____	______________________
____	______________________	____	______________________
____	______________________	____	______________________
____	______________________	____	______________________

Vocabulary Words for Unit

______________	______________	______________
______________	______________	______________
______________	______________	______________
______________	______________	______________
______________	______________	______________

Working Conditions

____

____

____

____

____

____

Student's Signature: ____

Teacher's Signature: ____

★ READING ACTIVITIES MENU ★

Student's Name: ____

Directions:

During the next _________ days, create your own menu of activities from the list below to do in place of the regular assignments.

Date(s)	**Activity**
__________	Create and perform a puppet show of the story or book.
__________	Interview another person who read the book.
__________	Write a letter to the author.
__________	Write another chapter.
__________	Write a different ending.
__________	Using a thesaurus, find synonyms for your 6 favorite words.
__________	Create a dialogue between 2 characters.
__________	Read other books by the same author. Compare/contrast.
__________	Read another book of the same type. Compare/contrast.
__________	Write a story or book of the same type which contains similar elements.

Include 3 free days. Add on days to the activities listed or create your own activities:

__________ ____

__________ ____

__________ ____

STRATEGY: USING THE STUDY GUIDE METHOD FOR READING EXTENSION

You can use the information, strategies, and forms in Chapter 4 to design a Study Guide with or without Extensions Menu to differentiate reading for gifted students. See the Animal Story and Biography study guides and extensions menus on pages 98–101 for examples of this method. Give the Product Choices Chart (page 80) to students who use the extensions menus so they can choose learning-style compatible ways to demonstrate what they are learning.

STRATEGY: USING TRADE BOOKS FOR SELF-SELECTED READING

Another way to extend reading instruction for gifted students is to let them read literature of their choosing, then discuss what they have read with each other and with you. This is generally the format gifted readers prefer for at least part of their reading time. They may all read the same novel, different books of the same genre or type, or books by the same author. You may decide to let each student read a completely different book. See Strategy: Individualized Reading starting on page 103.

Regardless of the approach you use, the emphasis should be on providing challenging reading activities for these kids. Following are several ideas you might have your students try.

- Locate inferences, cause and effect, etc.
- Find foreshadowing, personification, metaphor, or other literary elements.
- Analyze the theme and its relationship to other books.
- Analyze the bias of characters and/or the author.
- Create related writing activities.
- Rewrite certain events or create a new ending.
- Write a similar story.
- Write the same story, set in a different time period.
- Write a new ending.
- Write a new chapter to insert into the novel.
- Hypothesize on the validity of the content and events described.
- Hypothesize what would happen if different characters had interacted.
- Change one character in a significant way and draw a flowchart which predicts how this change would affect the other characters or the plot.
- Using cartoon format, create a dialogue between you and one of the characters in which you try to convince that person to behave differently.
- Create new possibilities for plot or character development.
- Share the story as a storyteller would.
- Read biographies about real people in similar situations to the one(s) described in the novel.
- Research the life of a famous person and write an original biography.
- Compare and contrast books by the same author.
- Compare and contrast books of the same genre.
- Create a dramatic reading or short play about the story.
- Create illustrations for a story or book that doesn't have them.
- Understand point of view and the presence of multiple perspectives in literature.
- Invent your own activity. Discuss it with the teacher before you start working.

Your gifted readers might also enjoy using the Author Extensions Menu on page 102. Remember to have them record their progress on a Daily Log of Extension Work (see page 78).

All Reading the Same Novel

1. Give the pretest on reading skills and vocabulary to anyone who wants to take it.

2. Offer students who already know 80 percent or more of the required skill work a Contract for Reading Skills and Vocabulary (see pages 92 and 94).

3. Help them agree on a novel they would like to read together by giving them information about several choices. The school or town librarian can assist you with this step.

4. Relate the vocabulary, writing activities, and other skill work to that novel. In some cases, you may be able to use selected pages from skill work the whole class is doing, instead of having to create new activities.

Text continues on page 103

★ ANIMAL STORY STUDY GUIDE ★

BE PREPARED TO:

1. Identify and discuss all of the elements in our story map as they appeared in this story.

2. Discuss the meanings of the vocabulary words for this story.

3. Describe the animal(s) that are important characters in this story. Include information about physical appearance, behavior, likes and dislikes, wishes, and the problem the animal(s) need to solve.

★ **CHECKPOINT:** ________________ **: Assessment for 1–3** ★
DATE

4. Create a dialogue between a human and an animal in this story in which the animal describes what he or she really wants. Continue by inventing a plan they form to make the animal's wish come true.

5. Explain the evidence from the story that shows a bond between humans and one or more of the animals.

6. Use a Venn diagram to chart the similarities and differences between an animal in the story and a "real" animal of the same species.

★ **CHECKPOINT:** ________________ **: Assessment for 1–6** ★
DATE

7. Make a chart that describes the human qualities each animal in the story possesses. (Anthropomorphism is a technique in writing that makes animals appear to have human characteristics.)

8. Illustrate in some manner some differences between wild and domestic animals of a certain species.

9. Prepare a want ad in which a human in the story advertises his or her need for an animal to help with a problem, OR in which the animal advertises for help from a human.

10. Create a brochure describing how a child should care for an animal in this story, if the animal were the child's pet.

★ **CHECKPOINT:** ________________ **: Final Assessment for 1–10** ★
DATE

ANIMAL STORY EXTENSIONS MENU

Write a first-person story in which the main character is an animal who tries to live with humans.	Do a research study about an organization that is working to save endangered animals from extinction. Plan a campaign to save an animal you admire.	Read 10 or more poems about animals. Write poetry about animals that interest you.
Read about people who have tamed and lived with wild animals. Describe the characteristics such people have in common.	**Student Choice**	Plan and present a debate about the merits of preserving a certain area for the use of its existing animals and plants. The other side of the debate would give reasons to develop the area into homes or shopping.
Pretend you're an archaeologist who has just discovered the remains of an extinct animal. Share information about how the animal lived, why it became extinct, and how it might have been saved from extinction.	Imagine that your family acquires an unusual animal as a pet. Present information about some of the joys and challenges of having the animal.	Create a composite animal with elements of several animals. Convince someone else that it's the best animal in the world.

★ BIOGRAPHY STUDY GUIDE ★

BE PREPARED TO:

1. Describe details from the subject's early years, including place and circumstances of birth, childhood, schooling, siblings, parents, and relatives who influenced him or her.

2. Describe details from the subject's adolescence, including hobbies, education, and memorable experiences.

★ **CHECKPOINT:** ________________: **Assessment for 1–2** ★
DATE

3. Describe the personal aspects of the subject's adult life, including relationships, commitments, and significant events.

4. Explain when and how the subject found his or her way to a chosen career. Include information about the people or events that influenced him or her.

5. Describe what qualities, circumstances, or events made this person important enough to have a biography written about him or her.

★ **CHECKPOINT:** ________________: **Assessment for 1–5** ★
DATE

6. Prepare a timeline of the subject's career, including both helpful events and setbacks.

7. Describe how the subject's life ended, as well as any awards or honors he or she received.

8. Give the meanings of any assigned vocabulary words.

9. Describe how the biography helped you better understand the events of the times in which the subject lived and worked.

10. Find some events in the biography that you think might not have happened as they were portrayed. Find another source of information about the subject and decide how accurate the portrayal is in the biography.

★ **CHECKPOINT:** ________________: **Final Assessment for 1–10** ★
DATE

★ BIOGRAPHY EXTENSIONS MENU ★

Create a bibliography of biographies in a specific category. *Examples:* women, astronauts, children, musicians, inventors, sports heroes, entertainers. Read those that look interesting to you. Find a way to get others interested in reading them.	Read 3 biographies in a specific category (see the box at the left). Illustrate the elements they have in common.	Illustrate the relationship between the subject's life and the time period in which he or she lived. Include information about specific events and how they influenced the person's life.
Describe gender or ethnic issues in biographies written for your age group during the past 10 years, and during the first 5 years of any previous decade.	**Student Choice**	Discover some things about which the subject would have been proud. Use these to create his or her obituary and epitaph.
Create an illustrated timeline showing major and minor events in the subject's life. Create a second timeline showing things the person might have wanted to do or accomplish.	Act out a biography of a person who was connected to a particular historical event your classmates are studying. Challenge your audience to guess the person's identity.	Use photography to illustrate the "snapshot method" of biography, in which you show common themes or elements found in 3 biographies.

★ AUTHOR EXTENSIONS MENU ★

Read interviews with the author. Write a short biography of the author based on that information.	Discover other things the author has written that don't follow the same style of the book you are reading.	Write something of your own in the same style as the author.
Write a letter to the author. (Get contact information from the publisher.) Give your reactions to the book and ask the author some questions about himself or herself.	**Student Choice**	Find out if the author has worked with other writers and/or illustrators. Compare the author's "working alone" style with his or her "working with others" style. Is there a difference? If so, describe it.
Read other books of the same type by different authors. Compare and contrast the styles of the various authors.	Learn the steps a person has to take to become a published author.	Research Children's Bestsellers lists published over the past 12 months. Find out how many books like the one you read were or are bestsellers.

Text continues from page 97

NOTE: Many companies have produced inexpensive and comprehensive prepackaged units for teaching novels. Check them out before you use precious planning time to come up with your own activities. See References and Resources at the end of this chapter.

5. Meet with this group in much the same way you would with a typical reading group. The main difference is that your discussions and activities will relate to the novel instead of the selection the rest of the class is reading. If you wish, you may prepare a Study Guide to help kids notice the most important elements. Students who finish the novel ahead of the others may use the remaining time to read other books by the same author or in the same genre.

Don't be surprised if the group studying the novel is much more enthusiastic than the group working with the assigned material. If this happens in your classroom, you may decide to let all students study a novel now and then instead of a designated unit. Most skills can be taught in any context, and you can use games to teach the vocabulary words students would otherwise miss. Some teachers use this method as a transition to a literature-based program, setting aside one day of the week for literature study while staying with the designated material for the other four days, or replacing one entire unit with literature-based reading.

Some students who read quickly and love to read can't resist sharing, even if it means giving away the ending of a novel or important plot twists along the way. To discourage spoilers, have them sign a Contract for Permission to Read Ahead (see page 93).

All Reading Different Novels by the Same Author

If you choose this option, you may want to use a cooperative learning format. Put the gifted students together in one group and suggest more complex novels. Removing them from the other groups will force the rest of the students to work more actively. Also, when gifted students are allowed to work in their own cooperative group, they are more likely to participate in cooperative activities than when they are in a group that slows down their reading pace and limits their preferred complexity of thought and discussion. For more about gifted kids and cooperative learning, see Chapter 8.

Meet with each group separately to discuss their particular novel. Discussions about the author's style may take place with the entire class. Use the Author Extensions Menu on page 102 to invite students to specialize in one aspect of the author's life and work.

All Reading Different Novels of the Same Genre

When you want all students to read different novels of the same type or genre—such as mysteries, science fiction, stories about animals, or biographies—use a Study Guide with or without Extensions Menu (see Chapter 4). The Study Guide itself serves as the differentiation tool, and the Extensions Menu may not be necessary, especially for kids in the primary grades. See pages 98–101 for study guides and menus you can use as is or adapt to meet your students' needs.

When you use the Study Guide method and allow kids to choose what to read, you can be sure that the Study Guide will help them know what to look for in their own selections. This is much more effective than telling kids to "go read other biographies of this person." For example, if your class is working on a unit on folk tales, your gifted readers can finish the designated selection at their own pace, then read other folk tales, even some from different countries. Class discussions would center around the characteristics of the genre, and students would contribute to the discussion based on their alternative reading.

STRATEGY: INDIVIDUALIZED READING

To meet the needs of gifted students (and give all students' interest in reading a boost), consider letting everyone read a different book. You'll want to have a variety of titles, topics, and reading levels available in the classroom. Several publishing companies distribute collections for this purpose. See References and Resources at the end of this chapter.

Initially, students should be free to browse through any books that interest them. Advise them to use the "Rule of Three" to select any book they actually plan to read. Tell them:

> Open the book to some page in the middle—preferably a page without pictures—and start reading. Whenever you come across a word you don't know, hold up one finger. When your count exceeds three words on one page, the book is probably too difficult for you to read independently. Go to another book and try again.

If you're concerned that students will choose books that are too easy, suggest that they try to read three consecutive pages from the middle of the book. If they don't find any unfamiliar words in that section, they should probably look for another book.

Have students keep track of what they read. There are many ways to do this. Two of my favorites are the Circle of Books and the Reading Response Sheet. Both are easy to understand and use.

The Circle of Books (page 105). When students finish reading a book, they place a tally mark in the appropriate section of the wheel. The marks help them (and you) to see if they are reading from a variety of categories or limiting themselves to one or two. Naturally, you may use other categories than the ones shown on the reproducible form.

The Reading Response Sheet (page 106). Students spend a few minutes at the end of each reading period jotting down their thoughts about and responses to the book they are reading. These might include their reactions to events and characters, predictions about upcoming events, character studies, rewritten chapters or endings, and so on. Completed pages may be collected to form a Reading Response Journal.

Students are also invited to write down an interesting word from their reading. You might suggest activities that will help them learn these words, or students might discuss their words when they meet with other students who are doing individualized reading.

> **CAUTION:** Vocabulary activities and writing activities can become very tiresome for prolific readers. If too much writing is required, gifted students might resist differentiated reading. Some students will appreciate not having to complete reading response sheets for every book they read.

Keeping Tabs on Individualized Readers

Schedule brief weekly conferences with students who are reading self-selected literature. Keep an ongoing Record Sheet for each student. See page 107 for a form you can copy and use.

1. In the far left column, record the date of each conference.

2. In the second column, record the title of the book the student is reading.

3. In the third column, make notes about the conference discussion. Here are some questions and suggestions to spark and guide your discussion:

- What is this story about?
- What techniques does the author use to "hook" you and draw you into the story?
- What's the best part of the story? Why? The worst/most boring part? Why?
- Find a good descriptive passage and read it to me.
- Which characters do you like? Which do you dislike? Tell why.
- How does the author get you to feel close to the characters?
- Which character is the most developed? The least developed?
- Say and define some of the interesting vocabulary words you found.
- Were there any parts of the book that didn't seem to belong?
- What did you admire about the author's style that you might use in your own writing?
- Was there anything confusing about the author's style? Explain.
- How would you change the book? The ending?

If you use the Recommended Books Chart (see page 109), you might also ask:

- What will you write about this book on the Recommended Books Chart?

4. In the far right column, note any tasks you ask the student to complete. These may be related to vocabulary development, story mapping, character study, or anything else you would normally use to teach a story.

Text continues on page 108

THE CIRCLE OF BOOKS

Each time you finish a book, put a tally mark in the appropriate section. Check to see if you are reading from a variety of categories or limiting yourself to just one or two.

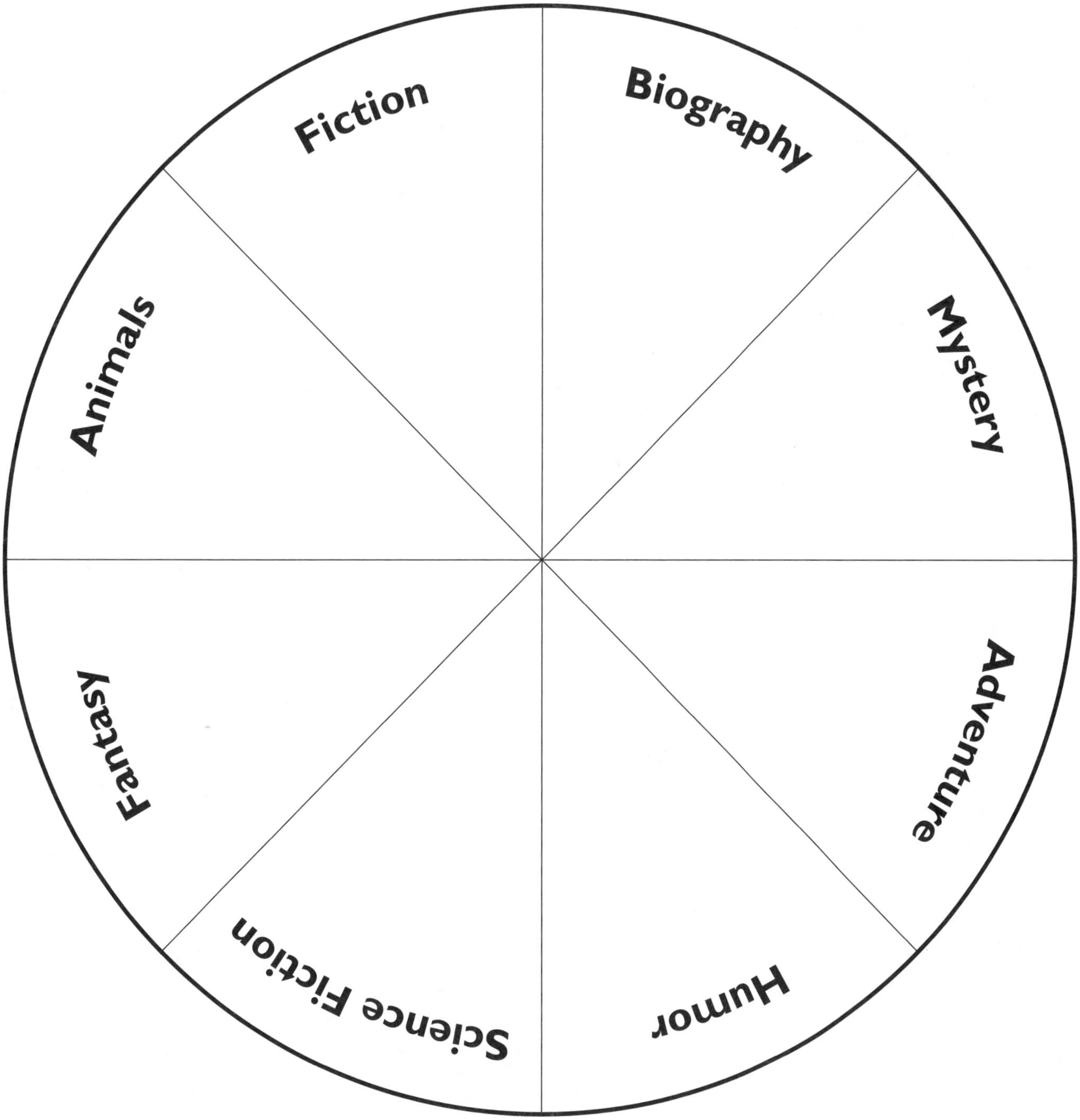

★ READING RESPONSE SHEET ★

Student's Name: ____

Title of Book: ____

Author's Name: ____

Today's Date: ____________________ Pages Read Today: ____________________
FROM TO

My reactions to today's reading: ____

____

____

____

____

What's really great about this book so far: ____

____

____

____

____

What I would like to change in this book: ____

____

____

____

An interesting word from this book: ____

TEACHER'S CONFERENCE RECORD SHEET

Student's Name: ____

Date	Book	Conference Discussion	Assigned Tasks

Text continues from page 104

5. Before the conference ends, write the date of the next conference in the far left column. This helps you keep track of when students are expected to return, and also makes it harder for students to "forget" to come to conferences for long periods of time. Keep all sheets in a 3-ring binder for easy access.

Tell students they must meet with you on their scheduled day regardless of whether they have finished their book. If they need additional conferences, have them sign up at a specified location.

Book Sharing

Provide one or more ways for students to share their books with one another. Avoid formal written book reports, since these generally have a negative effect on students' attitudes about reading. There are many alternatives to book reports that are far more creative and fun. Following are descriptions, instructions, and forms for three of my favorites. You might use one or all to structure regularly scheduled Book Sharing Time, during which students report verbally and briefly (about 2 minutes) about a book they are currently reading or have recently completed.

Before students start talking about a book they have read (or are reading), they should write the title and the author's name (or the book's call number) on the board.

Book Logos

1. Gather as many colors of paper as you have students in your room. Add a few extra colors so you're ready for new students. You'll need several sheets of each color.

2. Cut the sheets into 4G" x 5H" pieces (half the standard 8H" x 11" size).

3. Prepare two sample swatches of each color. Drop one of each into a "hat." All swatches should be the same size.

4. Have students select their colors by drawing swatches from the "hat." Tell them to write their name on their color and give it back to you.

5. Glue the appropriate matching swatch beside each student's name on a Book Logos chart. (See page 109 for an example.) Laminate the chart before displaying it, or the sun will quickly fade the colors.

6. Give each student a folder filled with a supply of his or her color paper. Label each folder with the student's name and the second color swatch.

7. Direct the students to make a logo for each book they finish reading. You might explain it this way:

> Cut out a shape from a piece of your paper that represents the essence of your book. This is your "logo" for that book. Using dark colored marker, print the title of the book and the author's name on your logo.

You might have prolific readers make a logo for every third or fourth book they read. If they have to make too many logos, they might get turned off to reading.

8. Display the logos around the room. When you run out of space, display them in the hallways.

Students may show their logos when they talk about their books to the class.

One year, my 27 fifth graders read 384 books! The logos were displayed in a line near the ceiling of the room, which eventually spilled out into the hall and wound its way around the entire floor. Imagine the lively conversations about books that were stimulated by the presence of these colorful logos. Furthermore, if students wanted to recommend certain books they had read to other students, they could easily locate the appropriate logo by its color.

This method of keeping track of the books your students read is certainly preferable to the traditional chart, which demonstrates (sometimes painfully) who the sluggish readers are for all the world to see. With the logos, an observer would have to work to add up the number of books read by any particular student. And since the purpose of the logos is to provide a forum for discussing books, nobody really cares about the numbers anyway.

Books I Want to Read

You know how frustrating it is to try to remember titles of books people have told you about. The Books I Want to Read method eliminates this frustration for your students. See page 110 for a form you can copy and use in your classroom.

1. Give all students a copy for the Books I Want to Read chart. Tell them to keep it in their desk or reading folder at all times. It *never* goes home.

★ BOOK LOGOS ★

(NOTE: The actual chart will show samples of the students' colors, not the names of the colors.)

Name	Color	Name	Color
Jason	Navy blue	Eric	Ivory
Tom	Red	Leandra	Gold
Kyoko	Gray	Joey	Violet
Susie	Yellow	Roberto	Neon yellow
Leshon	Orange	Elizabeth	Purple
Barbra	Pastel pink	Jim	Neon green
José	Brown	Julie	Neon pink
James	Black	Dimitri	Light blue
Alicia	Turquoise	Elena	Green

2. Tell students how to use the form. You might say:

   When I announce Book Sharing Time, take out your Books I Want to Read chart. Listen carefully as each speaker shares information about a book. Don't write anything while you're listening.

   When the speaker is done talking, decide if this is a book you'd like to read. If it is, write the call number or author's name and book title on your chart. If you want, you can jot down a few notes about the book.

   Whenever you go to the library or media center to choose a book, carry your chart with you. It will help you remember which books you'd like to read. When you finish reading a book, cross it off your list.

   When you run out of room on your chart, let me know and I'll give you a new one to staple to your old one.

Recommended Books

Using the example shown on page 111 as a model, create a large chart (at least 24" x 36") to post on a wall or bulletin board. Hang a pencil on a string nearby and watch the chart fill up with student recommendations. Encourage student to use soft voices at the chart, which is sure to become a center for discussion about books and authors.

VOCABULARY ACTIVITIES

Gifted kids usually love vocabulary activities, once they are introduced to the magic of words. All gifted students should have their own thesauruses for regular use in their writing.

To get your whole class hooked on words, bring in a copy of a "how-to-name-your-baby" book. Students will become fascinated with the history of their own names. Once they've been enticed by that, they're likely to be excited about studying the history of other words as well.

Working with the school or town librarian or with Internet resources, you can collect a variety of materials that help kids experience the delights of playing with words, understanding how words change through time, and learning how new words are added to our language. See References and Resources at the end of this chapter for several possibilities.

Vocabulary Builders

Look for books that help you teach one or more of the topics listed on the Vocabulary Builders chart on page 112. Introduce one category at a time, giving several examples. Then challenge students to come up with at least 10 more examples in the same category. Since gifted kids are highly competitive, they will work very quietly on these so nobody else steals their ideas!

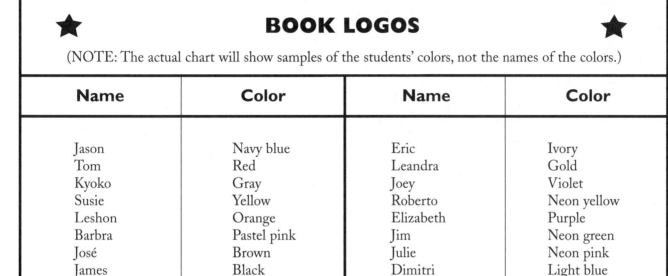

★ BOOKS I WANT TO READ ★

This list belongs to: ______________________________

Author's Name or Call Number	Title of Book	Notes

★ RECOMMENDED BOOKS ★				
My Name	**Title of Book**	**Author's Name or Call Number**	**Why I'm Recommending It**	**People I Think Would Like This Book**

Any and all of the activities described on the Vocabulary Builders chart can be modified and expanded. For example, students can transmogrify mottoes, proverbs, movie names, or book titles. They can even transmogrify stories or tales. Have them start by writing a one-page summary, then consult a thesaurus to put it in fancy words. This could be the basis of a class competition, with different groups working on different stories, folk tales, or fairy tales. When the groups are finished working, read their stories aloud to the class. The winning story is the one that takes the longest to figure out.

Etymologies

Word histories can be fascinating. It's fun to learn that "alligator" comes from the Spanish *el lagarto*—the lizard. Or that "fan" (as in sports fan) is short for "fanatic." Or that sideburns were named after General Ambrose E. Burnside, a general in the United States Civil War.

Give students copies of Etymologies Activities (page 114) and the Etymologies Chart (page 115). Invite them to select an activity from the list. Then have them find 10 or more words or phrases that fit their chosen category (names, places, sports, etc.). Turn them loose with unabridged dictionaries, college-level dictionaries, and other printed and Internet resources. Have students fill out an Etymologies Chart for each category they investigate. Explain that to complete the chart, they should write:

- The original word or phrase in the far left column.
- The original language of the word or phrase in the next column.
- The meaning of the word or phrase in the original language in the center column.
- Today's meaning of the word or phrase in the next column.
- An original sentence using the word or phrase in the far right column. (To make this more fun and interesting, students might write a rebus sentence.)

Super Sentences

The two Super Sentences included here (see pages 116 and 117) are from my book, *Super Sentences,* which includes 22 examples (11 from Level One, 11 from Level Two) that have been used in

★ VOCABULARY BUILDERS ★

1. ACRONYMS: Words made from the first letters of a list of words you want to remember.

Example: HOMES for the Great Lakes: Huron, Ontario, Michigan, Erie, Superior.

2. COINED WORDS: Words created to fill a need that no existing word serves. Many trademarks are coined words.

Examples: Kleenex, Xerox.

3. DAFFYNITIONS: Crazy definitions that make some sense.

Examples: Grapes grow on divine. A police uniform is a lawsuit.

4. ETYMOLOGIES: The histories of words, including their origins and changes through time and other languages.

5. EUPHEMISMS: More gentle ways of saying things that sound too harsh.

Example: "He passed away" instead of "He died."

6. FIGURES OF SPEECH: Expressions that mean something different as a whole than if you take each word literally.

Example: There are many skeletons in our family closet.

7. MALAPROPISMS: Words misused on purpose or by accident. They sound like the words you mean to say but have different, often contradictory meanings.

Example: "Complete and under a bridge" instead of "Complete and unabridged."

8. PALINDROMES: Words and phrases spelled the same forward and backward.

Examples: Otto, Madam, "Madam, I'm Adam."

9. PORTMANTEAUS: Words made by blending parts of other words.

Example: "Brunch" from "breakfast" and "lunch."

10. PUN STORIES: Stories that include as many puns as possible. Puns are plays on words.

Example: The pancakes were selling like hotcakes because they didn't cost a lot of dough.

11. SLIDE WORDS: Words slid together from abbreviations.

Example: "Jeep" from "GP" (a general purpose vehicle during World War II).

12. SUPER SENTENCES: Sentences made from very difficult vocabulary words.

13. TOM SWIFTIES: Statements that combine a word with its related adverb.

Example: "I just cut my finger!" cried Tom sharply.

14. TRANSMOGRIFICATIONS: Simple thoughts expressed in sophisticated or challenging words.

Example: "Scintillate, scintillate, asteroid minific" for "Twinkle, twinkle, little star."

15. ROOTS: Study the Latin roots of 10 words. Find words in other sources that have those roots.

many classrooms. This challenging vocabulary activity includes all levels of Bloom's Taxonomy.

1. Group students in pairs. Hand out copies of Super Sentence: Level One (page 116) or Super Sentence: Level Two (page 117).

2. Read the sentence aloud several times. Tell students to listen carefully and try to determine the parts of speech for the words in capital letters. They should write the part of speech above each word to make sure they select the correct dictionary entry when they go to look it up.

3. Tell students to work with their partners (using advanced or unabridged dictionaries) to complete the chart. Explain that they should list the "mystery words" (those in capital letters) in the far left column, write the pronunciation of each word in the center column (using the pronunciation key from the dictionary), then write the meaning of the word in the far right column—in their own words, not the dictionary definition.

4. Tell students that to complete this activity, they should be able to pronounce and define each "mystery word," read the sentence as it appears, and translate it into simpler words.

5. When the students are ready, bring the pairs together in a circle.

- The first student reads the sentence up to and including the first capitalized word.
- The next student starts where the first leaves off, and reads all words up to and including the next capitalized word.
- Students keep taking turns until someone asks to read the entire sentence aloud.
- When several students have read the sentence aloud, one or more should translate it and reread it using simpler words.

Students may make their own Super Sentences from vocabulary they are learning in books they are reading independently, or from newspapers, magazines, the Internet, or other sources.

Vocabulary Web

Educators at the College of William and Mary in Williamsburg, Virginia, have produced many self-contained literature units for students gifted in the language arts. Their Vocabulary Web Model is ideal for helping gifted kids study words in depth. The goal of the Web goes beyond simply learning a particular word. See page 118 for a completed Web and page 119 for a blank version you can copy and give to your students.

Students can work alone, but it's more fun to work in pairs. Assign words or have students choose their own words. Use one Vocabulary Web sheet for each word. Students write the word in the center circle, then work out from there—defining the word, finding synonyms and antonyms, writing a sentence using the word, giving examples, and analyzing the word. By the time they're finished, they have a thorough understanding of the word.

Give students the option of sharing their findings with the class or other appropriate audience.

BIBLIOTHERAPY

Bibliotherapy is guided reading that helps readers cope with and solve problems, understand themselves and their environment, build self-esteem, and meet the developmental challenges of adolescence. It can be especially powerful with gifted kids because of their love of reading, their ability to empathize, and their advanced grasp of literary devices including metaphor.

For gifted students, reading a story or novel about other gifted kids is a safe way to investigate, clarify, and validate their feelings. Confronting issues objectively through fictional characters gives them practice in dealing with their own real-life issues. Reading about characters who are like them, with similar abilities, emotions, and experiences, helps gifted kids know they're not alone.

Bibliotherapy involves more than handing books to your students and sending them off to read. Judith Wynn Halsted, author of *Guiding Gifted Readers from Preschool through High School,* notes that:*

> Rather than merely recommending a book to a child, it includes three components: a reader, a book, and a leader who will read the same book and prepare for productive discussion of the issues the book raises. To be effective, the leader must be aware of the process of bibliotherapy: IDENTIFICATION, in which the reader identifies with a character in the book; CATHARSIS, the reader's experiencing of the emotions attributed to the character; and INSIGHT,

* Halsted, Judith Wynn. "Guiding the Gifted Reader." ERIC Digest #E481 (1990).

Text continues on page 120

★ ETYMOLOGIES ACTIVITIES ★

1. First names, either gender.
2. Last names that describe occupations. *Examples:* Hooper, Smith, Taylor.
3. Places or things named after people. *Examples:* sideburns, Mansard roof, sandwich.
4. Native American words or names.
5. Foreign words in common English usage.
6. Words or phrases from sports. *Examples:* strike out, take a new tack.
7. Words or phrases from television and movies. *Examples:* commercial, Foley artist.
8. Words or phrases from art. *Examples:* Impressionism, fresco.
9. Words or phrases from architecture. *Examples:* flying buttress, Baroque.
10. Words or phrases from medicine. *Examples:* penicillin, anesthesia.
11. Words or phrases from music. *Examples:* concert, bebop.
12. Words or phrases from computers and the Internet. *Examples:* email, cyberspace.
13. Words or phrases from any other specialty or field of interest.
14. Words or phrases from a new category you create.

★ ETYMOLOGIES CHART ★

Category: ____________________

Word or Phrase	Original Language	Meaning in Original Language	Today's Meaning	Sentence

★ SUPER SENTENCE: LEVEL ONE ★

DIRECTIONS: Work with a partner to pronounce and define each "mystery word" (words in capital letters), read the sentence as it appears, and translate it into simpler words.

We live near a GROTESQUE, HIDEOUS, DETERIORATED old house filled with TORTUOUS, IMPENETRABLE hallways which give me EERIE, GHASTLY feelings of CLAUSTROPHOBIA and TREPIDATION, especially when I hear the FORMIDABLE CACOPHONY of BABBLING voices when no one else is there.

Word	Pronunciation	Meaning

Translation:

★ SUPER SENTENCE: LEVEL TWO ★

DIRECTIONS: Work with a partner to pronounce and define each "mystery word" (words in capital letters), read the sentence as it appears, and translate it into simpler words.

The TRUCULENT, OPPIDAN LICKSPITTLE SEQUESTERED himself from the BROUHAHA caused by the PUSILLANIMOUS MOUNTEBANK, and MACHINATED a MACHIAVELLIAN PREVARICATION to METE to himself some of the mountebank's LUCRE.

Word	Pronunciation	Meaning

Translation:

★ VOCABULARY WEB MODEL ★

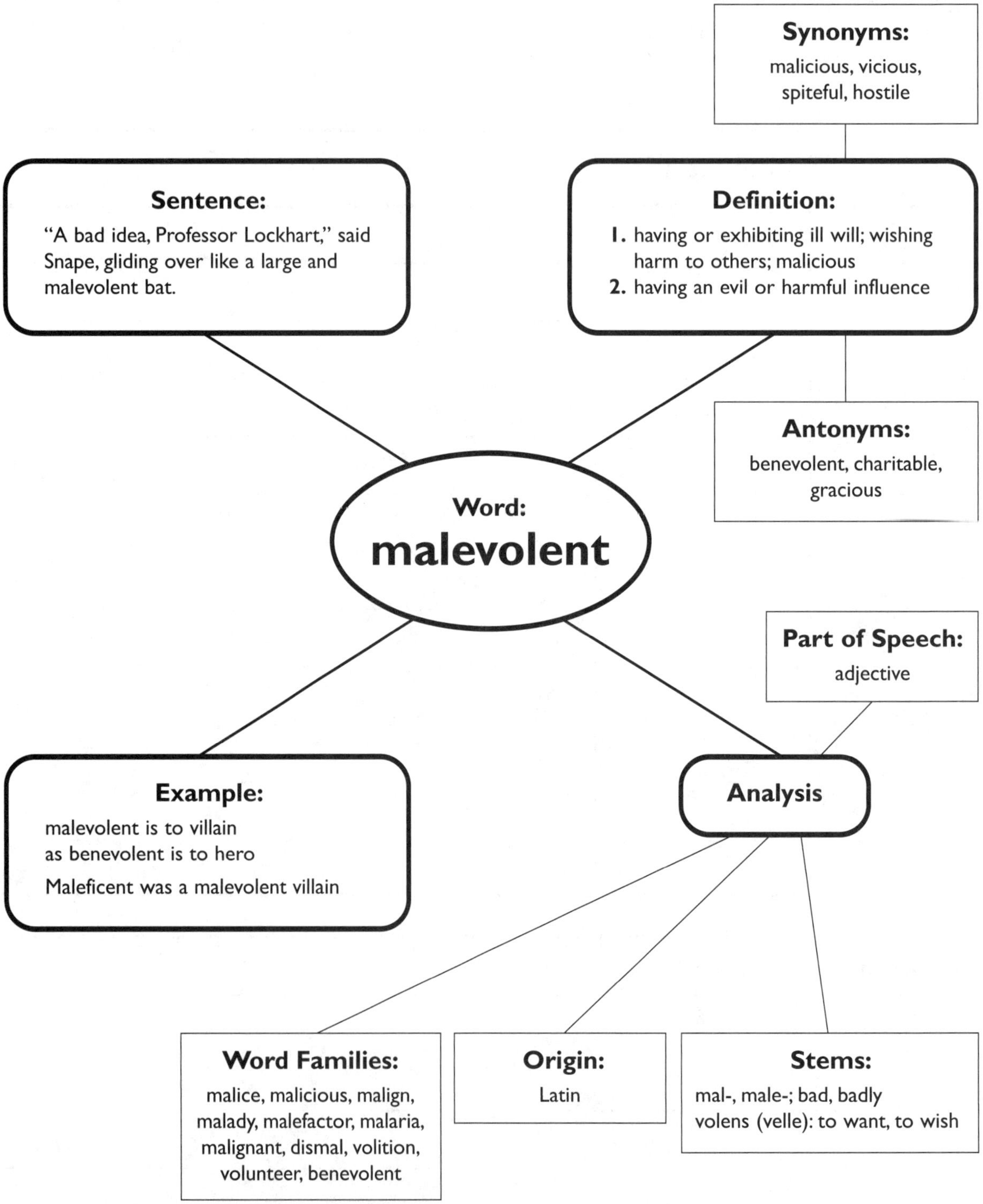
Synonyms:
malicious, vicious, spiteful, hostile
Sentence:
"A bad idea, Professor Lockhart," said Snape, gliding over like a large and malevolent bat.
Definition:
1. having or exhibiting ill will; wishing harm to others; malicious
2. having an evil or harmful influence
Antonyms:
benevolent, charitable, gracious
Word:
malevolent
Part of Speech:
adjective
Example:
malevolent is to villain as benevolent is to hero
Maleficent was a malevolent villain
Analysis
Word Families:
malice, malicious, malign, malady, malefactor, malaria, malignant, dismal, volition, volunteer, benevolent
Origin:
Latin
Stems:
mal-, male-; bad, badly
volens (velle): to want, to wish

Source: Center for Gifted Education, College of William & Mary, Williamsburg, Virginia.

★ VOCABULARY WEB MODEL ★

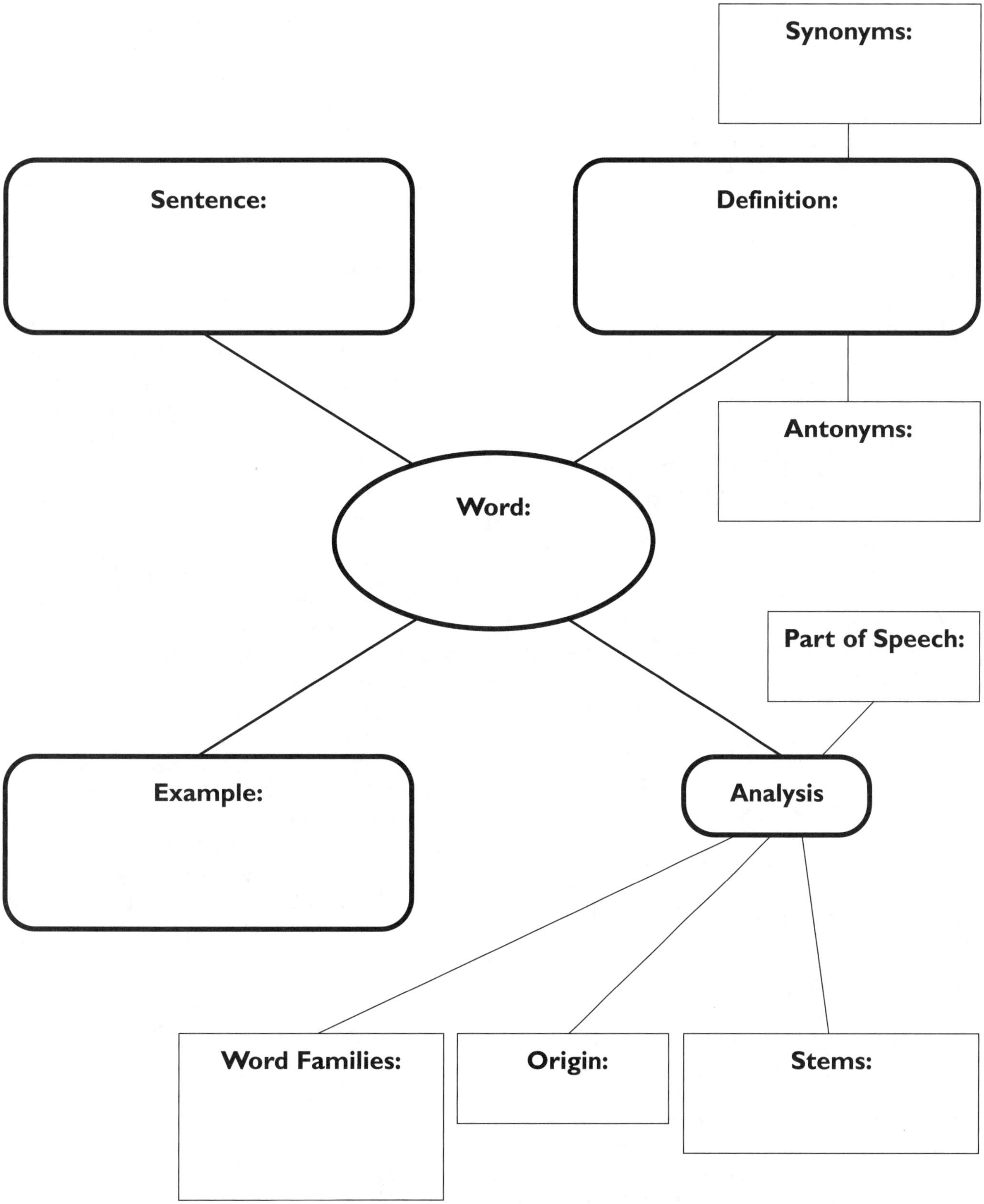

Text continues from page 113

the application of the character's experience to the reader's own life. The leader then frames questions that will confirm and expand on these elements.

If you plan to use bibliotherapy with your gifted students, start by finding suitable books. The characters and stories don't have to match your students' lives exactly, but they should have some things in common. Dr. Stephen Schroeder-Davis of Elk River, Minnesota, has prepared an annotated bibliography of books for gifted readers. (See References and Resources at the end of this chapter.) Librarians may be able to help you locate other books to offer your students. You'll want to become familiar with whatever your students read, either by reading the materials yourself or by using prepackaged units for individual novels. Then follow through with individual or group discussions.

WRITING FOR GIFTED WRITERS

Your outstanding writers, by the very nature of their sophisticated writing ability, need compacting and differentiation in their writing work. Many gifted students write stories, poems, and plays and keep them at home. Ask their parents about these writing projects, and invite the kids to keep an ongoing writing project in class and return to it whenever they buy back some choice time.

Since much of the writing done in school is skill work (spelling, grammar, and mechanics), you can use Most Difficult First (see Chapter 2) and Learning Contracts (Chapter 3) to make sure your gifted writers have opportunities to do work that is meaningful for them. For James, who was writing a book about the human body (see pages 41–43), I designed a contract for each type of writing the class was learning. The contracts allowed James to spend considerable class time on his book. His Contract for Expository Writing is shown on page 121. For students who are eligible for writing contracts but who don't happen to be writing books, the Expository Writing Extensions Menu (see page 122) offers several interesting choices. For other types of writing units, you might use the Study Guide method with or without Extensions Menu (see Chapter 4). Always have students record their progress on a Daily Log of Extension Work (see page 78).

Writing Activities Gifted Writers Enjoy

Many of the great ideas for writing activities you've come across or used over the years will delight your gifted students. Remember, gifted kids enjoy taking an idea and adapting it in some way to make it "their" idea. Here are several suggestions you might try in your classroom.

- Rewrite a story from a different character's point of view.
- Write opposing viewpoints papers. Argue two different sides of an issue.
- Write any kind of poetry you want. You can follow a form or not, use rhyme or not—whatever appeals to you. You can invent your own form.
- Listen to a piece of instrumental music—classical, jazz, world music, relaxing music, or whatever you choose. Write about it. How does it make you feel? What does it make you think about? What images do you see in your mind when you listen?
- Write a description of a work of art—a painting, sculpture, drawing, or photograph—you admire or dislike. Include your interpretation of what you think it's supposed to mean.
- Use the Internet to learn about a type of writing called technical writing. Study it, then produce a sample on a topic that interests you. Example: You might write a User's Guide to a favorite game or toy.
- Contact a writer you admire. Interview him or her in writing, using email or regular mail. Write a report about your interview.
- Choose a topic that interests you and write an essay about it at the start of the school year. Write an essay about the same topic in early May. Analyze your growth as a writer.

NOTE: Provide a rubric students can use to analyze and assess their own writing.

Another activity my students greatly enjoyed involves U.S. towns and cities with unusual names.

1. You provide a U.S. atlas and/or several state maps that list towns and cities by name.

2. Students search the atlas, maps, and/or Internet resources for unusual names and list at least 10.

★ CONTRACT FOR EXPOSITORY WRITING ★

Student's Name: *James*

✓ Concept

____ The topic is narrow enough to manage.
____ The topic sentence (first in the paragraph) clearly expresses the idea to be developed.
____ There are at least three details to support the topic sentence.
____ Each detail is related to the topic sentence.
____ The sequence of the details makes sense.
____ Proofreading is evident for grammar, punctuation, spelling, and other mechanics.

Extensions: ______________________________

____

Your Idea: *Work on "The Anatomy, Physiology, and Cetera of the Human Body" book*

Working Conditions

I will not bother anyone.

I will not call attention to myself.

I will work on the extension activities during the entire writing period.

Teacher's Signature: ______________ Student's Signature: ______________

3. Working individually or in small groups, kids choose one town, then write a story about how they think it got its name.

4. Students write a letter to the present mayor and town council, enclosing their story and asking for information about how the town really got its name.

Some town names I'll remember forever are Embarrass (Minnesota), Bowlegs (Oklahoma), Bugscuffle (Tennessee), Boring (Maryland and Oregon), Horseheads (New York), Rough and Ready (California, New York, and Pennsylvania), Dime Box (Texas), Double Trouble (New Jersey), What Cheer (Iowa), and Monkey's Eyebrow, Pippa Passes, and Mouthcard (all in Kentucky, a state famous for its colorful town names). Many of my students received replies to their letters and stories. I could imagine chuckle-filled discussions at local eateries.

EXPOSITORY WRITING EXTENSIONS MENU

Write an expository essay to submit to the editorial page of a local newspaper.	Develop a lengthy piece of writing of your own choosing. Contract with the teacher regarding feedback.	Prepare to speak at a government meeting to convince legislators to support your position.
Present a debate on a topic of your choosing with one or several other students to an appropriate audience.	**Student Choice**	Prepare to speak at a school board meeting to convince members to support your position on a school-related issue.
Evaluate the effectiveness of several expository paragraphs in a current nonfiction bestseller.	Write an expository paragraph in another language.	Rewrite a paragraph or page from a textbook to make the expository language more effective.

Getting Kids' Writing Published

Kids who enjoy writing and excel at it need opportunities to reach an audience beyond their classmates. School newsletters and newspapers are okay, but when you find a writer who's truly exceptional, you'll want to go further.

It's absolutely thrilling to become a published author, and there are several book and magazine publishers that welcome kids' writing. For a list of possibilities, see References and Resources at the end of this chapter. Students should contact publishers directly by writing formal letters of inquiry. (Your job is to coach them, not do it for them.) Some publishers' Web sites provide information about how to submit work for publication.

STRATEGY: THE GREAT FRIDAY AFTERNOON EVENT

The Great Friday Afternoon Event is language arts fun for the whole class. It's a way to celebrate language as well as provide welcome relief from the week's hard work. See page 124 for a handout you can copy and use with your students.

1. Divide the class into four heterogeneous teams.

- If you have more than 28 students, form more teams and create more categories of events, such as Choral Reading and Storytelling.
- On the handout, the teams are called A, B, C, and D, but you can allow your teams to choose their own names, slogans, etc.
- Each week, each team is responsible for a new category. Each week, each team has a new captain who's in charge of making sure that all students contribute their part to the team's Friday presentation.
- The teams stay together until all teams have presented all of the categories. Four teams stay together for 4 weeks, 5 teams for 5 weeks, and so on.
- After all teams have experience in all categories, you may want to change one or more of the categories. Or you may keep the same categories all year and have teams continue to rotate through them. Of course, you're free to use different categories than the ones I've suggested.

2. Make sure the teams understand their tasks as described on the handout.

3. Provide materials for students to use. Collect poems, plays, newspapers, news magazines, etc. Allow practice time during the week; help students rehearse. Invite parent volunteers to help collect the materials and come to the classroom to provide whatever assistance students need.

Although the teams are heterogeneous and all students contribute to the fun, gifted kids really enjoy this opportunity to showcase their talents. I usually combined this event with Book Sharing Time, during which students added to their Books I Want to Read list (see page 110). Then we played a competitive game to review what we've learned. I use Academic Bowl, described in Appendix A. Any other game show format will work just as well.

QUESTIONS AND ANSWERS

"How can I find the time to provide alternate activities when I don't have enough time to finish the required reading program?"

The alternatives described in this chapter are not offered in addition to the regular program. They are used instead of the regular program. The most common reason for using a prescribed program is because there's comfort in knowing you'll be teaching a complete curriculum. When you pretest skill or vocabulary work, you can allow kids who achieve at the required level to work on extensions instead of the regular curriculum. Even when the content is new and pretesting isn't possible, you can use study guides and extensions menus.

Invite grade-level colleagues to help you plan extensions menus. Work during lunch or common planning times. Don't forget the chocolate. (See pages 130–131.)

"How will parents feel if students aren't completing the required reading, or are skipping some skill work?"

Very few of the educational practices we use in today's classrooms even remotely resemble the way things were done in the schools today's parents attended. It's up to us to educate parents and keep them informed.

Whenever you implement a new strategy, send home a letter describing what you're doing. Bring parents up-to-date at open houses and parent-teacher conferences. Once parents see that their children are eager to go to school and learn, it's easy to convince them that your teaching methods are effective for their children.

THE GREAT FRIDAY AFTERNOON EVENT

How It Works:

1. The class is divided into 4 teams. Teams stay together for 4 weeks.

2. On Fridays, each team presents a different program to the class.

3. Teams rotate categories and captains every week.

4. After 4 weeks, all 4 teams will have presented all 4 types of programs.

	Poetry	Declamation	Play	Newscast
Week 1	A	B	C	D
Week 2	B	C	D	A
Week 3	C	D	A	B
Week 4	D	A	B	C

Poetry: Each team member reads or recites a poem. You can choose a poem by someone else or read a poem you have written.

Declamation: Each team member reads aloud or recites an excerpt or piece of prose writing. You can choose an essay, speech, book chapter, etc. by someone else or read something you have written.

Play: The team works together to read or act out a play or part of a play.

Newscast: The team works together to broadcast a 5–10 minute radio or TV show about a current or historical event.

"What about the truly precocious reader who is several years ahead of the others? Shouldn't that student have an accelerated program?"

Yes. For students who enter school reading several years ahead of their class, accelerated instruction may determine whether they keep their edge or slowly return to the level of their age peers. Remember to never accelerate students into out-of-level required reading materials without informing other people who might be affected in subsequent years. Any decision to place students in higher-level text materials in any subject must be made as a team. Your team might include other teachers, the principal, parents, and even some staff from the middle school or high school, since they will be affected by your actions.

Even if you can't use some required reading materials, very few trade books should be off limits, giving kids almost unlimited choices with real literature.

For more on the topic of acceleration, see Chapter 9.

"Isn't it important for all kids to participate in the regular writing program, since writing is such an important skill in so many areas of learning and working?"

Never forget the difference between the words "teach" and "learn." Your state or province only requires you to document what kids have learned. You only have to teach your assigned content to kids who have not yet mastered it. Keeping these principles foremost in your mind, you'll never have to worry whether extension activities in writing are appropriate for kids with advanced writing abilities.

SUMMARY

Gifted students usually prefer a reading program that offers choices about what they read and the activities they do. If you're not presently using a literature-based program with your entire class, the strategies described in this chapter will help you to better meet the reading needs of your gifted students. If you're already using real literature for much of your reading program, these strategies may help you to differentiate for your gifted readers. Gifted writers probably already know most of the writing skills you're planning to teach. They will benefit most from contracts and alternate activities.

REFERENCES AND RESOURCES

Reading and Vocabulary

Abromitis, Barbara. *New Directions in Vocabulary.* Rolling Meadows, IL: Blue Ribbon Press, 1992.

American Classical League, Miami University, Oxford, OH, (513) 529-7741 (www.aclclassics.org). Learning materials on Latin and Greek classical literature for kids of all ages.

R.R. Bowker, New Providence, NJ, (888) 269-5372 (www.bowker.com). Publishes *Best Books for Children, Best Books for Young Adult Readers, Children's Magazine Guides,* and many more selection tools for teachers and librarians.

Clearinghouse on Reading, English, and Communication, Bloomington, IN (http://reading.indiana.edu). An extensive online collection of lesson plans and literacy resources.

Collins, Norma Decker, and Nola Kortner Alex. "Gifted Readers and Reading Instruction." ERIC Clearinghouse on Reading, English, and Communication Digest #101 (EDO-CS-95-04), June 1995.

Enslow Publishers, Inc., Berkeley Heights, NJ, (800) 398-2504 (www.enslow.com). Publishes biographies and debate materials ("A Pro/Con Issue"); distributes Accelerated Reader materials.

Fromkin, David. *An Introduction to Language.* Fort Worth: Harcourt-Brace, 1997. Beginning information for kids interested in linguistics.

Fromkin, Victoria. *Linguistics.* Malden, MA: Blackwell Publishers, 1999. Information on the study of linguistics for kids interested in languages.

Funk, Charles Earle. *Thereby Hangs a Tale: Stories of Curious Word Origins.* New York: HarperCollins, 1993.

The Great Books Foundation, Chicago, IL, (800) 222-5870 (www.greatbooks.org). Their Junior Great Books program (www.greatbooks.org/programs-for-all-ages/junior.html) provides courses and materials for kids of all ages to study great literature from complex, higher-level perspectives.

Green, Jonathon. *Chasing the Sun: Dictionary Makers and the Dictionaries They Made.* New York: Henry Holt, 1996.

Halsted, Judith Wynn. "Guiding the Gifted Reader." ERIC EC Digest #E481, 1990 (www.eric.ed.gov).
—— *Some of My Best Friends Are Books: Guiding Gifted Readers from Pre-School to High School.* Scottsdale, AZ: Gifted Psychology Press, 1994.

International Reading Association, Newark, DE, (800) 336-READ (www.reading.org). Provides lists of books for various ages and interests; disseminates reading research; promotes literacy.

Language Arts Units for High-Ability Learners. Curriculum units for grades K–12 created by the Center for Gifted Education at the College of William and Mary (cfge.wm.edu) include *Journeys and Destinations* (grades 2–3), *Literary Reflections* (4–5), and *Autobiographies* (5–6). Available from Kendall/Hunt Publishing Company, Dubuque, IA, (800) 228-0810 (www.kendallhunt.com).

Libraries Unlimited, Santa Barbara, CA, (800) 368-6868 (www.lu.com). Request a Teacher Ideas Press catalog.

Morris, William, and Mary Morris. *Morris Dictionary of Word and Phrase Origins.* 2nd ed. New York: HarperTrade, 1988.

National Reading Styles Institute, Syosset, NY, (800) 331-3117 (www.nrsi.com). Marie Carbo materials for students who have trouble reading.

Thompson, Michael Clay. *Caesar's English: A Vocabulary Foundation for Elementary Students.* Unionville, NY: Royal Fireworks Press, 2000. Other books by Michael include *Classics in the Classroom, The Magic Lens,* and the *Word Within a Word* series, which helps kids increase their vocabularies exponentially through understanding Greek and Latin stems or roots. Contact Royal Fireworks Press, Unionville, NY, (845) 726-4444.

What's the Word? A multimedia vocabulary building course for grades 7 and up. From Vocabulary Enterprises, Addison, TX, (888) 44-LEARN (www.learnvocab.com).

Winebrenner, Susan. *Super Sentences.* Mansfield Center, CT: Creative Learning Press, 1989. Vocabulary building activities for ages 8 and up.

Prepackaged Units for Teaching Novels

Accelerated Reader software. Helps gifted readers K–12 with self-selected literature. From Renaissance Learning, Inc., Wisconsin Rapids, WI, (800) 338-4204 (www.renlearn.com).

Engine-Uity, Ltd., Phoenix, AZ, (800) 877-8718 (www.engine-uity.com). Ready-to-use units in literature and other content areas based on Bloom's Taxonomy.

Literature Connections Novel Guides. Complete teaching plans for many novels at many reading levels. From Holt McDougal, Geneva, IL, (800) 462-6595 (www.holtmcdougal.com).

Novel Units. Student packets and teacher guides keyed to particular works of literature, currently available for more than 550 titles. Request a catalog from Educyberstor, (800) 688-3224 (www.educyberstor.com).

Primaryplots 2: A Book Talk Guide for Use with Readers Ages 4–8 by Rebecca Thomas (1993); *Middleplots 4: Ages 8–12* by John Gillespie et al. (1994); and *Juniorplots 4: Ages 12–16* by John Gillespie et al. (1993). Guides for book talks and independent reading. Published by R.R. Bowker, New Providence, NJ, (888) 269-5372 (www.bowker.com).

Scholastic Reading Counts! A reading motivation and management program that helps you encourage and monitor independent reading in students K–12. From Scholastic, New York, NY, (800) 724-6527 (apps.scholastic.com/readingcounts).

Wordplay on the Web

About: The Human Internet (www.about.com). Type *Wordplay* in the search box for multiple sources, sites, and links.

FunBrain (www.FunBrain.com). Free games, activities, and word games for K–8 teachers and kids.

Grammar Lady (www.aacton.gladbrook.iowapages.org). Answers to grammar questions.

Oxford English Dictionary (www.oed.com). At this time you can't access the complete OED online without a subscription, but you can check the Word of the Day (with quotes and etymologies) and information about the dictionary.

Pun of the Day (www.punoftheday.com). A recent example: "200 years from the final buffalo hunt will be a bisontennial."

Vocabulary University (www.vocabulary.com). Vocabulary explorations and puzzles.

Wacky Web Tales (www.eduplace.com/tales). Word games for grades 3 and up.

Word Central (www.wordcentral.com). Fun stuff for kids based on the *Merriam-Webster Dictionary.*

Wordplay (www.fun-with-words.com). Anagrams, palindromes, spoonerisms, oxymora, mnemonics, etymology, word puzzles, and more.

Bibliotherapy

Dreyer, Sharon Spredemann. *The Best of Bookfinder: A Guide to Children's Literature About Interests and Concerns of Youth Aged 2–18.* Circle Pines, MN: American Guidance Service, 1993. Look for this in the library reference section. Find books by topic, author, or title.

Hebert, T.P. "Using Biography to Counsel Gifted Young Men." *Journal of Secondary Gifted Education* 6:3, 208–19, 1995. Biographies can help gifted young men deal with issues including underachievement, self-inflicted pressure in athletics, cultural alienation, and father-son relationships. The author suggests biographical works and strategies for using this approach, with case examples.

Schroeder-Davis, Stephen. Ask about his annotated bibliography of books for gifted readers. Contact him by telephone at (763) 241-3449 or email (sschroeder-davis@elkriver.k12.mn.us).

Writing

Grant, Janet E. *The Young Person's Guide to Becoming a Writer: How to Develop Your Talent, Write Like a Pro—and Get Published!* Minneapolis, Free Spirit Publishing, 1995.

Hoomes, Eleanor. *Create-An-Autobiography.* Hawthorne, NJ: Educational Impressions, 1999. One in a large series of how-to-write books from Educational Impressions, Hawthorne, NJ, (800) 451-7450. The series also includes *Create-A-Topia* (idealistic stories), *Create-A-Comedy* (humorous stories), *Create-A-Future* (science fiction), *Create-A-Monster* (horror), *Create-A-Fantasy* (whimsical stories), and *Create-A-Sleuth* (detective stories).

Melton, David. *Written and Illustrated By... A Revolutionary Two-Brain Approach for Teaching Students How to Write and Illustrate Amazing Books.* Kansas City, MO: Landmark Editions, 1985.

Mirriam-Goldberg, Caryn. *Write Where You Are: How to Use Writing to Make Sense of Your Life.* Minneapolis: Free Spirit Publishing, 1999. Inspiration, ideas, and resources for ages 12 and up.

Places Named (www.placesnamed.com). This hypertext collection of geographic and other reference information is perfect for the writing activity involving U.S. towns and cities with unusual names (see pages 120–121).

Simic, Marjorie. "Publishing Children's Writing." ERIC Clearinghouse on Reading, English, and Communication Digest #85 (EDO-CS-93-08), August 1993 (http://reading.indiana.edu).

Treetop Publications, Racine, WI, (800-255-9228) (www.barebooks.com). Publishes "Bare Books"—blank books for student authors to write in.

Whitfield, Jamie. *Getting Kids Published.* Waco, TX: Prufrock Press, 1994.

Writer's Digest, Cincinnati, OH, (800) 333-0133 (www.writers digest.com). Publishes *Writer's Digest* magazine and many books for writers including *Writer's Market;* holds writing competitions.

Places that Publish Children's Writing

About: The Human Internet (www.about.com). Type *Creative Writing for Kids* in the search box for multiple sources, sites, and links.

Children's PressLine, New York, NY (718) 755-6225 (www.cplmedia.org).

Creative Kids: The National Voice for Kids, Prufrock Press, Waco, TX, (800) 998-2208 (www.prufrock.com).

Henderson, Kathy. *The Market Guide for Young Writers: Where and How to Sell What You Write.* 5th ed. Cincinnati, OH: Writer's Digest Books, 1996. Market and contest listings for young writers ages 8–18. Look for the latest edition.

Highlights for Children, Honesdale, PA, (800) 255-9517 (www.highlights.com).

Knowledge Unlimited, Inc., Madison, WI, (800) 356-2303 (www.thekustore.com). Ask about their NewsCurrents Student Editorial Cartoon Contest.

Landmark Editions, Kansas City, KS, (913) 722-0700 (www.landmarkeditions.com).

Merlyn's Pen, Providence, RI, (800) 247-2027 (www.merlynspen.org).

New Moon: The Magazine for Girls and Their Dreams, Duluth, MN, (218) 728-5507 (www.newmoon.com).

Ranger Rick, National Wildlife Federation, Reston, VA, (800) 822-9919 (www.nwf.org/rangerrick).

RWT Junior (www.educyberstor.com/rwtjunior). This free Internet publishing program by ECS Learning Systems helps students learn more about writing skills and standards and get published online. For more information, visit the site.

Skipping Stones: A Multicultural Children's Magazine, Eugene, OR, (541) 342-4956 (www.skippingstones.org).

Stone Soup, Santa Cruz, CA, (800) 447-4569 (www.stonesoup.com).

Young People's Press Online, Toronto, ON, Canada, (800) 231-9774 (youngpeoplespress.com).

6

Planning Curriculum for All Students at the Same Time

Gifted students learn the same standards, themes, units and/or concepts as the rest of the class. They simply require regular opportunities to become engaged with learning activities that require more depth and complexity.

According to Dr. Sandra Kaplan, a professor at the University of Southern California's Rossier School of Education who teaches educators how to design challenging curriculum for gifted students, depth is when students can:*

- Understand the specific language used by specialists in a particular discipline.
- Learn as many details as possible, including traits, factors, variables, nuances, and elements that distinguish the topic being studied from other topics.
- Understand the patterns that keep recurring over time including prediction of continuing or changing patterns.
- Be aware of trends and their influences.
- Look for unanswered questions, including incomplete data, in the content being studied.
- Be aware of the rules that govern a discipline, including the stated and unstated causes related to existing explanations.
- Understand the ethics involved including discrepancies, inequities, injustices, bias, prejudice, and discrimination.
- Know the big ideas, including theories, generalizations, and principles, that govern the study of the discipline.

Complexity means the ability to:

- Make connections and understand interactions over time.
- Look at elements from several perspectives that include viewpoints from technicians, historians, futurists, critics, philosophers, and oneself.
- Make interdisciplinary connections.

At the same time you're creating instructional activities for the entire class, you can also develop extension activities for gifted students that provide more challenge. I have designed a curriculum development model you can easily use to develop learning tasks for all of your students simultaneously. It's based on the fact that kids learn best in their preferred learning styles.

- Auditory learners prefer tasks that allow them to work logically, analytically, and sequentially.
- Visual learners like learning from things they can see and study visually.
- Tactile-kinesthetic learners learn best from touching and feeling, and from moving as they learn.

If, during your planning stage for any unit of work, you design learning activities for all three types of learners at the same time you design extension tasks for gifted learners, all students will be able to select a task that allows them to learn the designated key concepts in a way that appeals to them.

You don't have to worry about matching the student with the right task. When you use the Curriculum Differentiation Chart described in this chapter, it's impossible for students to choose the wrong task. And, since the tasks are designed to

* Used with permission of Sandra Kaplan.

accommodate learning style differences, you can rest assured that everyone will find things they can do with enjoyment and competence.

All students should experience more complex learning once they have established a base of information. Gifted students can usually learn the basic information independently and apply it by spending almost all of their learning time with activities designed to really challenge them. The Curriculum Differentiation Chart includes extension activities especially for gifted learners. You should encourage your gifted students to choose these tasks instead of the others. If they insist on choosing a different task, let them. They'll still be learning the key concepts they need to know.

BLOOM'S TAXONOMY

Bloom's Taxonomy of Educational Objectives is the model I use to create challenging activities for gifted students. It describes six levels of thinking, arranged sequentially from least to most complex. Some of you may be familiar with the original version, but I prefer my adaptation, shown on page 133. In my version, Synthesis is considered the most complex level of thinking.*

1. **Knowledge** is simply recall. Students can say that they "know" something if they can recall it to recite or write down.

2. **Comprehension** means that students can say what they "know" in their own words. Retelling a story, stating the main idea, or translating from another language are several ways in which students can demonstrate that they "comprehend" or understand what they have learned.

3. **Application** means that students can apply what they have learned from one context to another. For example, they might use their knowledge of fractions to double a baking recipe, or they may be required to decide when to apply mathematical or social studies concepts to real-life situations.

4. **Analysis** means that a student can understand the attributes of something so that its component parts may be studied separately and in relation to one another. Asking students to compare and contrast, categorize, and/or recognize inferences, opinions, or motives would give them experience in analysis.

5. **Evaluation** gives students opportunities to judge what they have analyzed. My version of Bloom's model considers Evaluation after Analysis, since it's very natural to ask students to give their opinion or state a preference about something they are analyzing.

6. **Synthesis** requires students to create a novel or original thought, idea, or product. All of the activities we call "creative thinking" give students experience with synthesis. Also, when students can take bits and pieces of several theories or combine ideas from different sources to create an original perspective or idea, they are thinking at a synthesis level.

STRATEGY: THE CURRICULUM DIFFERENTIATION CHART

The Curriculum Differentiation Chart is a way to plan curriculum for all of your students at the same time, in the same place—literally on the same sheet of paper. It includes your descriptions of different learning tasks for auditory, visual, and tactile-kinesthetic learners, plus your extension activities for gifted students.**

Right now, you're probably thinking, "Where am I supposed to find time to design four different sets of learning tasks? Help!" I know it sounds daunting. The good news is, you don't have to do it alone.

When I give teacher training workshops, I ask teachers to work in "job-alike" groups, sitting together by common grade level or subject area. As they work together to plan differentiation opportunities for their students, they are amazed at how much they can accomplish in 20 minutes or less.

I first discovered this during my classroom teaching years and learned how to capitalize on it for everyone's benefit. When I wanted to plan an Extensions Menu or Curriculum Differentiation Chart, I would post a note in a conspicuous place on the day I wanted to work. My note usually said something like this:

* Bloom's original order is Knowledge, Comprehension, Application, Analysis, Synthesis, Evaluation.

** Teachers in my workshops have told me that the Curriculum Differentiation Chart ties both of my books together, *Teaching Gifted Kids in the Regular Classroom* and *Teaching Kids with Learning Difficulties in the Regular Classroom.* It allows them to plan a unit for all learners simultaneously—average, LD, and gifted.

I need help with some curriculum planning today during my lunch time. From 12:15–12:45. If you are available during this time, please come to my room and help with the brainstorming. P.S. I'LL BRING CHOCOLATE!

The "lunch-and-chocolate" approach soon becomes a habit for teachers who appreciate that many heads are better than one for all types of planning experiences.

Scenario: José

José was a third grader who had always found school work to be very easy. Recently he had developed some distracting behaviors. He had started turning his work in late, and much of it was sloppy and inaccurate. Even though José was capable of doing complex activities, his work always seemed to reflect his attitude of, "What is the least amount of work I can do and still stay out of trouble?" His favorite question was, "How many lines does this have to be?"

José's teacher recognized that he was bored by work that was too easy, and she decided to build some more challenging options into the upcoming unit on nutrition. She hoped that by offering José some choices with attractive incentives, he could function more like a gifted student should.

When she planned the next unit, she used the Curriculum Differentiation Chart shown on pages 134–135. All students could choose activities from the chart; the more capable kids could do fewer and more complex activities and skip the simpler tasks. José's eyes lit up when he heard the news, and his work in subsequent units was much more in line with his advanced ability.

How to Use the Curriculum Differentiation Chart

A reproducible Curriculum Differentiation Chart is found on page 136, but I don't expect you to use it as is. At 8H" x 11", there's not enough writing space, except for very brief notes. I suggest that you make your own charts on larger sheets of paper.

1. Look back at Preparing the Study Guide and Extensions Menu in Chapter 4 (page 69) for suggestions on determining key concepts and related topics.

2. Start each unit with an overview of the content. This is an essential step for some of your global thinkers, especially those with learning problems and gifted kids who are twice-exceptional (see Chapter 1, pages 18–22). You might use graphic organizers or survey the content and have students ask questions about what they notice in the survey.

3. Write the key concepts as statements in the far left column of the Curriculum Differentiation Chart.

4. Working *horizontally* across the chart, plan the differentiated tasks.

- The Products Choices Chart (see page 80) can help you design tasks that will appeal to auditory, visual, and tactile-kinesthetic learners. Feel free to add other products that support the key concepts and fit the learning styles.
- For ideas on how to phrase tasks, use the Trigger Words column in the Taxonomy of Thinking chart (page 133). Average and below-average students need considerable time with Knowledge and Comprehension tasks before they can move on to more complex tasks. I recommend that most of the tasks you design for your Visual and Tactile-Kinesthetic learners fall into the Knowledge, Comprehension, and Application categories. For the Extension tasks, use the Application, Analysis, Evaluation, and Synthesis categories. (Application is a "swing" category, depending on the complexity of the task.)
- All tasks on each horizontal line must teach the key concept on that line. After you write each task, check back to make sure this is the case. Confirm that if a student completed only that task and none of the other tasks on that line, he would still be learning the key concept.

IMPORTANT: After entering all of the key concepts, you should always work horizontally across the chart until you have completed all four columns for each key concept. This reinforces the idea that you're not finished planning until you've accommodated all types of learners. Once you've completed several charts, planning for differentiation with each new unit will become a habit.

5. If you need more than one extension task per key concept, create an Extensions Menu at the same time you're creating your Curriculum Differentiation Chart. See page 137 for a reproducible Nutrition Extensions Menu.

If you want to stretch this unit into other areas of the curriculum, create an Extensions Menu that allows for this, with one subject per square. See page 138 for a reproducible example.

6. Let all students choose the task they want to work on. They can choose anything that appeals to them, as long as it's on the same horizontal line as the key concept you're teaching. No matter what task they choose, they will learn the key concept.

Give students several days to work on their tasks. Then lead a discussion about what they have learned. Since students will have chosen different tasks and studied material from different sources, the discussion will be enhanced by variety.

7. To manage the students' extension activities, use the Independent Study Agreement (see Chapter 4) or the Personal Project Agreement (Chapter 7). Be sensitive to the fact that many gifted kids resist writing tasks. Writing slows down their thinking, and often it's not necessary for their mastery of a concept. Have students keep track of their progress using the Daily Log of Extension Work (see page 78).

> **NOTE:** Later in the unit, provide opportunities for all students to do higher-level tasks. They might select a culminating activity from the Extensions column or a task from the Extensions Menu, if you include one in your unit.

8. Decide how outcomes or grades will be determined. Use the Evaluation Contract (see page 77) or any other method of evaluating student projects. Be sure to tell students about the grading criteria you will use before they start working.

9. Plan the record-keeping procedures you will use. There are two parts to record-keeping. The first is making sure that students are working productively every day; the Daily Log takes care of this. The second is recording their grades.

- Students who work on tasks from the learning styles columns (Auditory/Analytic, Visual/Global, Tactile-Kinesthetic/Global) earn daily grades for their work.
- Students who work on extension activities may take several days to complete one task. In all available spaces in your grade book (or computerized grading program), enter the grade they earn for that task. This might require you to allow them to learn other key concepts on their own, without producing actual products related to each concept. As in the Study Guide method, these students would still be held accountable for assessments on all of the content at the same time the rest of the class is being assessed.

STRATEGY: LEARNING CENTERS

If you're comfortable using learning centers, you can transfer the learning tasks you created for the Curriculum Differentiation Chart to color-coded, laminated task cards for use in a learning center format. In addition to the task cards (perhaps arranged by key concept), a good learning center should contain:

- Clearly stated directions about how to use the center.
- Clearly stated objectives or purposes of the center.
- Interesting and inviting displays; enticing questions.
- Activities, resources, and materials that appeal to various learning styles.
- Instructions about how to choose tasks.
- Copies of the Product Choices Chart (page 80).
- Examples of what completed tasks should look like.
- Answer keys, if needed.
- Tips about where to go for help.
- A description of the rubrics and other evaluation criteria used to grade students' work.
- Instructions on how to store work between visits.
- Guidelines for students' behavior.
- Ideas of what to do when students finish ahead of others. *Example:* They might prepare additional task cards on the same or related topics.

Dariel McGrath took this idea one step further by encouraging gifted kids to create learning centers

Text continues on page 139

TAXONOMY OF THINKING

Category	Definition	Trigger Words	Products
Synthesis	Re-form individual parts to make a new whole.	Compose • Design • Invent • Create • Hypothesize • Construct • Forecast • Rearrange parts • Imagine	Lesson plan • Song • Poem • Story • Advertisement • Invention • Other creative products
Evaluation	Judge value of something vis-à-vis criteria. Support judgment.	Judge • Evaluate • Give opinion • Give viewpoint • Prioritize • Recommend • Critique	Decision • Rating/Grades • Editorial • Debate • Critique • Defense • Verdict • Judgment
Analysis	Understand how parts relate to a whole. Understand structure and motive. Note fallacies.	Investigate • Classify • Categorize • Compare • Contrast • Solve	Survey • Questionnaire • Plan • Solution to problem or mystery • Report • Prospectus
Application	Transfer knowledge learned in one situation to another.	Demonstrate • Use guides, maps, charts, etc. • Build • Cook	Recipe • Model • Artwork • Demonstration • Craft
Comprehension	Demonstrate basic understanding of concepts and curriculum. Translate into other words.	Restate in own words • Give examples • Explain • Summarize • Translate • Show symbols • Edit	Drawing • Diagram • Response to question • Revision • Translation
Knowledge	Ability to remember something previously learned.	Tell • Recite • List • Memorize • Remember • Define • Locate	Workbook pages • Quiz or test • Skill work • Vocabulary • Facts in isolation

CURRICULUM DIFFERENTIATION CHART

Unit: Nutrition

Key Concept	Auditory/ Analytic	Visual/Global	Tactile-Kinesthetic/Global	Extension
#1: Nutritional eating means that we include foods from the 5 major food groups in our daily food selection: the bread, cereal, rice, and pasta group; the vegetable group; the fruit group; the milk, yogurt, and cheese group; and the meat, poultry, fish, dry beans, eggs, and nuts group.	Describe the foods you would eat to maintain a balanced diet for 3 days. Include 3 meals and 2 snacks per day. Compute calories, fat grams, and the percentage of food in each food group for each day.	Find pictures of various foods and place them in the appropriate categories on a Food Groups Chart. With the pictures, create plans for 3 days' worth of balanced breakfasts, lunches, dinners, and snacks.	Draw pictures of food from all 5 food groups for 3 days' worth of meals, with 3 meals and 2 snacks per day. Create a pie chart to show what percentage of each day's food falls into each of the 5 major food groups.	Investigate how eating plans that don't take a balanced approach (examples: Atkins, Sugar Busters) claim to help people manage their weight while still providing good nutrition. Show which food groups these plans include and eliminate.
#2: For healthy, balanced eating, we should eat the recommended number of servings from each food group, and use fats and oils sparingly.	Keep a food diary for a week. Present your data to other students in a way that demonstrates your understanding of how to choose foods from all food groups.	Ask 6 students in your class to record everything they eat today and report the results to you in writing tomorrow. Make a chart showing how many food groups each student's choices included. Create a visual aid to show the results along with your recommendations for change.	Make models of correct serving sizes of some foods from all food groups. Demonstrate to other students how to choose correct serving sizes.	Hypothesize what happens to a person's body if he or she eats too much or too little over a period of several months. Explain how overeating and undereating affect bodily systems and functions.

#3: People who don't eat a balanced diet may lack energy and may be more likely to have weight problems or get sick.	Use the Internet to find several sources that explain how people's health is affected in countries where a balanced diet is difficult or impossible. Write a speech to convince people who don't eat a balanced diet to change their eating habits.	Draw a series of pictures illustrating how several months of unbalanced eating affect the body.	Prepare a skit showing how several months of unbalanced eating affect the body.	Hypothesize what would happen to a person's body if he or she omitted one entire food group from his or her diet for a period of several months. Be able to present evidence for your predictions.
#4: Junk food is high in calories and low in nutrients, so it doesn't fuel the body as well as nutritional foods. When people eat a balanced diet, they crave less junk food.	Listen to and/or watch food commercials for one evening. Compute the percentage of junk food ads compared to the percentage of ads that emphasize good nutrition. Predict the long-term effects on the eating habits of young people who get most of their food information from commercials.	Separate the groceries your family has at home into two categories: Junk Food and Nutritional Food. Draw pictures of the foods you find and place them in the appropriate categories. Highlight the category that has the most food items and the one that costs your family the most money each week.	Use the Internet to learn how eating too much junk food affects the body. Choose a way to share your findings with the class. If you like, make a videotape of your presentation.	Prepare a lesson on junk foods and present it to the class. Include information about why people crave junk foods, how junk foods affect the mind and body, and why they are a problem for many adults.
#5: Exercise has long-lasting, beneficial effects on the body, regardless of the degree to which one makes wise decisions about nutrition.	Locate at least two research studies on the benefits of exercise. Prepare a presentation tool that will communicate the recommended exercise program for children, young adults, adults, and seniors.	Prepare a multimedia presentation to illustrate several activities people can do to improve and maintain cardiovascular and muscular health.	Prepare a demonstration of aerobic and/or weight resistance programs that can help with weight control and overall good health.	Very few people in this country exercise regularly. Use the Internet to locate statistics on this issue. Interview one person your age and one adult to get their input on this problem. Hypothesize reasons people use to avoid exercise. Come up with a plan to entice non-exercisers to start exercising.

CURRICULUM DIFFERENTIATION CHART

Unit: ______________________________

Key Concept	Auditory/ Analytic	Visual/Global	Tactile- Kinesthetic/Global	Extension
# 1				
# 2				
# 3				
# 4				
# 5				
# 6				
# 7				
# 8				
# 9				
# 10				

★ NUTRITION EXTENSIONS MENU ★

Locate studies that have been done with babies who are allowed to choose their own foods from a high-chair tray. Discover the results and hypothesize the reasons for them. Should parents insist that their children eat balanced meals at all times?	Research the history of nutrition in the last millennium or over several millennia. Notice how the attitudes toward what people eat have changed over time. Hypothesize the reasons for these changes.	Investigate eating disorders. Discover the similarities and differences in overeaters and undereaters. Find information about treatment programs and their rates of success. Which "cures" seem to last for 5 years or longer?
Dietary supplements (for general health, weight control, and muscle strength) have become very popular in recent years. Investigate supplements and hypothesize reasons for their popularity. Discover some negative effects of various supplements.	**Student Choice**	Invite a panel of professionals from local agencies that offer physical fitness programs to speak to your class. Help students prepare questions to ask at the end of the panel's presentation. Moderate the panel.
Investigate the attitudes and behaviors of Americans and Europeans toward regular exercise and physical fitness from 1950 to the present day. Hypothesize reasons for the similarities and differences you find.	Design a menu of fitness activities that you think would appeal to people who are reluctant to exercise.	Project the eating habits of Americans in the year 2025. Include futuristic sources of food, such as products from aquaculture (food grown in oceans) and complete meals that are available in nontraditional formats.

NUTRITION EXTENSIONS MENU FOR OTHER SUBJECT AREAS

Science	Reading	Writing
• Find pictures in magazines that represent the food groups. Place them in categories on a chart. • Explain the concept of calories to the class. • Predict how people's eating habits may change by 2025.	• Read information on nutrition from several sources. • Create several challenging questions about nutrition for the class. • Read a novel or story about a person with an eating disorder. Give a talk about it to the class.	• Write a letter to your parent(s) describing good nutrition. • Write a story about a food-related topic. • Write about your need to eat in school during times other than lunch. Present your request to your teacher.
Talking • Interview your parents about your family's shopping/eating habits. Chart your findings. • Survey classmates about their eating habits. Chart your findings. • Prepare and present a debate about school lunches.	**Student Choice**	**Social Studies** • Clip articles about global or local food problems. Present a brief summary. • Show how advertising affects food choices. • Demonstrate how regional dishes rely upon regional agricultural products.
Mathematics • Determine your average daily caloric intake. Keep track of the calories you consume every day for a week and divide by 7. • Compute the percentage of your family's weekly income spent on food.	**Medicine** • Find information in medical journals or on the Internet describing the annual costs of people losing work time due to illness. Create a tool to share this information with the class. Hypothesize which problems may be related to poor nutrition.	**Politics** • Locate information about major candidates' positions regarding health care in this country. Hypothesize how their concerns may reflect nutritional issues.

Text continues from page 132

for other teachers as a Personal Interest Independent Study Project. (For more about these projects, see Chapter 7.) She taught Bloom's Taxonomy to her gifted students using my Build Blocks to Think chart, a kids' version of Bloom's model found on page 140. See pages 141 and 142 for Dariel's guidelines and examples of student-made learning centers.

To reduce congestion at the learning center, try this variation. Set up four centers around the same unit: auditory, visual, tactile-kinesthetic, and extension. Let all students choose the task they prefer. They'll still be working on the same key concepts, and that's what really matters. The centers don't have to be elaborate. They can be located on bookshelves or small tables.

Regardless of the format you choose, pull the kids back for a large-group discussion after they have had a few days to gather information about a key concept. Use the Name Card method (see pages 11–13) for optimum participation and learning. Gifted students who have opted to learn a key concepts more independently and are working on tasks from the Extension Menu may be excused from some of these discussions.

Students' grades should be a combination of the work they do on the tasks they choose and more formal assessments of what they have learned. Credit can be given for following behavior guidelines and working conditions. Content from mastered units can be used for Academic Bowl games, described in Appendix A.

STRATEGY: THE SOCRATIC SEMINAR

Challenge your students' thinking with the Socratic Seminar, a time-honored question-and-discussion format. You might use it with your whole class or with small groups of high-ability learners as a differentiation tool. It's an outstanding way to move content from recall to true understanding, and all students benefit from it. Gifted kids love it because it gives them lots of opportunities to think and share their thoughts with others. You can use the Socratic Seminar to discuss literature, history, current events, school or community issues, or hypothetical situations.

1. After students have learned enough about a topic to think and speak intelligently about it, schedule a seminar. Plan about 30 minutes to start, then longer time periods as students become more comfortable with the process.

2. Have 12–15 students sit in a circle. The rest of the class forms a second circle, ideally with another facilitator. If this isn't possible, students take turns sitting in an "inner circle" as active participants and an "outer circle" as observers.

3. Explain the rules of discussion.

- Students speak directly to each other, not to you.
- They take turns contributing.
- They aren't required to raise their hands, as long as they can handle the intricacies of talking to each other in this way. If not, raised hands may be in order.
- When they give an answer or offer an idea, they should also give evidence to support it. Evidence might come from what the student has read or learned, or from personal experience. Each bit of evidence should be clearly identified by its source.
- When referring to something another person said previously, they should use the person's name, not "He said..." or "She said...." (You may have to model this and give students practice ahead of time.)
- Students may challenge each other's statements in nonaggressive ways. Again, they should use names, not pronouns. *Example:* "I disagree with what Kari said, because the book says on page 32 that...."

If it seems that students aren't listening well, try asking them to briefly summarize what the previous speaker said (using the speaker's name) before making their own contribution.

4. Ask an open-ended question—one for which there is no single or correct answer. Here are some examples, in no particular order:

- Why do you think _______ happened? Could it have been prevented? Under what circumstances might the outcome have changed?
- What feelings, emotions, or events might have caused the people to behave the way they did?
- How do you think you would behave under similar circumstances?
- Are you saying _______? (Restate or paraphrase what speaker has said.)

Text continues on page 143

★ BUILD BLOCKS TO THINK ★

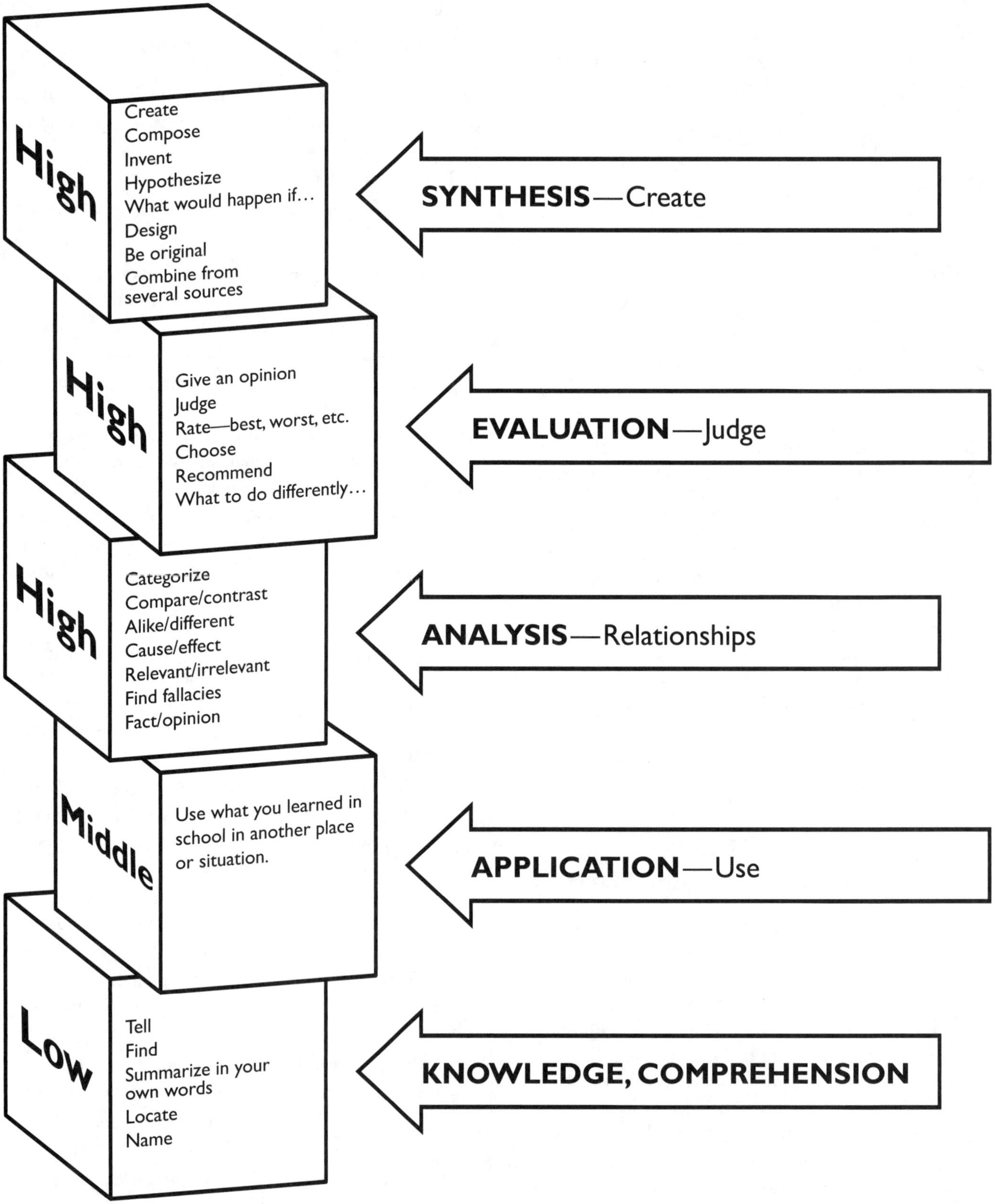
High
Create
Compose
Invent
Hypothesize
What would happen if...
Design
Be original
Combine from several sources
SYNTHESIS—Create
High
Give an opinion
Judge
Rate—best, worst, etc.
Choose
Recommend
What to do differently...
EVALUATION—Judge
High
Categorize
Compare/contrast
Alike/different
Cause/effect
Relevant/irrelevant
Find fallacies
Fact/opinion
ANALYSIS—Relationships
Middle
Use what you learned in school in another place or situation.
APPLICATION—Use
Low
Tell
Find
Summarize in your own words
Locate
Name
KNOWLEDGE, COMPREHENSION

★ GUIDELINES FOR CREATING STUDENT-MADE LEARNING CENTERS ★

1. Form a committee of at least two students.

2. Gather references. Research your topic.

3. Make a list of vocabulary words related to your topic.

4. Using the vocabulary words, create puzzles and games. Make copies. Create answer keys when necessary.

5. Create learning activities at all levels of Bloom's Taxonomy. Use your Build Blocks to Think chart.

6. Create a Bloom symbol for each activity card.

7. Copy the activities onto cards. Use marker. Include the appropriate Bloom symbol on each card. Laminate the cards if possible.

8. Find or make pictures, diagrams, photos, charts, and clippings to decorate the learning center. Prepare titles.

9. Arrange everything for display on poster board or in a one-gallon plastic bucket (such as an ice-cream container). Put cards and puzzles in plastic folders.

- The committee presents the learning center to a class.

- Students sign a contract to do a certain number of activities and puzzles within a given time frame. Rewards are given on completion. *Examples:* computer time, bonus points, free time, etc.

- The class has an exhibition to display students' projects. Invite parents and other classes to visit.

EXAMPLES OF STUDENT-MADE LEARNING CENTERS

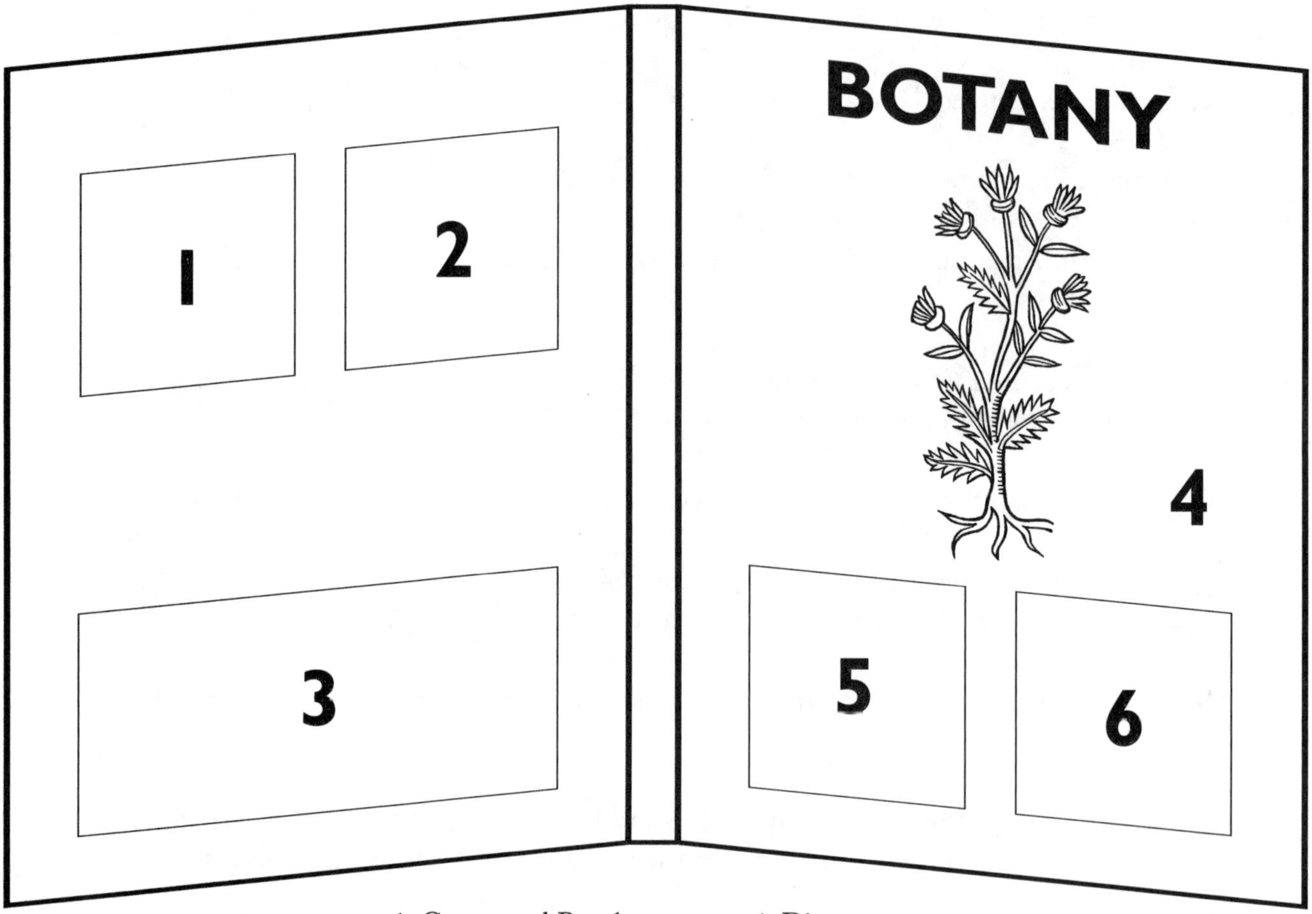

1. Games and Puzzles
2. Trivia Questions
3. Plastic Pockets with Activity Cards
4. Diagram
5. Photograph
6. Clipping

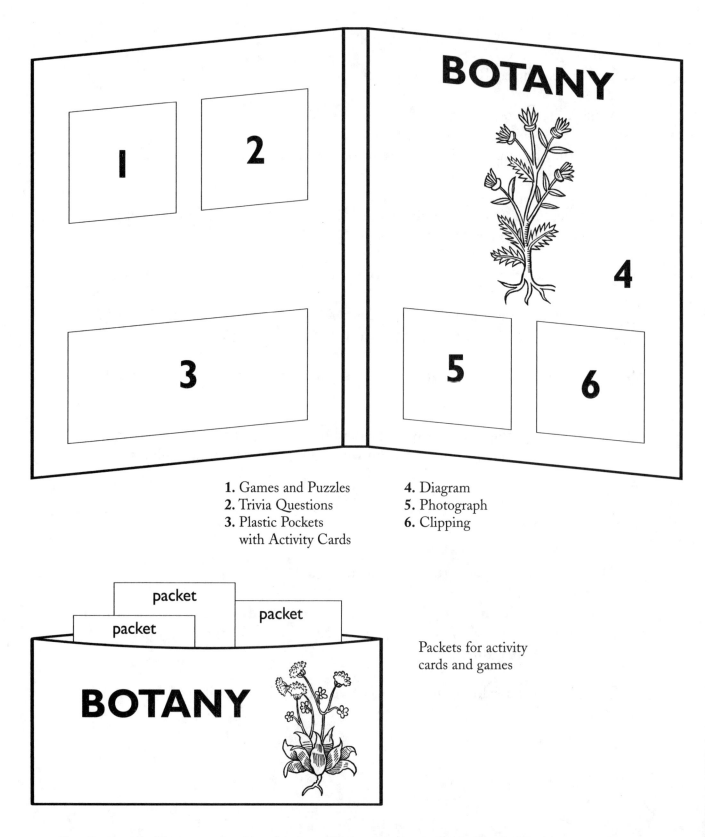

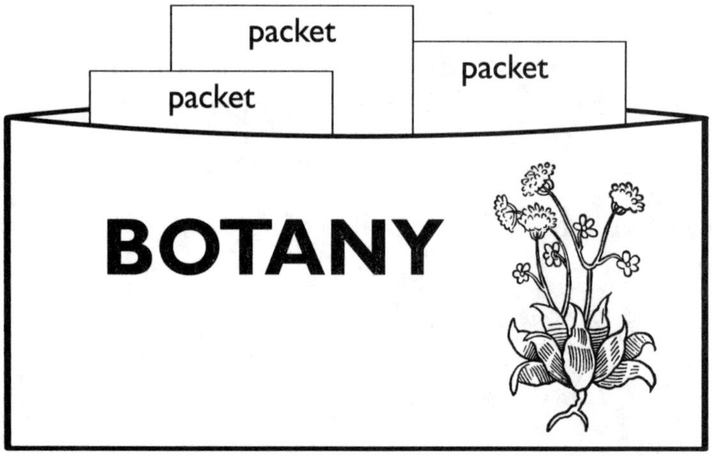

Packets for activity cards and games

Used with permission of Dariel McGrath.

Text continues from page 139

- Tell us more about _______.
- How is what we're discussing similar to _______ [another topic the group has discussed]? How is it different?
- Would anyone like to speak to the other side of this point of view?

From time to time, have students find something in the actual text that supports their statements or opinions.

5. Wait 1–2 minutes for someone to reply. Be patient and resist the urge to jump in. If no reply is forthcoming after 2 minutes, tell students that they may talk quietly to one other person to generate ideas.

Your hardest task as teacher/facilitator is to stay out of the discussion. Your role is to ask questions that keep the discussion going, not to give your opinion or declaration of what is correct.

6. Allow 5–10 minutes for reflection on the Socratic Seminar process. Invite students' suggestions on how to make the next seminar even better.

This process may take a long time to get comfortable and seem truly useful, but don't lose heart. The results are worth the wait. For more information about Socratic seminars, see References and Resources at the end of this chapter.

QUESTIONS AND ANSWERS

"How can I create these alternate activities when I hardly have time for everything I already have to do?"

This question has been partially answered on page 123, but I know it's the "biggy" for overworked teachers. Differentiation is not about adding responsibilities to your already crowded schedule. Rather, it represents a holistic way of teaching that, in many classrooms, has replaced more traditional methods of treating subject areas separately. Time and again, strategies designed to benefit gifted students have found application with all students. If you try these methods with one unit, you'll probably discover that you enjoy teaching this way, since it allows you to be more creative while simultaneously guaranteeing that your students will still be mastering the standards for which you're responsible. Creating all your units to incorporate differentiation will soon become your natural, preferred way of planning.

Differentiated units based on Bloom's Taxonomy are available from several publishers, including Engine-Uity and Thinking Caps, Inc. See References and Resources at the end of this chapter.

"What if some students complete the extensions before the rest of the class is done with their work?"

Prepare and use an Extensions Menu for the unit, similar to the ones found on pages 137 and 138. Invite interested students to become resident experts on a topic they want to learn more about (see Chapter 7). When you allow some students to become resident experts on topics related to the unit you're teaching, this enhances the experience for everyone.

Another strategy that works well is to teach Bloom's Taxonomy directly to those early finishers, then have them create learning center tasks for other teachers. They should start by interviewing the teachers and getting a list of topics for which the teachers want tasks created. See Strategy: Learning Centers starting on page 132 to learn how Dariel McGrath and her students did this.

You might also have students use Build Blocks to Think (see page 140) to create Bloom's-type questions for you to use for discussions or tests. Once students have learned the language of the taxonomy, they can be directed to create a certain number of questions by category.

Students might also create questions for the Academic Bowl game in Appendix A. Be sure they provide the answers, too!

"How can I translate these different activities into grades?"

You may already have rubrics students can use to decide the grade they want to work for before they begin any work. If not, try my Evaluation Contract (see page 74). I also recommend John Samara's Product Guides and Bertie Kingore's Portfolio Assessment tools. See References and Resources at the end of this chapter.

"Why should I offer alternate activities for my one or two gifted students, while my colleague next door is doing the same for her one or two gifted students? This doesn't seem very efficient."

There is a way to group gifted students without having to "track" everyone else. It's called cluster grouping. Only one teacher per grade level is primarily responsible for differentiating the curriculum for gifted students, and the gifted students are clustered in that teacher's class as part of a heterogeneous group. Clustering allows gifted students to enjoy alternate activities together. They no longer have to choose between working with the class on less challenging activities or working alone. For more about cluster grouping, see Chapter 8.

SUMMARY

In this chapter, you have learned how to plan curriculum units that reach and teach all of your students. You have learned to design learning tasks that are responsive to different styles of learning and different levels of ability. You have learned how to manage a classroom in which students are working on different tasks simultaneously.

The first time you use the methods described here, the process may seem tedious and time-consuming. As you use these methods again and again, you'll actually spend less time on each unit plan. Your reward will be the positive response from students and their parents for the exciting learning opportunities available in your classroom. Rather than trying to find one way of teaching that meets all kids' needs, you'll be using one way of planning to challenge and excite all of your students.

REFERENCES AND RESOURCES

General

Beecher, Margaret. *Developing the Gifts and Talents of All Students.* Mansfield Center, CT: Creative Learning Press, 1995. Planning units that meet the needs of all students on a learning continuum.

Bloom, Benjamin, et al. *Taxonomy of Educational Objectives: Handbook of the Cognitive Domain.* New York: Longman, 1984. The original source of Bloom's Taxonomy.

The Curry/Samara Model (CSM) of Curriculum, Instruction, and Assessment. Teaches how to develop unit plans using Bloom's Taxonomy. Developed by James Curry and John Samara. Contact the Curriculum Project, Austin, TX, (800) 867-9067 (www.curriculumproject.com). Ask about Samara's Product Guides, which can eliminate the problem of gifted kids doing shoddy work on their projects.

Kingore, Bertie. *Implementing Portfolios.* Austin, TX: Professional Associates, 1997. Keeping track of students' projects and assessment tools for their work.

Tomlinson, Carol. *How to Differentiate Instruction in Mixed-Ability Classrooms* and *The Differentiated Classroom: Responding to the Needs of All Learners.* Alexandria, VA: ASCD, 1995 and 1999. These books show teachers how to differentiate the curriculum for all students who can benefit from differentiation opportunities.

Van Tassel-Baska, Joyce. *Planning Effective Curriculum for Gifted Learners.* Denver, Love Publishing, 1992. A comprehensive approach to planning and implementing differentiated curriculum for gifted students.

Materials Based on Bloom's Taxonomy

Engine-Uity, Ltd., Phoenix, AZ, (800) 877-8718 (www.engine-uity.com). Ready-to-use units in literature and other content areas based on Bloom's Taxonomy.

Royal Fireworks Press, Unionville, NY, (845) 726-4444. Request their catalog of materials to implement Bloom's Taxonomy in primary classrooms.

Social Studies School Service, Culver City, CA, (800) 421-4246 (www.socialstudies.com). Multiple catalogs of materials to support social studies learning.

Socratic Seminars

Augsburg Paideia Group. Training in the Socratic teaching method. Augsburg College, Minneapolis, MN, (612) 330-1000 (www.augsburg.edu/paideia). Or contact director Anne Kaufman by telphone at (612) 330-1188 or email (kaufman@augsburg.edu).

Letts, Nancy. Training in eliciting high-level thinking in all students through Socratic seminars. Contact Jeremy Redleaf by telephone at (914) 525-5766 or email (jeremy@nancyletts.com).

Metzger, Margaret. "Teaching Reading Beyond the Plot." *Phi Delta Kappan* 256 (November 1998), 240–246, 256. This teacher gives very specific guidelines for using the Socratic Seminar to make reading comprehension more interesting and complex.

7

"I'm Done. Now What Should I Do?"

As you have no doubt ruefully observed, gifted students often finish an activity before the rest of the group. This may produce considerable anxiety for you, especially since you now know that extra credit work may not be the answer. You have learned that most gifted kids don't need to be spoon-fed activities to keep them busy. They just want some time to do things that are interesting to them without having to account for their work in a formal sense or follow a teacher's arbitrary timeline.

If you have tried the Most Difficult First strategy described in Chapter 2, you've already discovered how easy it is to allow some students to do whatever they want with time they buy back. Some kids like to read. Others may be in the middle of writing stories and will eagerly return to them. Some may use their time to daydream, which is essential to problem-solving and creative thinking. Others may be curious about a topic or idea and would love to spend some school time exploring it.

Gifted students tend to get passionately interested in topics that are not connected with the school curriculum, which is one reason why school is often frustrating for them. They are seldom given opportunities to learn the things they want to learn. Even when they are, those opportunities may not be very satisfying. The teacher says, "Well, do a report on it"—with the underlying message, "Make sure it's done well, looks great, and that you use your time wisely." When we speak of using time wisely, we usually mean looking busy. We expect students to be reading something, writing something, or doing something else observable to indicate that they are staying on task.

The impression students get is that all learning done in school must be for a reason and must result in a formal product, usually a report. However, we adults frequently enter bookstores or other people's homes and browse through books, idly wondering if we would like to know more about a certain topic at a later time. We would be offended if a bookstore owner posted a sign proclaiming, "NO BROWSING ALLOWED!" Why not provide opportunities for students to browse in school?

Maybe you have—and maybe you've been frustrated by gifted kids who lost interest in a topic shortly after they chose to investigate it. Many student researchers don't know how to get past traditional research methods into those that truly challenge and interest them. We want gifted students on independent study to experience how research can change the way they think and learn. We want them to discover how to synthesize information from many sources, to build on what they learn, to make connections between what they know and what they are learning, and to emulate adult researchers by using research methods that go way beyond simply looking something up.

The strategies described in this chapter will help you structure meaningful and exciting independent study options for your gifted students. You'll feel less anxious about letting kids spend school time on topics that passionately interest them. These strategies are appealing to students and easy to manage for you.

STRATEGY: THE INTEREST SURVEY

What if a student needs a topic but can't think of one? Here's where an Interest Survey can be very helpful. You'll find a reproducible survey on page 147.

Interest surveys allow you to learn things about your students that may not typically come to your attention. You may wish to survey all of your students at the beginning of every school year. (For younger kids, you may want to send the survey home so the parents can help fill it out.) Besides giving you insights into the kinds of things your gifted students may want to study in depth, the survey can also help you motivate reluctant learners. Raymond Wlodkowski, an educational psychologist and expert on motivation, has found that one of the quickest ways to motivate students is to discover what they are interested in outside of school, then spend a short time each day talking with them about their interests. Watch for dramatic, positive changes in a relatively short period of time.

STRATEGY: THE PERSONAL INTEREST INDEPENDENT STUDY PROJECT

We can assume that many gifted kids have a desire to learn about some topic in great depth. (Remember James, who was writing a book about the human body? See pages 41–43.) We can give them a way to pursue their interest in school. To distinguish this approach from the curriculum-related independent study described in Chapter 4, I call it the Personal Interest Independent Study Project.

Using the Interest Survey and conversations with parents and former teachers, help students identify topics of personal interest to them. Topics don't have to be related to any of the prescribed curriculum. Encourage students to select something they may be working on at home. Reassure them that you won't interfere with their ideas, creativity, or product choices. Sometimes gifted kids resist bringing their topics of passionate interest to school because they fear the teacher will take control.

Allow time for students working on personal interest projects to get together to chat, share resources, and brainstorm ways to solve problems in their research. Plan to spend some time with these kids as a group so they perceive you are interested in their projects and value the time they spend on them. If time is short, consider meeting in the hall as the rest of the class does Sustained Silent Reading or works on reading activities. Kids on independent study are already avid and skilled readers; it won't hurt them to substitute these meetings for silent reading periods.

Personal Interest Independent Study Projects for the Primary Grades

Even young gifted students relish opportunities to pursue topics of their choosing. For students in the primary grades, personal interest projects may be relatively unstructured.

Independent study with visual aids, like the "transparency talk" described in the scenario that follows, is a fairly unstructured and developmentally appropriate way for primary students to explore and share their areas of interest.

- Students enjoy it because they are allowed to investigate large amounts of information without immediately being expected to report on everything they learn. Most are willing to create more formal projects on specific subtopics later, when they have had the chance to satisfy their curiosity. The expectation that visual aids will be included in the presentation relieves them of the burden of doing too much writing.
- Teachers enjoy it because kids learn how to work on the same project for several days or weeks, relieving them of the responsibility for providing numerous shorter activities for those students who are always "done" and don't know what to do next.

For additional suggestions, see Acceptable Student Projects on page 148. See page 166 for a project especially suited to primary students.

★ INTEREST SURVEY ★

1. What kinds of books do you like to read?
2. How do you get the news? What parts of the newspaper do you look at regularly?
3. What are your favorite magazines or Web sites?
4. What types of TV programs do you prefer? Why?
5. What is your favorite activity or subject at school? Your least favorite? Why?
6. What is your first choice about what to do when you have free time at home?
7. What kinds of things have you collected? What do you do with the things you collect?
8. If you could talk to any person currently living, who would it be? Why? Think of 3 questions you would ask the person.
9. If you could talk to any person from history, who would it be? Why? Think of 3 questions you would ask the person.
10. What are your hobbies? How much time do you spend on your hobbies?
11. If you could have anything you want, regardless of money or natural ability, what would you choose? Why?
12. What career(s) do you think might be suitable for you when you are an adult?
13. If you could spend a week job-shadowing any adult in any career, which would you choose and why?
14. Tell about your favorite games.
15. What kinds of movies do you prefer to see? Why?
16. Imagine that someday you will write a book. What do you think it will be about?
17. Describe 10 things that would be present in a perfect world. Describe an invention you would create to make the world a better place.
18. What places in the world would you most like to visit? Why? Tell about your favorite vacation—one you've taken or wish you could take.
19. Imagine that you're going to take a trip to another planet or solar system. You'll be gone for 15 years. List 10 things you will take with you to do in your spare time.
20. What questions do you think should be on this survey that aren't already on it?

★ ACCEPTABLE STUDENT PROJECTS ★

For primary students:

1. Draw or trace pictures that represent learning onto transparencies. Show them to an audience and narrate them.
2. Show your learning on a graphic map or chart. You might use a story map, character chart, or advance organizer.
3. Survey others. Transfer the information to a chart or graph.
4. Create a game that others can play to learn the information you researched.
5. Create a mobile, diorama, display, or other visual representation of your learning.
6. Create dictionaries for specific topics. Or translate words into another language.
7. Draw attribute webs. Write brief topic ideas on the spokes of the web.

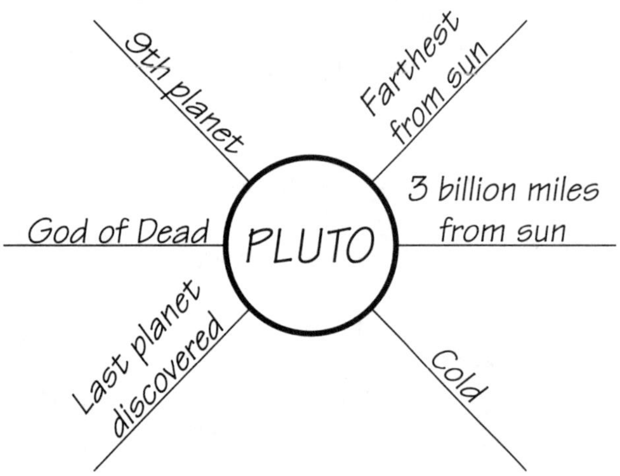

For students in all other grades:

1. Choose an idea from the primary section above.
2. Make a filmstrip on blank filmstrip material. Narrate your filmstrip.
3. Create and present a puppet show.
4. Create a radio or television broadcast, video production, or Web page.
5. Hold a panel discussion, round-robin discussion, or debate.
6. Write a diary or journal of an important historical event or person. Write a speech a person might have made at the time.
7. Create a time line of events. They might be personal, historical, social, or anything else you choose.
8. Working with several other students, create a panel discussion about a historical topic. Or play the roles of historical figures reacting to a current problem of today.
9. Create an invention to fill a personal or social need.
10. Present biographical information about a person from the past or present, dressed as that person.
11. Write a song, rap, poem, story, advertisement, or jingle.
12. Create a travel brochure for another country or planet.
13. Create an imaginary country from papier-mâché. Locate essential features.
14. Make a model. Describe its parts and the functions of each.
15. Create a chart or poster to represent synthesis of information.
16. Write a script for a play or a mock trial.
17. Write a journal of time spent and activities completed with a mentor.
18. Collect materials from a lobbying or public service agency. Summarize the information. (*Tip:* Use the Internet or the *Encyclopedia of Associations* found in the reference section of most public libraries.)
19. Write to people in other places about specific topics. Synthesize their responses.
20. Create a learning center for teachers to use in their classrooms.
21. Rewrite a story, setting it in another time period, after researching probable differences.
22. Gather political cartoons from several sources. Analyze the cartoonists' ideas.
23. Critique a film, book, television show, or video program. Write a letter to the editor and send it to your local newspaper.
24. Write a how-to manual for people who need instruction on how to do or use something.
25. Contact publishers to find out how to get something you've written published.
26. Come up with your own ideas.

Scenario: Alexa

Alexa entered second grade reading at a sixth-grade level. She was comfortable with math concepts at about the third-grade level. She was placed in a third-grade room for reading and math, but stayed with her second-grade teacher, Mr. Romero, and her age peers for all other subjects and activities. She also read five to eight books a day, which she kept hidden in her desk.

Mr. Romero asked Alexa why she kept her books out of sight, and Alexa responded that her first-grade teacher often became unhappy when she wouldn't "do her reading"—meaning the assigned reading tasks and skill work. Alexa was so busy reading at her challenge level that she didn't have time to "do her reading." Mr. Romero encouraged Alexa to spend time reading, hoping that the child would discover a topic she would want to pursue in some depth. But Alexa seemed content to do the same second-grade work the other students were doing, even though she had clearly mastered the concepts they covered.

One day in early October, Mr. Romero kept Alexa in from recess and took her to the school library, thinking that might pique her curiosity about some topic. Most of the books on display were about Halloween and Thanksgiving. Alexa noticed a book about ancient Rome and asked why it was being featured. Mr. Romero said the most important words any teacher can say when working with gifted students: "I don't know, but I can probably help you find out." A bookmark indicated a section on how the ancient Roman celebration of the harvest festival contributed to the American celebration of Thanksgiving. Alexa was enthusiastically interested. "Did any other ancient civilizations have similar customs?" she wanted to know. "Let's find out," her teacher suggested.

Twenty minutes later, Alexa left the library with six books, each on a different ancient civilization. She also had six large note cards, six blank transparency sheets, and a quick lesson in how to make transparencies. Her task was to select one civilization at a time, browse through books and other resources on that civilization until she found a picture representing a harvest celebration, transfer it to a blank transparency, and color it. She would also jot down phrases and information about the civilization on a note card, using one card per civilization. Each time she finished her work with one civilization, she would give the transparency and note cards to Mr. Romero for safekeeping. She would then go on to explore other civilizations, preparing transparencies and note cards, with the eventual goal of sharing her findings with the class in a "transparency talk." To record Alexa's progress, Mr. Romero prepared the Compactor shown on page 150.*

During the next several weeks, Alexa became so interested in her project that she chose to do almost none of the regular second-grade work. Instead, she continued to read about ancient civilizations—but without taking notes. Mr. Romero watched, amazed, as Alexa simply synthesized her reading into the pictures she created on the transparencies.

On the day of her talk, Alexa used the overhead projector to share with her classmates what she had learned. Unfortunately, Mr. Romero had forgotten to set a time limit, so Alexa went on for 42 minutes about how the people in six ancient civilizations celebrated their harvest festivals. Although her classmates were courteous, they nearly knocked out a wall getting to recess when her report was over.

Remember that Alexa had taken no notes. She had kept all of the information in her head. That's part of what being gifted is all about: abilities to think and remember that go way beyond those of one's age peers.

What if Alexa had wanted to share something with the class before researching all six civilizations? That would have been fine. What if she had wanted to switch to a different topic after researching two civilizations? That also would have been fine. The teacher already had ample evidence that Alexa had mastered the expected standards. Such evidence allows much more flexibility for project work.

When Alexa's parents heard about her project, they wanted to help. Mr. Romero suggested that they take Alexa to various places in the community (libraries, museums) to find more information on her topic than was available at school. Alexa and her parents documented her "differentiated homework" on a Daily Log of Extension Work (see page 78).

* The Compactor is introduced and described in Chapter 2.

THE COMPACTOR

Joseph Renzulli and Linda Smith

Student's Name: *Alexa*

Areas of Strength	Documenting Mastery	Alternate Activities
Reading	*Passed end-of-book test for second-grade book*	*Placed in third-grade group for reading*
Math	*Passed end-of-book test for second-grade book*	*Placed in third-grade group for math*
Second-grade skill work	*Advanced abilities and placement in reading and math*	*Will become a resident expert on harvest festivals of ancient civilizations*
Writing	*Superior writing ability—stories collected in portfolio*	*Will write a chapter book*

STRATEGY: THE TOPIC BROWSING PLANNER

When we ask students to select a topic for a project, we usually insist that they do it quickly. Then we encourage them to narrow large topics down to smaller, more manageable subtopics. This leads to situations in which gifted kids start a project with great enthusiasm, but lose interest quickly and stop working on it. That's because we have forced them to choose something they already know quite a lot about.

How can students decide on a subtopic before they have a chance to explore the larger topic? Given the speed with which information is growing and changing, we should be encouraging gifted students to explore a topic in depth before requiring formal feedback on a small part of it.

When kids are allowed extended time periods for browsing, they learn that really good ideas may come later in the process of searching for a topic. This relieves some pressure on perfectionists, who can relax about the need to find the perfect topic quickly.

The Topic Browsing Planner creates opportunities for students to pursue topics that interest them. It invites them to discover topics they never knew existed, any one of which may become the focus of in-depth research. The work is done in school, after they have completed their compacted work and instead of the work the rest of the class is doing. Students can buy back time for browsing by demonstrating mastery of certain concepts on a pretest, by completing the Most Difficult First problems on an assignment (see pages 35–38), and/or by carefully finishing compacted assignments long before other students.

Scenario: Rahul

By the end of the first day of school, Rahul was "done" with fourth grade. It was painfully clear to his teacher that there was little or nothing in the planned curriculum that represented new learning for him. Worse still, his class had more than its share of struggling students. No wonder his constant refrain was, "I'm done! Now what should I do?"

Although Rahul was obviously precocious, his parents didn't want him promoted to a higher grade. Therefore, it was up to the teacher to find an interesting, ongoing task that would keep him busy and learning—without creating extra work for her.

She took Rahul aside one day and said, "I've noticed that you often finish your work very quickly and you have a lot of time on your hands. Would you like to use some of that time to investigate a topic you're interested in?" Rahul's instant response was, "Yes! Antarctica." The teacher said, "That sounds like a very interesting topic. Let's start a Topic Browsing Planner on Antarctica and see what resources can be found."

The teacher contacted the school and town librarians, who began gathering information from many different sources. Rahul's parents agreed to help with the search, and that became a way to differentiate Rahul's homework. Soon Rahul was loaded down with books, pamphlets, filmstrips, magazine articles, and Internet resources.

The teacher moved Rahul's desk close to a bookcase and gave him part of a shelf to store his reference materials. Whenever Rahul had time left over after finishing his compacted work, he could simply reach over to his shelf and retrieve something else to browse through.

At the start of this experience, Rahul had asked the teacher, "How much work" (meaning writing) "will I have to do?" She had said, "You may use the first several weeks to explore your topic before you start taking notes or worrying about a formal project." Relieved, he became thoroughly engrossed in learning about Antarctica.

Rahul's Topic Browsing Planner, found on page 152, shows the results of 10 days of browsing. Whenever he discovered subtopics he found interesting, he recorded them. Eventually he became fascinated by the subtopic of how global warming affects icebergs and, by extension, other bodies of water. When he learned that an international committee had been formed to study the problem, and that a scientist from his own city was on the committee, Rahul added him to his list of possible interview subjects. To see how melting ice affects stationary objects, he designed an experiment using melting ice cubes. By the time Rahul officially selected a subtopic to focus on, he was eager to learn more about it.

How to Use the Topic Browsing Planner

Every personal interest project (or potential project) should start with a Topic Browsing Planner. Reproducible forms are found on pages 153 and 155. The Resources Record Sheet (page 154) may be copied on the back of the planner. A simpler version of the planner for primary students is on page 155.

1. Help students select topics to investigate. Make sure the students understand that the topics don't have to be related to the curriculum.

Explain that they will eventually choose a subtopic to focus on and a project to work on, but they shouldn't worry about that yet. For now, they should select something in which they are passionately interested.

2. Give students copies of the Topic Browsing Planner and Daily Log of Extension Work (see page 78) and explain how to fill them out.

Unless you're using the primary version of the planner, call students' attention to the Resources Record Sheet on the back. Tell students that you don't expect them to complete all of the sections or use all of the resources they list. The purpose of the form is to help them keep track of sources they may want to consult or return to as their project progresses.

3. Tell students that they are not to take any formal notes for a period of 5–10 days. Instead, they should use that time to browse through all of the information they can find on their general topic of interest.

4. Enlist the services of school and public library personnel. Provide places for students to store the resource materials they accumulate.

5. Be available to guide students through the same process of exploration, discovery, and delight that Rahul experienced.

Some students may already know their way around the library, the Internet, and other resources. Others may need help discovering the wealth of information available to them. Give everyone a copy of the Resources Suggestions list on page 156. Even experienced researchers might not think of contacting a travel agency or seeking out a historical reenactment group. Students can use the blank lines to add other resources they find and recommend.

6. After students are finished browsing, meet with them and help them choose subtopics to focus on.

Text continues on page 157

★ TOPIC BROWSING PLANNER ★

Student's Name: *Rahul* Date: *10/18*

General Topic to Explore: *Antarctica*

On a separate sheet of paper, list the things you already know about this topic. Staple that list to this form.

Subtopics I May Want to Learn More About:

Animals of Antarctica

Plants of Antarctica

Scientific Expeditions

Female Antarctic explorers

Penguins

Movies about Antarctica

How global warming affects icebergs and how that affects other bodies of water

Professionals I Might Interview:

Dr. Carlos DeMarco, scientist, Shedd Aquarium, Chicago

My mom's friend's son Tim, who just returned from 6 months on a science team in Antarctica

Experiments or Surveys I Might Conduct:

Effects on stationary objects of changes in water levels

Differences in resistance to cold of men and women

Specific Subtopic I Will Focus My Project On:

How the increased rate of the melting of the polar ice caps is affecting bodies of water—and people—all over the globe

Teacher's Signature: *Judy Lynch*

Student's Signature: *Rahul Patel*

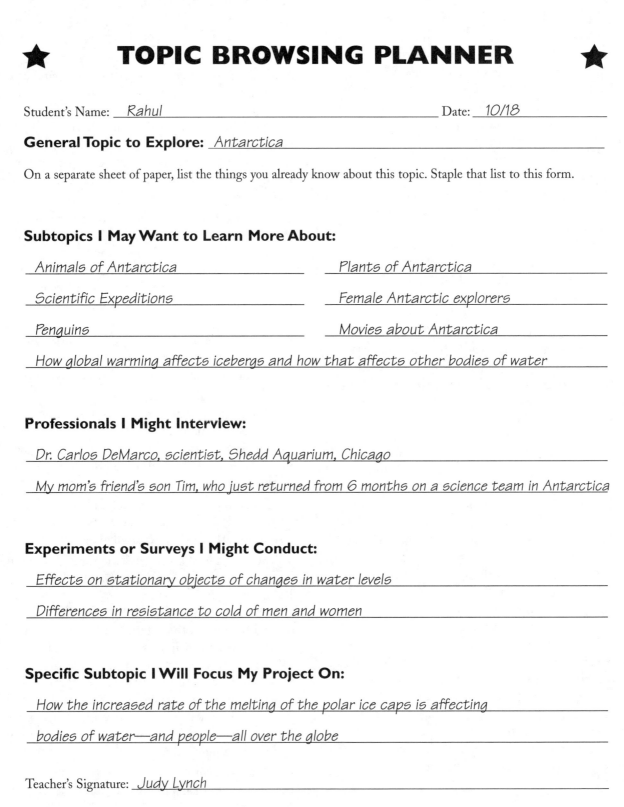

★ TOPIC BROWSING PLANNER ★

Student's Name: ______________________________________ Date: _______________

General Topic to Explore: ____

On a separate sheet of paper, list the things you already know about this topic. Staple that list to this form.

Subtopics I May Want to Learn More About:

__________________________________ __________________________________

__________________________________ __________________________________

__________________________________ __________________________________

__________________________________ __________________________________

Professionals I Might Interview:

____

____

____

Experiments or Surveys I Might Conduct:

____

____

____

Specific Subtopic I Will Focus My Project On:

____

____

Teacher's Signature: ____

Student's Signature: ____

★ RESOURCES RECORD SHEET ★

Sources of Information	**Specifics** (call number, author's name, publication date, Internet address, etc.)	**Title**	**Where I Found It**
Books (reference books, biographies, histories, first-person accounts, etc.)			
Periodicals (magazines, newspapers, newsletters, etc.)			
Internet Resources (Web sites, newsgroups, online encyclopedias, Internet magazines, etc.)			
Other Sources (TV, radio, etc.)			

★ TOPIC BROWSING PLANNER FOR PRIMARY GRADES ★

Student's Name: ____ Date: ________________

General Topic to Explore: ____

On the back of this paper, list the things you already know about this topic.

Subtopics I May Want to Learn More About:

____

____

____

____

Specific Subtopic I Choose to Learn More About:

____

____

How I Will Share What I've Learned with the Class:

____

____

Teacher's Signature: ____

Student's Signature: ____

★ RESOURCES SUGGESTIONS ★

Books
Almanacs
Atlases
Biographies
Dictionaries
Encyclopedias
First-person accounts
Histories
Nonfiction books
Reference books
Yellow Pages

____

____

Internet Resources
Chat rooms
Internet magazines
Newsgroups
Online encyclopedias
Web sites
'Zines

____

____

Libraries and Archives
Company libraries/archives
County records
Indexes to free materials
Indexes to periodicals
Library archives
Maps
Microfiche/microfilm
Newspaper files/archives
Public libraries
Reference libraries
School libraries
Specialized libraries
Specialized bibliographies
Specialized encyclopedias
State records

____

____

Organizations
Chambers of Commerce
Clubs
Encyclopedia of Associations
Groups
Teams
Troops
Professional associations

____

____

Other
Documentaries
Field trips
Films
Videos

____

____

People
Experts in the field
Faculty members
Family members
Friends
Friends' parents
Government officials
Historical reenactment groups
Neighbors
Parents
Professionals in the field
Senior citizens
Teachers
Youth group leaders

____

____

Periodicals
Brochures
Catalogs
Diaries
Journals
Magazines
Newsletters
Newspapers
Trade magazines

____

____

Places
Antique shops
Art galleries
Businesses
Cemeteries
Colleges and universities
Historical sites
Historical societies
Houses of worship
Living history sites
Museums
Schools
Smithsonian Institution
Travel agencies
Weather stations

____

____

Software
CD-ROM encyclopedias
Databases
Simulation programs

____

____

Text continues from page 151

STRATEGY: THE RESIDENT EXPERT PLANNER

Once students choose a subtopic they want to learn more about, they're ready to move on to the next stage of the Personal Interest Independent Study Project: becoming a "resident expert."* A reproducible Resident Expert Planner is found on pages 160–161. (Copy the second page on the back of the first page.) A simpler version for primary students is on page 162. See also the Independent Study Option for the Primary Grades: The 4C Booklet on page 166.

How to Use the Resident Expert Planner

1. Help students identify a topic they want to pursue in depth. Explain that they will have the opportunity to really get into their topic, and they will be expected to share what they learn with the class or other appropriate audience.

Identifying the topic is simple. The specific subtopic from the Topic Browsing Planner becomes the main topic for the Resident Expert Planner.

For example, let's say a student is interested in the general topic of life in other countries around the world. He might browse his way through various countries, then decide he's most interested in learning more about life in Russia. Eventually he may choose to focus on life as a child in Russia. That becomes the specific subtopic of his Topic Browsing Planner and the topic of his Resident Expert Planner.

2. Have students break down their main topic into 6 subtopics. For each subtopic, they should come up with 3 questions to ask. (If you're using the primary version of the planner, your students will come up with 4 subtopics and 2 questions each.)

Conduct several direct instruction lessons on how to write questions that are specific rather than too broad. Give students a few days to think about and write their subtopics and questions. This might take more browsing time, during which students may return to some of the sources they consulted earlier. They might also consult other sources they listed on their Resources Record Sheet.

For example, the student who chooses to focus on life as a child in Russia might come up with these subtopics and questions:

1. **Daily Life**
   a. What are children's routines at home?
   b. What are their chores and responsibilities?
   c. What types of foods do they usually eat?
2. **Family Life**
   a. What might their parents do for a living?
   b. How many brothers and sisters might they have?
   c. Do extended family members live nearby or far away?
3. **School**
   a. What days and times do they go to school?
   b. What subjects do they study?
   c. What kinds of teaching methods are used in Russian schools?
4. **Religion**
   a. What are the main religions in Russia?
   b. What type of religious education might a child have?
   c. What religious holidays are celebrated?
5. **Government, Laws, and Economy**
   a. What type of government does Russia have? How has it changed in recent years?
   b. What are some rules and laws in Russia?
   c. What are the country's main imports and exports?
6. **Recreation**
   a. What do families do together for fun?
   b. What are the main government or state holidays?
   c. How do Russians like to spend their vacations?

NOTE: Some students invariably announce that they want to pursue more than 6 subtopics. Suggest that they start with that number and expand their search later.

* Chapter 4 discusses another type of "resident expert"—one whose independent study project is related to the curriculum.

3. Once students have their subtopics and questions, it's time for them to start taking notes. Teach them the Note Card method described in the following section.

NOTE: Be flexible about the note-taking requirement. Remember that some gifted students (like Alexa; see page 149) can learn a great deal of information and later share it with an audience without writing anything down.

4. You may want students to keep track of the resources they use and prepare a written bibliography. If so, choose a simple format and teach it to them. Provide plenty of examples and practice time. Show students how to use 5" x 7" note cards, recording one reference on each card. Once the research is done, it's easier to alphabetize a stack of cards than a long list of notes on paper.

Tell students to record only those resources they actually use, not those they simply read or consult. Explain that even when they take a lot of notes from a single source, they only need to make one card for that source.

IMPORTANT: Please don't make this requirement too tedious. We don't want kids spending hours recording reference source information and preparing lengthy, detailed bibliographies. You might ask younger students to record only 2 books, 1 encyclopedia (or other reference book), 1 article, and 1 Web site. Older kids will be relieved if you allow them to limit the number of sources that require formal citations.

5. Work with students to identify the materials and supplies they need. They may already have good ideas from the time they spent browsing their general topic.

6. Help students plan how they will report on their project. Give them copies of the Product Choices Chart on page 80.

7. Have students keep track of the work they do on their personal interest projects. The Daily Log of Extension Work on page 78 is an excellent tool for this purpose. It also makes students accountable for being productive.

You may decide to let students do part of their project at home, as a way to differentiate their homework. They should note this on their Resident Expert Planner and use a separate Daily Log to record their progress at home.

You might also use the Check-Off Sheet for Resident Expert Project on page 163. Students fill in each square with a brief description of part of their project. As each part is completed, they mark an X in the box for that square and record the date they finished that task.

Don't insist that they do the parts in any particular order. As long as they get them done, it really doesn't matter. Global learners may actually do better if they plan their project backwards from the last step to the first.

Don't set a time limit for any part or step. As long as students follow the working conditions, the amount of time they spend on a project isn't important.

8. Work with the students to identify any potential problems they might encounter while working on their projects. Help them brainstorm possible solutions.

The Note Card Method

Some gifted students are not efficient or effective note-takers. They tend to write down too much, and they may have trouble organizing their information. The Note Card method can help them stay organized and be more selective about the information they will record.

You'll need a supply of 5" x 7" note cards in 6 different colors (or 4 for primary students). *Example:* white, blue, green, pink, yellow, violet.

1. Give each student 18 cards—3 each of the 6 different colors. Have them decide which color goes with which subtopic on their Resident Expert Planner. They might choose yellow for subtopic 1, green for subtopic 2, and so on.

2. Tell them to label each card with a subtopic and a question. *Examples:*

1. Daily Life

a. What are Russian children's routines at home?

3. School

b. What subjects do Russian children study in school?

3. Explain that whenever they come across information about the first question under their first subtopic, they should record it on the card with that label. Similarly, whenever they come across information about the second question under their third subtopic, they should record it on the card with that label...and so on. *Tip:* Prepare some sample cards in advance and pass them around as you explain this process. It's easier to show it than to tell about it.

When students try to research one subtopic at a time in several sources, things can quickly become very confusing. They have trouble remembering which books they've consulted, and there's no way to record interesting information about other subtopics they notice along the way. With the Note Card method, it's okay if one source yields information about several subtopics. Students can easily switch cards and keep taking notes without interruption. Plus they only have to use a source once. When they put it aside, they're done with it, because they've pulled everything they want from it.

4. Tell students that each note should be 1 or 2 lines long—no longer. Each note should be a phrase—no capital letters on the first word, no ending punctuation.

These simple instructions minimize copying. (Be very clear that nothing should be copied word-for-word from another written source.) Kids are more likely to make notes selectively and put information in their own words. Teach them how to write phrases; sometimes just subjects and verbs are enough.

5. Remind students to check each note carefully to make sure it belongs on a particular card. They should pay close attention to the subtopics and questions written at the top of each card.

The Personal Interest Independent Study Project Agreement

The Personal Interest Independent Study Project Agreement on page 164 is similar to the Independent Study Agreement on page 75. It is an official contract between you and the student, designed to teach kids how to behave responsibly while working independently.

Hold a meeting for all kids who have decided to become resident experts. Give everyone a copy of the agreement and have them follow along as you read it aloud. Make sure students understand that if they fail to meet the conditions, the logical consequence is that they will have to return to the teacher-directed group for the remainder of the unit.

You may share the agreement with students' parents, but their signatures aren't required, since most of the work will be done in school. Students should bring their agreements to workplaces outside the classroom (the library, media center, resource room, other classrooms) but should never take them home. Keep the signed agreements and the completed Daily Logs from both school and home in the students' compacting folders.

Evaluating Students' Project Work

My strong feeling is that if students are willing to work on personal interest independent study projects without grades, we should encourage that attitude. It would be nice to see intrinsic motivation surface now and then. However, it's more than likely that kids will want grades. If they do, use the Evaluation Contract described in Chapter 4, page 74, and have students choose the grade they plan to work for. The only two choices available should be A or B. Why would anyone want to do an independent study for a lower grade?

Letting Students Evaluate Their Own Work

Whether or not a grade is attached to a personal project, you might ask kids to evaluate themselves on the process skills of doing research. Create a checklist of desired project behaviors and abilities and ask students to complete it every two weeks or so. Or use the Self-Evaluation Checklist on page 165. Ratings should be simple pluses (+) and minuses (–). If you want, you can add your feedback, using a different color writing tool. Discrepancies between a student's self-evaluation and a teacher's evaluation can lead to better understanding about the expectations for future projects and improved performance on current projects.

Text continues on page 166

★ RESIDENT EXPERT PLANNER ★

Student's name: ______________________ Date project work begins: ______________________

My topic: ______________________ I am contracting for a grade of: ______________________

My 6 subtopics and 3 questions for each:

1. ______________________
a. ______________________
b. ______________________
c. ______________________

2. ______________________
a. ______________________
b. ______________________
c. ______________________

3. ______________________
a. ______________________
b. ______________________
c. ______________________

4. ______________________
a. ______________________
b. ______________________
c. ______________________

5. ______________________
a. ______________________
b. ______________________
c. ______________________

6. ______________________
a. ______________________
b. ______________________
c. ______________________

more ☞

RESIDENT EXPERT PLANNER continued

Materials or supplies I need for my project:

What I need:	Where to get it:
____________________	____________________
____________________	____________________
____________________	____________________
____________________	____________________

The format I will use for my report: ____________________

The part of the project I will complete at home (optional): ____________________

____

____

Potential problems:	Possible solutions:
____________________	____________________
____________________	____________________
____________________	____________________

Student's signature: ____________________ Teacher's signature: ____________________

★ RESIDENT EXPERT PLANNER FOR PRIMARY GRADES ★

Student's name: ____________________ Date project starts: ____________________

My topic: ____

My 4 subtopics and 2 questions for each:

1. ____________________ **3.** ____________________

a. ____________________ a. ____________________

b. ____________________ b. ____________________

2. ____________________ **4.** ____________________

a. ____________________ a. ____________________

b. ____________________ b. ____________________

Materials or supplies I need for my project:

What I need:	Where to get it:

How I will give my report: ____

Student's signature: ____________________ Teacher's signature: ____________________

★ CHECK-OFF SHEET FOR RESIDENT EXPERT PROJECT ★

Student's name: ______________________ Topic: ______________________

☐ ________ DATE COMPLETED	☐ ________ DATE COMPLETED	☐ ________ DATE COMPLETED
☐ ________ DATE COMPLETED	☐ ________ DATE COMPLETED	☐ ________ DATE COMPLETED
☐ ________ DATE COMPLETED	☐ ________ DATE COMPLETED	☐ ________ DATE COMPLETED

★ PERSONAL INTEREST INDEPENDENT STUDY PROJECT AGREEMENT ★

Read each condition as your teacher reads it aloud. Write your initials beside it to show that you understand it and agree to abide by it.

Learning Conditions

______ I will spend the expected amount of time working on my Personal Interest Independent Study Project.

______ I will complete all required forms and keep them at school.

______ If I want my project to be graded, I will complete an Evaluation Contract and work at the agreed-upon level.

______ I will leave my project to participate in designated whole-class activities or lessons as the teacher indicates them—without arguing.

______ I will keep a Daily Log of my progress.

______ I will share progress reports about my project at regular intervals with the class or other audience. Progress reports will be 5–7 minutes long. Each will include a visual aid and a question for the class to answer.

Working Conditions

______ I will be present in the classroom at the beginning and end of each class period.

______ I will not bother anyone or call attention to the fact that I am doing different work than others in the class.

______ I will work on my project for the entire class period on designated days.

______ I will carry this paper with me to any room in which I am working on my project, and I will return it to my classroom at the end of each session.

______ **I understand that I may keep working on my project as long as I meet these Learning and Working Conditions.**

Teacher's Signature: ____

Student's Signature: ____

★ SELF-EVALUATION CHECKLIST ★

	Student	Teacher
During My Research:		
I selected a topic that held my interest.	______	______
I understood the Working Conditions.	______	______
I followed the Working Conditions.	______	______
I worked well independently.	______	______
I asked for help when I needed it.	______	______
______________________________	______	______
______________________________	______	______
______________________________	______	______
For My Report to the Class:		
I created an interesting question for the class to answer.	______	______
I had someone listen to my report before giving it to the class.	______	______
I was able to explain what I learned to others.	______	______
My report had an attention-grabbing beginning.	______	______
My report was well-organized.	______	______
I spoke loudly and clearly with good expression.	______	______
I made frequent eye contact with others.	______	______
I held the class's attention during my report.	______	______
I answered questions clearly.	______	______
______________________________	______	______
______________________________	______	______
______________________________	______	______

Text continues from page 159

INDEPENDENT STUDY OPTION FOR THE PRIMARY GRADES: THE 4C BOOKLET

To help younger children develop their resident expert and research skills, create Browsing Boxes on a variety of topics.* Or ask parents to create them; this is a great project for volunteers.

You'll need several fairly large boxes with lids, like the ones used to store files or hold several reams of paper. Label each box with a specific topic. Gather books and other types of reference materials on those topics and store them in the boxes. The materials should be suitable for a wide range of reading abilities. School or public librarians can help you find these materials. Ask public librarians for "extended loan" privileges so you can keep them for longer periods of time.

Students select one of the available topics and peruse the materials in that box to learn more about it. They use a 4C Booklet to record their research and plan a way to share it with others.

A 4C booklet can be 4 sheets of writing paper stapled together, or a large sheet of drawing paper folded into 4 sections, or any other format that works for you and your students. Label each sheet or section as in the figure below.

Students work on their projects while you teach grade-level content to kids who need direct instruction. The 4C booklet is not homework. It replaces the regular school work that is not challenging for some students. Kids working on 4C booklets can record their progress on a Daily Log of Extension Work (see page 78).

* Used with permission from Connie Webb, McMinnville Public Schools, McMinnville, Oregon.

QUESTIONS AND ANSWERS

"What if a student who needs to do an independent study can't find a topic to work on?"

Suggest that he spend a few days writing down questions that pop into his head for which he doesn't know the answers. Those questions can become topics for study. Or send him to the library to browse the books in the nonfiction section. Any books he finds interesting can lead to possible topics.

THE 4C BOOKLET

C1: COLLECT facts, words, ideas, and pictures about your topic.	**C2:** COMPARE your topic to something else. Look for similarities and differences, advantages and disadvantages, relationships, ways to classify or categorize, or something else you can compare.
C3: CREATE a way to share what you have learned about your topic.	**C4:** COMMUNICATE your findings with the class or other appropriate audience.

"What if a student decides that she doesn't want to pursue her subtopic after finishing a Topic Browsing Planner?"

Simply file the completed planner in her compacting folder and let her move on to something else. Or, if this makes you uncomfortable, tell your students that you expect them to study one subtopic in depth for every three planners they complete. If they resist, try to find out why. Perhaps they are reluctant to get up in front of the class to make progress reports. Find a mutually acceptable way for them to share their information. For example, you might allow them to videotape their reports and play the video for the class.

"Won't other students also want to browse and share what they learn with the class?"

Of course they will. Why not take some Friday afternoon, after the class has met most of the criteria you have set for the week, and let everyone browse through some topic for an hour or so? Leave time near the end for students to share what they have learned, briefly and informally. Or use those mini-reports as mini-rewards for when the class finishes a session early, or the kids have been particularly wonderful on a given day during that week. Most kids love to do a mini-transparency talk, sharing only one picture that describes what they have learned.

"What should I do if students who are working on these special activities become disruptive?"

You probably already know what to do. The response to this situation is always the same. Ask the students to rejoin the class and participate in the regular activities. Tell them that their behavior indicates that they would be more productive in teacher-directed situations.

Whenever students take advantage of an opportunity to do alternate activities, whether it's a Learning Contract (Chapter 3), Study Guide (Chapter 4), or Personal Interest Independent Study Project (this chapter), start by making sure they know what to do and have adequate resources and skills for the task. Decide in advance on the working conditions and explain them in careful detail. Have students sign an agreement to abide by the working conditions. Attach the agreement to their contract, guide, or planner so they can refer to it often.

For ideas and examples of working conditions, see Julie's Learning Contract on page 48, Working Conditions for Alternate Activities on page 51, either Independent Study Agreement in Chapter 4 (pages 75 or 76), and the Personal Interest Independent Study Project Agreement on page 164. Please be selective. Even though Working Conditions is a reproducible form, I hope you won't simply photocopy it every time one of your students chooses a special activity or independent study. You may find that some of your students need fewer or different working conditions to stay on track.

Sometimes, if gifted students find themselves working alone on a project, they will misbehave on purpose to manipulate themselves into a position where they won't appear so "different." Most kids prefer not to be singled out by having to work alone. Allow kids working on personal interest projects to work together, even if their topics are different.

"What happens if students refuse to work on their planners and insist on just sitting and vegetating during their choice time?"

As the teacher, you will make it clear that they have only two choices: Either they can develop an independent study project of some kind, or you can assign them more "regular work." Doing nothing isn't an option.

"What if a student never finishes the project related to his personal interest topic?"

Celebrate! Why would you want the project to be finished? You and the student would then have to go through the process of choosing another topic! James, the gifted writer from Chapter 2 (pages 41–43), worked on his book about the human body for the entire school year and beyond.

Real expertise is an endless journey, and gifted kids are often driven to become real experts on a topic that interests them passionately. People who make their living as researchers often spend many years on a single project. So relax. There's nothing wrong with a project that goes on forever, as long as the student meets the working conditions and is willing to share progress reports now and then to document his progress.

"How can I justify using the time it takes to create and monitor independent study activities when there's so much pressure on me to bring below-level students up to par?"

Imagine how much less guilty you'll feel when you're no longer holding fast learners back to the same pace required by students who don't find learning easy. When gifted kids are working on independent projects, you'll actually have more time to work with needy students. Any time you spend teaching gifted kids to work well independently pays off large dividends. It reduces the stress you may feel because gifted students and their parents are so frustrated with the learning pace of the classroom. When you know all kids are really learning, you can feel better about your own effectiveness as a teacher.

SUMMARY

When we excuse gifted kids from regular class activities so they can pursue topics that interest them, we must trust that they will use that time productively—provided we have taught them the expected behaviors. Students will be more successful at independent study if procedures and expectations are clearly explained before they begin their work. Gifted kids are usually so relieved and happy to discover that there is a place in school for their passionate interests that they are eager to meet the required working conditions.

REFERENCES AND RESOURCES

See also the References and Resources for Chapter 4.

Active Learning Systems, Epping, NH, (800) 644-5059. Developers of IIM (Independent Investigation Method), which helps children of all ages research and present information on any subject.

Alternative Learning Publications (ALPS), Greeley, CO, (800) 345-ALPS (www. alpspublishing.com). Many resources for facilitating independent projects and teaching kids to do in-depth research.

Baum, Susan. *Chi Square Pie Charts and Me.* Unionville, NY: Trillium Press, 1987.

Black, Kaye. *Kidvid: Fun-Damentals of Video Instruction: Grades 4 Through 12.* Rev. ed. Tucson, AZ: Zephyr Press, 2000. Helps kids produce their own videos.

Blandford, Elizabeth. *How to Write the Best Research Paper Ever.* Dayton, OH: Pieces of Learning, 1998.

Boyce, Linda N. *A Guide to Teaching Research Skills and Strategies (Grades 4–12).* Williamsburg, VA: Center for Gifted Education, 1997. Available from the College of William and Mary, Center for Gifted Education, Williamsburg, VA, (757) 221-2362 (cfge.wm.edu).

Creative Learning Press, Inc., Mansfield Center, CT, (888) 518-8004 (www.creativelearningpress.com). Their materials on research and thinking skills raise independent study into more complex and abstract realms.

Doherty, Edith, and Louise Evans. *Self-Starter Kit for Independent Study.* East Windsor Hill, CT: Synergetics, 1983.

Draze, Dianne. *Project Planner: A Guide for Creating Curriculum and Independent Study Projects,* San Luis Obispo, CA: Dandy Lion Publications, 1990.

Encyclopedia of Associations: National Organizations of the U. S. Farmington Hills, MI: Gale Group, updated often. A fabulous resource for free material for student researchers from national headquarters of thousands of companies in the United States. Look for it in a public or university library. Also from Gale: *Encyclopedia of Associations: International Organizations.*

Facts On File, Inc., New York, NY, (800) 322-8755 (www.factsonfile.com). Request their catalog of reference books, CD-ROMs, and databases.

Grun, Bernard. *The Timetables of History: A Horizontal Linkage of People and Events.* New York: Simon & Schuster, 1991. See page 87 for more *Timetables* books.

"A Pro/Con Issue" Series. From Enslow Publishers, Inc., Berkeley Heights, NJ, (800) 398-2504 (www.enslow.com). Resources for debates.

Institute for the Advancement of Philosophy for Children. A curriculum that teaches reasoning and judgment to advanced thinkers of all ages. Publications include *Harry Stottlemeier's Discovery* and *Lisa.* IAPC, Montclair State University, Upper Montclair, NJ, (973) 655-4277 (www.montclair.edu).

Invent America! Alexandria, VA, (703) 684-1836 (www.inventamerica.org). A K–8 creativity and problem-solving program that helps kids learn by inventing

Kingore, Bertie. *Portfolios: Enriching and Assessing All Students: Identifying the Gifted Grades K–6.* Austin, TX: Professional Associates, 1993.

Knowledge Adventure, Torrance, CA, (800) 545-7677 (www.knowledgeadventure.com). Resources for multimedia presentations.

Leimbach, Judy. *Primarily Research, Primarily Reference Skills, Primarily Problem Solving,* and *Primarily Creativity* aid primary kids in independent learning. From Dandy Lion Publications, San Luis Obispo, CA, (800) 776-8032 (www.dandylionbooks.com).

Macrorie, Ken. *The I Search Paper.* Portsmouth, NH: Boynton-Cook, 1988.

"Opposing Viewpoints" Series. From Greenhaven Press, Farmington Hills, MI, (800) 877-4253 (www.galegroup.com/greenhaven). Resources for debates.

Pollette, Nancy. *Research Reports to Knock Your Teacher's Socks Off.* Dayton, OH: Pieces of Learning, 1997.
—— *Research Without Copying.* Dayton, OH: Pieces of Learning, 1991.

Primary Education Thinking Skills and *Primary Education Thinking Skills 2 (PETS).* Available from Pieces of Learning, Marion, IL, (800) 729-5137 (www.piecesoflearning.com).

Product Guide Kits by John Samara. These excellent tools help kids prepare high-quality products. Every school should have them. Available from The Curriculum Project, Austin, TX, (800) 867-9067 (www.curriculumproject.com).

Rice, Donna. *How to Manage Learning Centers in the Classroom.* Westminster, CA: Teacher Created Materials, 1997. (888) 343-4335 (www.teachercreated.com).

Rube Goldberg Machine Contest (www.rubegoldberg.com). Students build complex machines to perform simple tasks. The contest is "designed to pull students away from their matter-of-fact way of looking at a problem and send intuitive thought spinning into a chaos of imagination." For more information, contact Rube Goldberg Inc. at (203) 227-0818.

Russell, Susan J., and Rebecca B. Corwin. *Statistics: The Shape of Data.* White Plains, NY: Dale Seymour Publications, 1997. Data-gathering techniques for elementary students.

Russell, Susan J., and Karen Economopoulos. *Does It Walk, Crawl, or Swim? Sorting and Classifying Data.* White Plains, NY: Dale Seymour Publications, 1997. Data-gathering techniques for elementary students.

Schurr, Sandra. *Signaling Student Success: Thematic Learning Stations.* Westminster, CA: Teacher Created Materials, 1996. (888) 343-4335 (www.teachercreated.com).

Schuler, Sandra L. *Checklists for Super Student Projects.* Parsippany, NJ: Good Apple, 1997. A comprehensive assistant for 38 projects for many types of learning styles. Evaluation guidelines are included.

"Science Project Ideas" series. Books by Robert Gardner that help kids with project-type learning include *Science Project Ideas About Animal Behavior, Science Project Ideas About Rain,* and *Science Project Ideas About the Moon.* From Enslow Publishers, Inc., Berkeley Heights, NJ, (800) 398-2504 (www.enslow.com).

Starko, Alane, and Gina Schack. *Looking for Data in All the Right Places.* Storrs, CT: Creative Learning Press, 1992

Strichart, Stephen, et al. *Teaching Study Skills and Strategies to Students with Learning Disabilities or Special Needs.* Boston: Allyn & Bacon, 1998.

WebQuest (webquest.org). A WebQuest is an inquiry-oriented activity in which some or all of the information that learners interact with comes from resources on the Internet. The Web site includes an overview, readings, training materials, and examples.

8

Grouping Gifted Students for Learning

When students are grouped for learning, gifted kids require different considerations than their age peers. There is much evidence that struggling students do better today, in heterogeneous classes, than they did previously, when they were "tracked" in low-ability groups. But the evidence about gifted students is just the opposite. Their long-term achievement may suffer unless they are purposefully grouped together for at least part of each school day.

The practice of grouping high-ability students has been challenged in an educational climate that opposes ability grouping in general. However, the research of James Kulik, Chen-Lin Kulik, John Feldhusen, and Marcia Gentry clearly demonstrates that gifted students consistently benefit from being with students of similar ability.

We can accomplish our goal of allowing gifted youngsters to work together through the careful use of two practices: cooperative learning and cluster grouping. This chapter describes both in detail. Although their benefits are interrelated, I have chosen to discuss them separately.

COOPERATIVE LEARNING

Cooperative learning has been suggested as one response to the challenges inherent to teaching a class with a wide range of ability. In some schools, gifted students who have already mastered grade-level curriculum are expected to become teachers for their peers who need help with the material. This is grossly unfair to the gifted students, who may be denied consistent opportunities to make forward progress in their own learning.

Cooperative learning is an educational practice that is generally accompanied by some gains in achievement and profoundly improved social interaction behaviors for boys and girls. Since the demands of the adult workplace often require all people to work in groups from time to time, cooperative learning skills are valuable for all students, including those who are gifted. Remember that on-the-job groups are rarely totally heterogeneous in nature. In most cases, team members have common training and experience.

Gifted students may have much to lose and little to gain from traditional cooperative learning practices. As you'll see, it's not difficult to create appropriate cooperative learning experiences for your gifted students.

Scenario: Kim Liu

Kim Liu was a very unhappy sixth grader. His science teacher used cooperative learning almost all of the time, and Kim Liu had exhibited some decidedly uncooperative behaviors in his group. Most often, he insisted on doing his work alone, sulked when he was forced to join the group, and refused to carry out the jobs to which he was assigned.

Sometimes, he would act as though he had decided to participate in the cooperative learning activity, but he would soon take over the group, regardless of his assigned job, and try to boss the others into doing things his way. At other times, he simply told his teammates the answers so he could get some relief for a few minutes at the end of science class. Kim Liu's teacher was using a lot of energy trying to come up with ways to convince him to cooperate. No strategy seemed to work, and almost everyone involved was totally frustrated.

During this period, Kim Liu's teacher attended one of my workshops on teaching gifted kids. She was startled to hear me describe children whose reactions were similar to his. Using guidelines presented in the workshop and detailed in this chapter, she was able to help Kim Liu and her other gifted students develop a more positive attitude about cooperative learning, which made everyone concerned much happier.

Cooperative Learning and Gifted Kids

You may recall that earlier in this book, I suggested that you never ask anything of gifted kids that you wouldn't want someone to ask of you. Let's look at what this really means.

Imagine yourself at the first class meeting of a graduate course you need to take. Your professor is explaining how anxious she is to try out a new method she has just learned called cooperative learning. One course requirement, which will count for 51 percent of your grade, will be a group project. To save time, she has divided the class into groups alphabetically. You'll have the chance to meet with your new "friends" for 30 minutes at the end of class to plan your group project.

Visualize yourself at the first meeting of your group. Monitor your inner reflexes as you discover a slacker in your midst. If you're a student who's proud of your perfect graduate record of all A's, you know you'll do everything you can to make sure your record isn't threatened by this person, who is already enumerating the various reasons why she can't work very hard on this project.

Nod your head if you know that you're probably going to become a little bossy with these folks. Nod if you realize that you're most likely going to end up doing much more than your fair share of the work.

With cooperative learning, we often create situations in which some students have to do just what we would try to avoid. And we criticize them for responding exactly as we would respond.

Most training in cooperative learning directs teachers to set up completely heterogeneous groups. Cooperative learning trainers teach that a group of four students would ideally include one high achiever, two average achievers, and one perceived low achiever. Many experts in cooperative learning contend that all students, regardless of their ability, realize achievement gains from participating in heterogeneous cooperative learning groups. They claim that high-ability students don't suffer, and that gifted students actually understand concepts better when they explain them to other students.

Author, educator, and researcher Robert E. Slavin has observed that "Gifted students working in heterogeneous cooperative learning groups are no worse off than they are in more traditional classrooms." Statements such as this imply that it's perfectly acceptable to consistently place gifted students in heterogeneous groups for learning. But consider this little-known fact about Slavin's research: It systematically excluded the top 5 percent of the student body, meaning that his studies never actually included gifted students! His data, then, is accurate for high achievers, but not for gifted kids. One must also question how much learning typically happens for gifted students in traditional classrooms. "No worse off" is not synonymous with "better off."

Furthermore, out-of-level tests are rarely (if ever) used to document cooperative learning experts' achievement claims for gifted students. When a student starts a particular course of study with a standardized test score in the 95th–99th percentile and moves up only a few percentage points, then naturally it's going to look as though the student hasn't lost any ground. At the same time, it's extremely difficult to measure whether the student has made any gains. Achievement gains for gifted students can be adequately measured only with tests normed for students at a more advanced level, where they have some growing room.

In cooperative learning studies which actually questioned gifted students about their attitudes toward cooperative learning, the majority of those interviewed agreed they did not really dislike cooperative learning per se. They just resented being taken advantage of in cooperative learning groups. Many adults can surely relate to that.

When the learning task requires lots of drill-and-practice, or when some students are having significant trouble learning new concepts, it's highly likely that gifted students in heterogeneous cooperative learning groups will spend most of their time tutoring the other students. They may actually do more teaching than learning. With the increased pressure in many states to bring the least capable students up to the levels of learning required by state standards, the practice of using gifted kids to teach others may appear even more attractive.

The implied message gifted students receive from always being placed in heterogeneous cooperative learning groups is that once they master the grade-level content, there's nothing left for them to learn. Most teachers would not consciously choose to send such a message.

When the cooperative learning tasks are problem-centered and open-ended, and the teacher has enough training to make sure gifted kids are not being taken advantage of in any way during the cooperative group work, heterogeneous cooperative groups may be defensible for part of the learning time. However, many gifted kids don't prefer group work, so they should have the option to decline it, at least some of the time. There are many jobs in the real world where people work alone successfully.

Gifted students can benefit from learning how to work cooperatively with other students. Cooperative learning experiences can specifically teach them the important social interaction skills they frequently lack, while allowing them to enjoy the company of their age peers. The real question is not whether gifted students belong in cooperative learning groups. Rather, the question is under what conditions they can benefit from cooperative learning and learn the social skills they need to succeed later in life.

STRATEGY: PLACING GIFTED STUDENTS IN THEIR OWN COOPERATIVE LEARNING GROUPS

When gifted students are removed from heterogeneous cooperative learning groups and placed together in their own group with an appropriately challenging task, their experience with cooperative learning is much more satisfying than when they are forced to tutor and/or coach other students in heterogeneous groups. Especially for tasks that focus on drill-and-practice, it is desirable to place gifted students in separate groups to work on more difficult tasks. The rest of the class is arranged in heterogeneous groups, with the "high" in the group being a very capable student, although not necessarily gifted.

Teachers may fear that when the gifted students are working in their own groups, the other groups will lack appropriate role models. Nothing could be further from the truth. Educational researcher, author, and Purdue professor Dale H. Schunk has documented that for one person to serve as a viable role model for another, there can't be too much difference in their abilities. This concept makes sense when you compare it to almost any other learning process. For example, if you're learning to downhill ski, you're more likely to gain confidence by watching novices fall and get up unharmed than by watching hotshots fly down a Black Diamond slope.

David A. Kenny and his colleagues at the University of Connecticut in Storrs studied heterogeneous cooperative learning groups in fourth grade. Although they didn't observe any negative effects on gifted kids in these groups, their research showed that simply having gifted kids in a group doesn't lead to increased achievement by other kids in that group. Further, they found that the other students experienced lower self-esteem. Although non-gifted students may appear to rely on gifted kids for assistance, knowing that they can't do the task more independently reduces their self-confidence.

It is often true that high-ability kids make much more patient coaches than highly gifted students. When gifted students in heterogeneous cooperative learning groups try to explain something to the others, it's as if they are speaking a foreign language. Their listeners may nod their heads in agreement, but they may also feel intimidated, and they won't ask questions for fear of looking foolish or dumb. Meanwhile, the gifted students feel increasingly frustrated about how long it takes the others to understand an idea they grasped at once. Since the gifted students have probably not had instruction in how to teach, they may resort to just giving the answers. Since the other kids may feel daunted in the presence of gifted kids, they may rely on the gifted students to simply tell them the answers. No one benefits from this experience.

You may have seen ample evidence in your own classroom that cooperative learning can be problematic for gifted students. They are the students who are most likely to complain about having to do cooperative learning. It is their parents who tend to be most negative about cooperative learning, because they worry that their children's own learning time will be severely limited.

After one second-grade teacher placed her gifted students in their own cooperative learning group, it took her class almost a full school week to adjust. One group approached her and declared they couldn't do any work today because "we need

Josephine!" Finally, the teacher's firmness paid off. As the students realized they were not going to be "saved" by the return of the most capable students, all of the groups got to work, completed their tasks, and began cooperating to learn, instead of counting on the gifted students to lead them to success.

Most teachers who have removed gifted students from heterogeneous groups report that they are very pleased with the results. They observe their gifted students moving quite happily through the more difficult material, learning to cooperate on tasks few can do alone. Teachers are especially thrilled when they see new academic leadership emerging in the other groups.

Several books on cooperative learning have included the refreshing notion that it might be all right to allow certain students who feel passionate about not working in groups to work alone, at least for part of the time. Elizabeth Cohen in *Designing Groupwork,* and James Bellanca and Robin Fogarty in *Blueprints for Thinking in the Cooperative Classroom,* have all concluded that it's reasonable to expect that we will encounter students who truly hate working in groups, and it's okay to let them work alone at certain times. Roger and David Johnson, co-directors of the Cooperative Learning Center at the University of Minnesota, have written, "There are times when gifted students should work in cooperative learning groups, there are times when they should work with each other, and there are times when they should work alone."

When you think about it, most people seek out cooperation only when they need assistance. We prefer to work alone on tasks we can do easily without help from others. If we want gifted students to learn how to cooperate, we must make sure they are working on tasks difficult enough to create a need for cooperation. The kids themselves must perceive that cooperation is necessary. Difficult tasks can inspire such a perception.

SUMMARY: COOPERATIVE LEARNING OR HETEROGENEOUS GROUPS?

How can you decide when it's best to place your gifted students in their own cooperative learning groups, and when heterogeneous groups would probably be better for everyone? Here are two approaches you might try.

1. Assess the type of cooperative learning task that has been assigned.

When the task is drill-and-practice (math computation, studying for a recall-type test, answering comprehension questions about a story or novel the class is reading), and you have evidence that some students have mastered that material, place those kids together in their own group and assign them a more complex task. *Examples:* They might read an advanced novel, work on advanced problem-solving techniques in math, write story problems for the rest of the class, or work on resident expert projects in small groups.

For tasks that focus on critical thinking, the development of concepts and generalizations, or problem-based learning, placing gifted students in heterogeneous groups may be perfectly appropriate. Such experiences may be richer when a variety of viewpoints is represented. Any open-ended activity with many possible answers or solutions lends itself to heterogeneous grouping. So does any subject in which the content is new for everyone, including the gifted students. Hands-on science experiments and current events discussions are other good choices for cooperative learning experiences with heterogeneous groups.

2. Ask yourself three key questions.

- Does the task require input from different types of learning styles and different perspectives?
- Is the subject matter new for all students?
- Is it likely that the gifted students will be engaged in real learning rather than continuous tutoring?

If you can answer yes to all three questions, then heterogeneous cooperative learning groups are probably appropriate. If you answer no to one or more of the questions, then it may be better to place the gifted students in a separate group to work on the same kind of content from a more challenging perspective. All other students would work in heterogeneous groups comprised of one of the strongest remaining students, one student who may find the task difficult, and one or two students of average ability. As you circulate among the cooperative groups at work, let your observational skills tell you whether your gifted students have been placed where they belong.

CLUSTER GROUPING

I realize how often you have asked yourself these questions while reading this book:

- How am I ever going to find the time to implement these strategies?
- Is it fair to put myself out for just one or two students who need this kind of attention when their grades seem to indicate that they're doing just fine in school?
- Isn't it better to spend my time with the kids who really need me?

In most schools, when teachers and principals meet to set up classes for the following year, the gifted students are separated from each other so all classes can have one or two of the "best kids." This practice creates the "just one or two students" dilemma that troubles many teachers.

You know how hard it is for gifted students to be true to their abilities when they're a minority of one in a heterogeneous classroom. They will often pretend to be less capable than they really are just to fit in with the other kids. A method that addresses this situation is sorely needed. The one I strongly support is to group the identified gifted kids at a grade level into a cluster of learners with similar abilities and needs, and to place them together in the classroom of a teacher who has had some training in compacting and differentiation and is comfortable using those strategies. All of the arguments used earlier about cooperative learning apply to the logic of purposefully clustering gifted kids together.

Another issue makes cluster grouping increasingly imperative. During the 1990s, education focused primarily on the learning needs of students who could not meet state standards. Pressure on individual classroom teachers and school administrators was intense and will likely continue until all students can demonstrate mastery of at least minimum standards.

With so much attention aimed at students with learning difficulties, much less attention has been paid to students who have already demonstrated mastery. The attitude among some teachers has been to not worry about high-achieving students at all and to spend the bulk of their time with "the kids who really need me." For many gifted students, being in a heterogeneous classroom has been an excruciating experience.

As an educator, I fail to understand why American education has to choose between meeting the needs of one group while sacrificing the needs of another. School and district mission statements don't claim to serve only certain groups of students. The promises of a good education are made to all. Yet, in daily practice, gifted kids get less teacher attention and less opportunity to work on personally challenging curriculum than anyone else in the class. We must find and use ways that will eliminate the short-shrifting of public education for gifted students.

There is a way to have it all: to continue grouping gifted students together (because they learn better in homogeneous groups) while simultaneously grouping the rest of the students in heterogeneous groups (because that seems best for them). The structure that provides optimum grouping practices for all students is cluster grouping. It provides a sensible alternative to the stampede to eliminate ability grouping for everyone and replaces it with the notion that grouping by achievement for gifted students is defensible and can be accomplished without a return to "tracking" as we used to know it.

Scenario: Third Grade at "Adams School"

Six children at "Adams School" had been identified as gifted at the end of second grade. As the teachers and principal met to set up the classes for the three third-grade sections, they considered how to group the gifted students. The traditional method called for them to divide the six gifted students evenly, placing two in each of the three classes so all teachers would have their fair share of the brightest students. Under this system, all three teachers would have to develop appropriate compacting and differentiation opportunities for the gifted students. Furthermore, the gifted students would be in the minority in all three classes.

The teachers and principal knew that there might be times when these students felt isolated and uncomfortably different from their classmates. So they decided to try something else. Instead of separating the gifted students, they formed a cluster group of all six and placed them in the otherwise heterogeneous class of one teacher who had some training in how to teach the gifted. Knowing that at least six students would benefit from any compacting and differentiating opportunities she created, the teacher felt justified in taking the time to develop them.

When the gifted kids found themselves in a group of others with similar abilities and interests, they started taking risks to experience learning activities that were different from what the rest of the class was doing. They were also more willing to take advantage of the differentiation opportunities because they would have learning companions for those tasks.

QUESTIONS AND ANSWERS ABOUT CLUSTER GROUPING

Most educators have many questions about clustering—so many, in fact, that the rest of this chapter is devoted to answering the ones I most frequently hear. If you like the clustering concept, and if you think it might benefit your students, you may decide to share this information with your principal, who in turn may decide to share it with other administrators or school board members.

Schools that cluster-group gifted students are on their way to providing something that sounds almost impossible to achieve in our current educational climate: a full-time gifted education program that requires only minimal funds to support it. The program is full-time because gifted kids are having their learning needs met every day in every subject area. It requires only minimal funds because it's part of the regular classroom program and utilizes many of the same materials purchased for other learners at that grade level. Best of all, it prevents gifted kids from becoming the group which benefits least from heterogeneous grouping.

IMPORTANT: It's not enough to simply cluster gifted kids together. It's essential that the program be carefully monitored by a principal or gifted program coordinator to ensure that consistent compacting and differentiation are taking place.

"How does cluster grouping work?"

Using a combination of local and standardized identification criteria, gifted students are identified in the spring at every grade level. Sometimes the identifying group is comprised of the gifted education specialist and a screening committee; sometimes it includes the building principal and the teachers of the grade level the students are leaving and the one they are about to enter. In most schools, the identified group represents no more than about the top 5 percent of the grade level.

These students are placed in a cluster of four to six students and assigned to a teacher who has had some special training in the teaching of the gifted. The rest of the students in that class are heterogeneously mixed. The other teachers also have heterogeneous mixes of students, but they don't have any of the identified gifted students.

What if there are more than six identified students at a grade level? Larger clusters may be allowed, or two clusters could be formed. In middle or junior high schools, where there are not enough qualified gifted students to form a separate class for them in the areas of their strength, students may be clustered in one specific class period, along with a heterogeneous mix of others.

NOTE: The concept of "enrichment clusters" developed by Dr. Joseph Renzulli is not the same as the cluster grouping concept described in this chapter. Enrichment clusters are designed to bring enrichment experiences to all students in a school every now and then. Clustering gifted children means they are grouped together full-time and placed in otherwise heterogeneous groups for the entire school year.

"How should students be identified for cluster groups?"

The most important criteria is that students should have demonstrated ability in reading and/or math which exceeds grade level expectations by one full year or more. Schools should use whatever methods they wish to identify such students. For example, they might give potential candidates next year's end-of-the-year tests in reading and math during the spring or summer. For students from kindergarten through grade 2, the *Brigance Diagnostic Inventory of Essential Skills* can determine the instructional level in most subject areas.

Standardized, norm-referenced tests should be used for inclusion purposes only and to identify the percentage of students who need the cluster grouping option. If a student performs well on local tests but not so well on standardized tests, she should not be excluded based on the standardized test data alone.

If a student can demonstrate more than 70 percent competency on advanced content from higher-level curricula, that evidence should supersede any standardized test data. Gifted students often score much lower on group tests of ability or IQ than they would on an individual intelligence test administered by a trained tester. One reason is they take too much time with each item, considering its many facets and ramifications, and losing precious minutes in the process.

If 9 percent of the students at a particular grade level score above the 95th percentile on standardized tests in reading and math, you would cluster 9 percent of the kids at that grade level, not the arbitrary 5 percent often cited on national identification guidelines.

If a student scores high on standardized tests but gets poor grades because he "doesn't complete his work," the test results would be more important than his classroom work or his grades.

Teachers' and parents' observations of precocious behaviors may also be used as identification tools. Be careful that students who don't complete their work aren't automatically disqualified. You learned in Chapter 1 that there are many reasons for this beyond the assumption that the child doesn't know how to do the work. These reasons include perfectionism, frustration, and being twice exceptional.

In summary, always give more weight to the data that points toward inclusion in the cluster group, whether that data includes demonstrated mastery, observations, or standardized tests.

"How should all students at a grade level be assigned to classes if the school clusters gifted students?"

If you're worried that classes without gifted kids will suffer, please don't. A three-year study of cluster grouping at the elementary level by Marcia Gentry* documented improved achievement at all grade levels in which clustering was done, including classes where there were no gifted clusters. One factor that accounted for that improvement was the unique way in which students were grouped into classes.
In the spring, when class placements were made, students were sorted into the following five groups:

I. Gifted
II. Above Average
III. Average
IV. Below Average
V. Significantly Below Grade Level

Classroom A, taught by a teacher with some training in gifted education, was assigned the cluster group of gifted students and some students from groups II–IV. All other classes got a range of students from groups II–V.

This grouping method reduced the range of achievement in each classroom. It freed the cluster teacher to spend more time with the cluster kids, instead of being pulled away by the needs of those students who were significantly below grade level.

Tip: For this method to achieve the desirable outcomes, be absolutely certain that there are enough students from group II in each non-cluster class, even if it means putting no group II students in the gifted cluster.

"What if we have ten to twelve gifted students at a grade level?"

Some advocates of cluster grouping believe that there's nothing wrong with larger clusters. My experience indicates that each cluster should have no more than four to six students in a class of 25–30 kids. If you have 10–12 gifted students, I recommend creating two clusters for two classrooms. You might group kids who are very advanced in math in one cluster, and those whose exceptionality is more related to reading in the other.

"What about gifted students who move into the district during the school year? Should they be placed in the cluster group?"

First, you need to be sure that they meet the same criteria used to select kids for the existing cluster group. If they do, and if their placement in the cluster class won't disrupt the balance in enrollment between all classes at that grade level, go ahead with the placement. If that's not possible, try to place these students with a teacher who has had some training in basic compacting and differentiation strategies and is willing to use them. This ensures that the special learning needs of these students will be met, even though they aren't yet in the cluster group.

"Where should we place students who are gifted in one subject area but very average in other subject areas?"

Place them in the same classroom as the cluster group, but without designating them cluster members. Then, when you offer the same options to the whole class that you offer to the gifted cluster,

* Gentry, Marcia L. "Promoting Student Achievement and Exemplary Classroom Practices Through Cluster Grouping: A Research-Based Alternative to Heterogeneous Elementary Classrooms." Research Monograph 99138. Storrs, CT: NRC/GT, University of Connecticut, 1999.

group any students who demonstrate eligibility for differentiating opportunities with the other eligible students.

"Isn't cluster grouping the same as tracking?"

No, they are different. In a tracking system, all students are grouped by ability for much or all of the school day, and students tend to remain in the same track throughout their years in school. In cluster grouping, only gifted students are grouped together in their areas of strength because they learn better that way. Students of all other ability levels are grouped heterogeneously because research indicates that this may be the best arrangement for them. Cluster grouping allows gifted kids to learn together while avoiding permanent grouping arrangements for students of other ability levels.

"Isn't it elitist to provide programming for gifted students?

No, it is not. Elitism means giving special treatment to one group of students while withholding similar services from other students. Gifted education has been accused of being elitist because often children from minority groups are inadequately represented in gifted programs. When teachers learn how to provide opportunities for all students (including gifted students) to be challenged by rigorous and interesting curriculum, elitism doesn't occur. In fact, the more gifted education strategies regular classroom teachers learn, the likelier it becomes that more students, not just those identified as gifted, will reap the benefits of a challenging curriculum.

Related concerns about equity are also misleading. Equity doesn't mean that all students should have the same learning experiences. It means that all students should have an equal opportunity to make progress in their own learning. Reverse discrimination can occur when gifted students are always placed in heterogeneous groups, where it's unlikely that their learning experiences will be consistently challenging. It's not equity when all students in a mixed-abilities classroom are presented with the same level of difficulty.

Finally, elitism is alive and well in American education. Gifted athletes always receive special treatment as a privileged group in their school. I'm not promoting elitism or condemning athletics. I simply would like critics of gifted education to acknowledge that athletics is a gifted program. If our culture can openly support giftedness in bodily-kinesthetic abilities, we ought to be able to offer similar support in other categories of learning in which some youngsters clearly excel.

"Won't the creation of the cluster group rob the other classes of academic leadership?"

This issue has been of serious concern to classroom teachers for at least the 10 years I have been supporting this practice. Interviews with cluster teachers reveal some very interesting evidence which can help to allay this concern. The reality is that "new cream rises to the top" in classrooms which don't have a cluster of gifted students. New academic leadership emerges. Students who have never been classroom stars now find that role possible, comfortable, available, and challenging

This result was documented most recently in the Gentry study (see page 177 and the References and Resources at the end of this chapter). The numbers of students nominated for cluster groups increased each year as teachers recognized new leaders in their classrooms. Furthermore, there were measurable achievement gains across the board at the grade levels that were studied. The data suggest that cluster grouping gifted students may actually lead to higher test scores for other kids as well.

The only conditions under which this concern about equal achievement in all sections of a grade level may become relevant is if schools ever have to report achievement data by individual classrooms, or if teachers' pay is tied to the scores their students make on high-stakes tests. If and when these conditions occur, the practice of clustering gifted kids will be moot.

When the people in charge of setting up class groups remember that the second-highest group of students should not be grouped in the same class as the gifted cluster, there should be many kids in other classes who can act as positive role models and get good scores on important tests.

"Won't the presence of the cluster group in one teacher's class intimidate the other students in that class? Won't it have a negative effect on their achievement?"

No to both questions. When the cluster group is kept to a manageable size, the general achievement level improves for all students in the cluster-group classroom. This suggests the exciting possibility that when teachers learn how to provide what gifted students need, they also offer many of the same opportunities to the entire class, thus raising the level of learning for all students.

The positive effects of cluster grouping may be shared with all students over several years by rotating the cluster teacher assignment among staff who have had the necessary training in compacting and differentiating the curriculum for high-ability students. Computerized scheduling programs can ensure that all students are in a cluster-group classroom at least once during their elementary school experience.

"Won't the cluster teacher have a range of ability in his or her classroom that's too wide to teach?"

No, not if the class sections are set up carefully. If there are more than two sections of classes at a grade level, the teacher who takes the cluster group of gifted students does not also receive the neediest learners. That group of students is usually distributed among all other sections of the grade level.

In some districts where special education teachers work daily to co-teach with regular classroom teachers, students with special education needs are purposefully clustered. Under these circumstances, it may be acceptable to place gifted and special needs kids in the same classroom. Because the special education teacher is also available, the regular teacher may be able to spend more time with the kids in the gifted cluster.

If there are only two sections of a grade level, the teacher who has the gifted cluster is also assigned some of the neediest learners. Keep in mind that under all conditions, with or without using cluster grouping, teachers will have a range of ability in their classrooms. So we may as well provide the gifted kids with the comfort and challenge of each other's company, since this offers clear benefits for them.

"What special skills or training do cluster teachers need?"

Since gifted students are as far removed from the norm as students with significant learning difficulties, teachers need special training in how to teach children with exceptionally high ability. The strategies described in this book can actually provide training for cluster teachers. All teachers of gifted children should know how to do the following:

- Recognize and nurture behaviors usually demonstrated by gifted students of various cultures and backgrounds.
- Facilitate a classroom climate in which individual differences are valued and accepted.
- Create conditions in which all students will be stretched to learn.
- Allow students to demonstrate and get full credit for previously mastered material.
- Provide opportunities for faster pacing of new material
- Plan differentiated learning tasks for all who need them.
- Incorporate students' passionate interests into their independent studies.
- Facilitate sophisticated research studies by students.
- Provide flexible grouping opportunities so students are sometimes working with the entire class and sometimes in small groups or independently.
- Accept the fact that students are at different levels in their learning and need constant opportunities to work at those various levels.
- Be flexible in their teaching style and comfortable allowing kids more flexibility in their learning behaviors.
- Always let their sense of humor be a guiding force in their classroom.

"How can teachers make sure that gifted kids don't dominate class discussions or activities?"

Use the Name Card method described on pages 11–13. This will not only alleviate that potential problem, it will also dramatically improve the quality of classroom discussions and increase the level of participation for all students. Even the most capable students prefer this method to traditional hand-raising because they get to share their answers to all the questions with their partner, who is also a highly capable learner. Teachers love it because it eliminates forever the physical gyrations gifted kids exhibit as they try to get in their two cents' worth for every question, and it significantly reduces blurting behaviors.

Also keep in mind that when the most capable learners are working with each other in their own small groups, or even independently, they are physically removed from some of the large-group activities. This provides more opportunities for other students to shine in class activities and discussions.

"Are cluster students automatically eligible for all compacting and differentiation opportunities offered by the teacher? Can other students ever participate in these activities?"

No student is ever automatically eligible or ineligible for compacting or differentiation opportunities.

All students in the class have a chance to qualify for differentiation unit by unit.

"Won't other teachers be resentful if they aren't the cluster teacher?"

Not if they know their chance is coming. All teachers who wish to be cluster teachers should be given their turn on a rotating basis, with each turn lasting two years. During the first year, teachers work very hard to implement the newly-learned strategies; they should have at least one more year to enjoy the fruits of their labors. Meanwhile, other teachers can receive the necessary training. After two years, the cluster group is assigned to another trained teacher. Eventually, every teacher who wants to be a cluster teacher has the opportunity to do so.

"How are records kept of the progress made by students in cluster groups?"

Differentiated Learning Plans (see pages 186–187 and 188) and Cumulative Record Forms (pages 187 and 190) should be kept for all cluster students. The information on these forms should be shared with parents at conferences.

"Won't parents be unhappy if their child isn't in the same class with the clustered gifted students?"

Most school districts that use cluster grouping keep a low profile about it. Administrators simply regard it as one more criteria to consider when deciding how to set up classes for instruction. However, this doesn't mean that parents will remain unaware that cluster grouping is going on. There are three ways to calm their fears on this score.

1. Remind parents that there will still be plenty of positive role models in all classrooms, because the other groups will be totally heterogeneous. For parents who insist that their children be placed in the same classroom with the cluster, explain that their kids might actually be better off as the newly-emerging leaders in one of the other classes. You might provide supporting facts and findings from the Gentry study. See References and Resources at the end of this chapter.

2. Communicate that the district is providing adequate staff development for all teachers. Emphasize that everyone is learning strategies designed to improve the educational experience for gifted kids. This lets parents know that they have the right to request—and expect—appropriate opportunities for their children regardless of the teachers they are assigned to.

3. Be sure to rotate the cluster teacher assignment every two years or so. This sends parents the clear message that there are many teachers in a school who can and do teach gifted students.

"What evidence is available from schools that already use cluster grouping for gifted students?"

If you or your administrator would like to communicate with other schools who are using cluster grouping successfully, contact me to request a document called the "Cluster Network," a list of names and telephone numbers. You may reach me through my Website (www.susanwinebrenner.com).

"Should cluster grouping practices replace our district's current program components in gifted education?"

No. Cluster grouping should supplement existing program components. The complaint many teachers (and parents) have about most gifted programs is that they comprise only a small percentage of the student's learning time. Adding cluster grouping to a comprehensive program already in place is a beneficial, cost-effective option.

If your school must choose between resource-room programs or cluster grouping, my recommendation is to go with the cluster groups. This greatly improves the chances that gifted students will receive appropriate learning opportunities on a daily basis. Unless your district has a gifted education specialist, however, cluster teachers may not get the coaching and assistance they need to provide the best possible classroom program for their gifted kids.

"Isn't it better for gifted kids to be grouped together in self-contained classes for the entire school year?"

Yes, that is the best arrangement for gifted kids, provided the district is large enough to get political support for such a practice. Gifted students in self-contained classes are more likely to "stay gifted" and remain true to their ability. Gifted kids have characteristics and needs, such as competitiveness, that are often not facilitated in mixed-abilities classes. However, when self-contained classes are not going to happen, cluster grouping is the next best thing, in my opinion.

"What are the disadvantages of cluster grouping?"

There may be pressure from parents who want their children placed in a cluster classroom, even if they aren't eligible for the cluster group. Parents who move into the district during the school year and learn that their gifted children can't be placed in the cluster classroom might be unhappy. To address these situations and others that may arise, administrators should:

- Provide training for all staff in compacting and differentiation so parents can expect those opportunities to be available in all classes.
- Require parents to provide written documentation of their child's exceptional learning abilities and their need for curriculum differentiation instead of simply requesting the placement by phone.
- Rotate the cluster teacher assignment every two years among trained teachers so parents understand that many teachers are capable of teaching gifted students.
- Rotate all students into cluster classrooms over a period of several years.
- Reference the Gentry study, which documents the benefits of placing high achievers in non-cluster classrooms. See References and Resources at the end of this chapter.

SUMMARY: HOW GOOD IS CLUSTER GROUPING?

In 1999, the Gentry study reported measurable positive outcomes of clustering gifted students. Other studies continue to document the benefits of grouping gifted kids together in their areas of strength for at least part of each school day. They include:

1. The cluster group is taught by a teacher who has been trained to differentiate the curriculum for gifted students.

2. The students in the group enjoy consistent interaction with their intellectual peers. Instead of doing differentiated activities alone, they have someone to share the experience with. This is very reassuring. It also teaches them that they are not the smartest thing since sliced bread and there are still some things left to learn.

3. The cluster teacher has several identified gifted students to differentiate for, rather than just one or two. This is much more efficient in terms of teacher time and effort.

4. New academic leaders emerge among the students who are not in the cluster classroom. Positive role modeling is still very much in evidence. Nobody suffers because the gifted students are somewhere else.

5. Achievement can improve for all kids in the grade levels that use cluster grouping, not just in the classroom with the cluster students.

6. The district has a totally cost-effective way to meet the needs of gifted students. No additional funds are required except for teacher training.

7. Perhaps the most exciting benefit is that all staff receives excellent staff development. Specialists in gifted education have known for years that the strategies designed for gifted students benefit many other students as well. Since trained cluster teachers are free to use the strategies they learn with all students, a district's entire program reaps the rewards.

8. Cluster grouping provides gifted students with something their parents have always been told the district could never afford: a full-time gifted program. Every day—not once or twice a week for an hour or two—these students are in a situation where a trained teacher is compacting the curriculum and providing challenging learning experiences. This becomes a regular occurrence instead of a rare opportunity.

It appears that there are no significant disadvantages to clustering gifted students, and more advantages than we could ever hope to buy with the amount of money generally designated for gifted education. The only caution to keep in mind is that simply placing gifted students in cluster groups won't make appropriate education happen for them. Purposeful staff development is essential. The teachers who receive the cluster groups must be trained to teach them the way they need to be taught. Furthermore, the cluster program must be supervised by the gifted education coordinator or administrators to ensure that consistent differentiation is available.

REFERENCES AND RESOURCES

Research and Practice on Cooperative Learning As It Affects Gifted Students

Bellanca, James, and Robin Fogarty. *Blueprints for Thinking in the Cooperative Classroom.* Arlington Heights, IL: Skylight Publishing, 1991. Many strategies for using cooperative learning.

Cohen, Elizabeth. *Designing Groupwork: Strategies for the Heterogeneous Classroom.* New York: Teachers College Press, 1994.

How to develop sophisticated, complex cooperative learning tasks that can challenge all students in cooperative learning groups.

Coleman, Mary Ruth, et al. "Cooperative Learning and Gifted Students: Report on Five Case Studies" (ERIC Document 365008, 1993) and "Cooperative Learning and Gifted Students: A National Survey: Short Report" (ERIC Document 359717, 1993). Order online (askeric.org) or call the ERIC Document Reproduction Service (EDRS) at (800) 538-3742.

Cooperative Learning Center, University of Minnesota, Minneapolis, MN, (612) 624-7031 (www.co-operation.org). This research and training center has been part of the University of Minnesota's College of Education for over 20 years. Roger T. Johnson and David W. Johnson are the co-directors. The Web site includes a Cooperative Learning Q&A, essays, newsletters, and more.

Johnson, Roger T., and David W. Johnson. "What to Say to Parents of Gifted Students About Cooperative Learning." Edina, MN: *The Cooperative Link* 5:2, 1989. This article quotes the Johnsons as saying that it's okay to sometimes group gifted students in their own cooperative groups, and to allow them to work alone as well.

Kenny, David, Francis Archambault, and Bryan Hallmark. "The Effects of Group Composition on Gifted and Non-Gifted Elementary Students in Cooperative Learning Groups." Research Monograph 97116. Storrs, CT: NRC/GT, 1995. More research to help teachers create appropriate groups for cooperative learning activities.

Matthews, Marian. "Gifted Students Talk About Cooperative Learning." *Educational Leadership* 50:2, 48–49, October 1992. Dr. Matthews interviewed gifted students for their opinions about cooperative learning. The consensus was they didn't dislike cooperative learning per se; they resented being placed in situations where other students took advantage of them and expected them to do the bulk of the work.

Mills, Carol, and William Durden. "Finding an Optimal Match: A Reasonable Response to the Use of Cooperative Learning, Ability Grouping, and Tracking." *Gifted Child Quarterly* 36:1, 11–16, Winter 1992.

Robinson, Ann. "Cooperation or Exploitation: the Argument Against Cooperative Learning." *Journal for the Education of the Gifted* 14:1, November 1990. This was written during the time when the gifted education community was responding to the frustration of gifted kids and their parents that many cooperative learning situations were robbing gifted students of working at their own challenge levels for much of the learning time.

Sharan, Yael, and Shlomo Sharan. *Expanding Cooperative Learning Through Group Investigation.* New York: Teachers College Press, 1992.

Slavin, Robert. "Ability Grouping, Cooperative Learning, and the Gifted." *Journal for the Education of the Gifted* 14:1, 3–8, Fall 1990.

Research and Practice on Ways to Group Gifted Learners Together

Allan, Susan. "Ability Grouping Research Reviews: What Do They Say About Grouping and the Gifted?" *Educational Leadership* 48:6, 60–65, 1991. This article is good to use with administrators because it was published in a journal they respect.

Brigance Diagnostic Inventory of Basic Skills. Use this tool with students in the primary grades to document their advanced learning ability in order to place them in cluster groups and to know the level at which they need to be taught in almost all subject areas. Available from Curriculum Associates, North Billerica, MA, (800) 225-0248 (www.curriculumassociates.com).

Coleman, Mary Ruth. "The Importance of Cluster Grouping." *Gifted Child Today* 18:1, 38–40, January–February 1995.

Feldhusen, John. "Synthesis of Research on Gifted Youth." *Educational Leadership* 46:6, 6–11, 1989. Documents the benefits of grouping gifted students together.

Fiedler, Ellen, Richard Lange, and Susan Winebrenner. "In Search of Reality: Unraveling the Myths about Tracking, Ability Grouping, and the Gifted." *Roeper Review* 16:1, 4–7, 1993. Addresses the commonly expressed myths about grouping and builds a rationale for grouping gifted students together for at least part of their learning time.

Gentry, Marcia L. "Promoting Student Achievement and Exemplary Classroom Practices Through Cluster Grouping: A Research-Based Alternative to Heterogeneous Elementary Classrooms." Research Monograph 99138. Storrs, CT: NRC/GT, 1999. This document describes how cluster grouping gifted students has positive benefits on all students at any grade level where cluster grouping is used. Read an abstract and conclusions online (www.gifted.uconn.edu/nrcgt/gentry.html).

Hoover, Steve, Michael Sayler, and John Feldhusen. "Cluster Grouping of Gifted Students at the Elementary Level." *Roeper Review* 16:1, 13–15, 1993. More evidence of the benefits of cluster grouping for gifted students.

Kulik, James A., and Chen-Lin Kulik. "Ability Grouping and Gifted Students." In Nicholas Colangelo and Gary A. Davis, *Handbook of Gifted Education,* 2nd ed. (Needham Heights, MA: Allyn & Bacon, 1996), 178–196.

Rogers, Karen B. "Grouping the Gifted and Talented." *Roeper Review* 16:1, 8–12, 1993.
—— "The Relationship of Grouping Practices to the Education of the Gifted and Talented Learner." Research-Based Research Document (RBRD) 9102. Storrs, CT: NRC/GT, 1991.

Schuler, Patricia A. "Cluster Grouping Coast to Coast." *National Research Center on the Gifted and Talented Newsletter,* Winter 1997. Storrs, CT: NRC/GT. Results of a research study examining the actual practice of cluster grouping in the U. S.

Schunk, Dale H. "Peer Models and Children's Behavioral Change." *Review of Educational Research* 47, 149–174, 1987.

Teno, Kevin. "Cluster Grouping Elementary Gifted Students in the Regular Classroom: A Teacher's Perspective." *Gifted Child Today* 23:1, 44–49, January–February 2000. A teacher documents the benefits of cluster grouping for gifted students, other students, and teachers.

Winebrenner, Susan, and Barbara Devlin. "Cluster Grouping of Gifted Students: How to Provide Full-time Services on a Part-time Budget." ERIC EC Digest #E538, August 1996. This document, an earlier version of the Questions and Answers included in this chapter, is available online at the ERIC Web site (www.eric.ed.gov).

9

Et Cetera: Related Issues

This chapter considers topics that are important to meeting gifted students' learning needs but don't require separate chapters of their own. Each addresses a question I'm often asked at workshops and conferences.

- How can we deliver gifted education services to our students?
- How can we manage a differentiated program for gifted students and keep useful records?
- Under what circumstances is acceleration recommended? What types of acceleration are available?
- What qualities are needed by teachers who work with gifted children?
- How can we secure appropriate extension materials for our gifted students?
- What about pull-out programs?
- How is the role of the gifted education specialist changing?
- How can gifted education advocates win support from parents?

PROGRAM DELIVERY OPTIONS

Identifying gifted kids and providing services to them has always been a "chicken-egg" situation. Why identify gifted kids if programming isn't available? How can we design programming for gifted kids if we don't know who they are? Should we identify all of our gifted kids in all categories of giftedness, or only those who will benefit from a program we can actually offer?

One answer to all of these questions (and the dilemma they represent) is to design a program that has several components. The best type of program for gifted students combines regular in-class compacting and differentiation with regular out-of-class opportunities to meet and learn with other gifted students. I suggest that your program include as many of the following components as you can possibly arrange.

In-class experiences:

- Compacting and differentiation
- Pretesting
- Most Difficult First
- Learning contracts and study guides
- Tiered tasks of various difficulty levels
- Extensions centers
- Independent study
- Flexible grouping
- Cluster grouping
- Acceleration
- Grade-skipping
- Great Books
- Advanced course material

Out-of-class experiences:

- Gifted kids meet in groups
- Attention to social-emotional needs
- Field trips
- Working with mentors

- Career information
- Academic competitions
- Advanced technology
- Summer programs for gifted kids
- Advanced forms of independent study
- Dual enrollment/early entrance to college
- Internet resources
- Invent America; Invention Convention
- Destination ImagiNation*
- Science and learning fairs

Most of the in-class experiences listed are described in this book. To arrange the out-of-class experiences, work with your colleagues, your students' parents, and community resources. Make sure your gifted students know that there are many options available to them and many people who are willing to help them.

PROGRAM MANAGEMENT AND RECORD-KEEPING

Although only a few states require Individualized Education Plans (IEPs) for identified gifted students, it's a good idea to keep track of differentiation opportunities over time. Careful record-keeping is vital whenever you do something new and different.

Creative Collaboration

Teachers and administrators in McMinnville, Oregon, have come up with a method called Creative Collaboration to ensure that plans for differentiation are done right and carried out effectively.** The goals are to help gifted students become highly motivated, responsible, and autonomous lifelong learners and to help teachers become more effective, creative, and self-confident when teaching bright students. Tips for success include:

- Make sure the timeline and schedule are as user-friendly as possible for all concerned.
- Engage in conversations, interviews, and kid-watching to gather as much information as needed.
- Try to perceive problems as opportunities.

1. The gifted education specialist interviews identified gifted students one-on-one. During the interview, the specialist asks the student:

- What are your strengths?
- What are some things that you have difficulty with?
- On a scale of 1 (low) to 5 (high), how self-directed are you at school? How self-directed are you at home?
- If you could improve school for yourself, what would you do or want others to do?
- How do you go about solving personal or school problems for yourself?
- What do you see yourself doing or being involved in at your school in the future and also as a career person?

2. A written plan is created that combines the information from the interview with any other data being used in the identification process. A good plan includes:

- The student's educational strengths and needs.
- Agreed-upon goals.
- Teaching strategies.
- Learning activities.
- Materials and resources.
- Tools to assess the plan's ongoing effectiveness.
- Role assignments for all those involved including the classroom teacher, gifted specialist, principal, counselors or social workers, parents, mentors, and educators from the next school the student will attend.

3. The plan is implemented and monitored to keep the momentum going and make sure that the details are being followed. If necessary, the plan is adjusted.

The Differentiated Learning Plan

When working with gifted students, I prefer the term Differentiated Learning Plan (DLP) to Individualized Education Plan (IEP). Page 188 shows one version of a DLP. In some schools, this form is used as a group DLP for all students who are placed

* Formerly Odyssey of the Mind. See References and Resources at the end of this chapter.

** From a paper presented at the Association of Supervision and Curriculum Development (ASCD) Annual Conference, New Orleans, March 2000. Adapted and used with permission of the McMinnville Public Schools, McMinnville, Oregon.

in a gifted cluster. For ideas on what to record on the form, consult the section on differentiating content, process, products, environment, and assessment on pages 5–6. For information about cluster-grouping gifted kids, see Chapter 8.

The Meeting Record Sheet on page 189 may be copied on the back of the DLP or stapled to it. Use it to record information from every meeting about a student's differentiated learning plan.

Keeping Track of Students' Work from Year to Year

The Gifted Student's Cumulative Record Form on page 190 provides an ongoing record of the alternate activities in which gifted students are engaged. Teachers can learn about the projects students have completed in earlier grades and use this information to plan for the current year. The form helps teachers provide consistency from one grade level to the next, and it also gives some assurance that appropriate compacting opportunities will be available for students as they move through the grades.

1. Prepare one form for each gifted student. If school policy permits the use of the cumulative record folder, this form should be kept there. If not, it should be passed along from one teacher to the next.

2. Use the form to briefly describe all compacting opportunities, personal project work, and other differentiation provided to the student during the year.

3. Consult the form several times each year to establish some scope-and-sequence for a student's differentiated experiences, and to encourage the student to become engaged with a variety of topics rather than returning to the same topic year after year.

ACCELERATION

From time to time during our teaching career, we meet students who are described as profoundly gifted. Their intelligence is so far advanced, even when compared to other gifted kids, that most of the strategies described in this book don't come close to providing the challenges they need. The only reasonable response to their unique ability is to accelerate the content they will learn or accelerate the students themselves. We can allow them to work with curriculum designed for students in higher grades, or we can permit them to skip some or all parts of a particular school year.

Acceleration makes most people very uncomfortable. Caring parents and teachers are very concerned about the social adjustment of children who skip some years of school. They express sincere concerns that kids will be too short to go to the prom or too young to get a driver's license at the same time as their friends. Dire predictions are made that these youngsters will most likely have a miserable adolescence.

What was your adolescence like? Was it a happy, productive time or were you mostly miserable? I've often said that if someone were to offer me eternal life, but I'd have to repeat my adolescence, I would decline! One of the things that works against gifted kids is the culture's insistence that they spend the bulk of their time with youngsters their own chronological age. Yet very few adults have friends who are the same age as themselves. As adults, we choose friends on the basis of many criteria, with age being the least important.

Furthermore, with the decline in the rigor in American curriculum over the past decades, due in part to the increasing range of ability in most heterogeneous classrooms, staying with one's age group may be even more painful for highly gifted kids than before. The time has come to put aside irrational fears and worries and look at the research on this topic.

The work of Dr. Julian Stanley (creator of the Academic Talent Search) and other researchers has given us 20 years of data about students who have experienced acceleration. The researchers have unequivocally concluded that for highly gifted children, the long-term benefits of acceleration far outweigh any disadvantages. Although these kids may experience a rough time in adolescence, when they are physically smaller and less socially adept than their peers, by the time they reach college they are more likely to be well-adjusted and productive than similar kids who did not experience acceleration. It can be very misleading to predict how a child will function in a group of older students by looking at the way he or she is presently behaving. Many times, I have seen gifted kids move into a higher grade level and begin to model their behavior after that of the older students, becoming more mature and serious than they had been in the lower grade.

Text continues on page 191

DIFFERENTIATED LEARNING PLAN

Student's Name: ______________________ Grade: ______________________

Teacher's Name: ______________________ Date Plan Begins: ______________________

Student's learning strengths

____

____

____

Student's areas of interest

____

____

____

Learning Goals and Needs	Extended Learning Experiences	Resources	Results/Comments

Student's signature: ______________________ Teacher's signature: ______________________

Parent's signature: ______________________

MEETING RECORD SHEET

Student's Name: ______________________ Grade: ______________________

Teacher's Name: ______________________ Date Plan Begins: ______________________

Date	Topic(s)	Suggested Change(s)

GIFTED STUDENT'S CUMULATIVE RECORD FORM

Student's Name: ______________________________

Date of Birth: ____________________ Year/Age/Grade Student Was Identified as Gifted: ____________

Grade Level	Year and Teacher	Compacting Opportunities	Independent Project Work

Text continues from page 187

In 1999, an extremely helpful and long-needed publication came on the scene: *Iowa Acceleration Scale: A Guide for Whole-Grade Acceleration (K–8).* It summarizes the research in this area and makes concrete recommendations to help determine which students should experience acceleration and which should not. See References and Resources at the end of this chapter.

There are four ways in which a student may be accelerated: through early entrance to kindergarten, grade-skipping (or double promotion) in elementary school or high school, completing two grades in one year, or working ahead in a particular subject.

Early Entrance to Kindergarten

If you suspect that your preschool child might be gifted, arrange to have an IQ test administered by a trained psychologist. You can find one by calling the Psychology Department of any university. Ask them to use the *Stanford-Binet Intelligence Scale, Form L–M,* rather than the newer *Fourth Edition.* The *L–M* has no ceiling, and kids with very high IQs can be accurately identified with this test. You may have to pay for this testing, but it yields very useful information. Having the proper data can help you advocate properly for your child during his or her school experience. Of course, you should not share the actual IQ score with your child or anyone else.

Dr. John Feldhusen and his colleagues at Purdue University have researched the issue of early entrance to kindergarten.* They recommend that a child being considered for early entrance should:

- Be within six months of the approved entering age.
- Have been tested and evaluated by a trained psychologist.
- Be more mentally mature than is expected for his or her age.
- Have the necessary academic skills.
- Be physically healthy and well-adjusted socially and emotionally.
- Want to go to school at this time.
- Not come from a family that puts a high value on competitive sports, since the child might always be too small or not strong enough to earn a place on teams. (This is not a concern if the child is large for his or her age.)

The receiving teacher must be agreeable to the idea, and the placement should be made on a trial basis of about six weeks. At the end of that time, all parties should meet to decide how well the placement is working. Most often, the arrangement continues, but in rare cases, it is decided that the child should leave kindergarten and wait until his or her age peers begin school. Some counseling may be useful to help the child understand that this doesn't represent a personal failure, but most kids who have had this experience don't seem to suffer any permanent damage.

Although many states have a policy requiring a uniform kindergarten entrance age, the local Board of Education usually has the discretion to make exceptions. Alternate methods for grouping and instruction, including entrance into school at various times during the year (not just September) and multi-age classes, are available in some districts with year-round school calendars. These options could be beneficial for precocious gifted students. Don't hold a gifted youngster back to start kindergarten at an older age, even if the child is a boy and doesn't seem particularly adept in social situations. Part of kindergarten is learning how to behave in socially acceptable ways.

Grade-Skipping Past Kindergarten

When considering grade-skipping, keep these guidelines in mind:

- Students who are accelerated should be able to demonstrate that they have mastered at least 70 percent of the present year's curriculum. They should be expected to continue achieving in the top 10 percent of the receiving grade level.
- Procedures must be available to help the students learn material that is new to them but was taught in the earlier grades.
- The students themselves should be part of the acceleration plan and should want the change to happen. I recommend that students spend time visiting the receiving class before being asked for their decision about moving ahead.
- Avoid moving students during the year before they move to another building. They would miss the transition activities designed to make them com-

* Used with permission of John F. Feldhusen.

fortable in the new building. However, acceleration at the beginning of a year when the child has moved to a new school is usually very successful.

- Acceleration into the same grade level of an older sibling is not generally successful unless there are many sections of that grade level. Siblings should not be placed in the same classroom unless there is no alternative.
- Concern over physical characteristics, motor coordination, and social-emotional development are not generally valid. Students who are good candidates for acceleration generally can compensate in these areas with great success.
- A written implementation plan is essential and must have the input of the receiving teacher as well as the present teacher.
- Use the *Iowa Acceleration Scale* for a concrete method to identify which students are good candidates for grade acceleration.

My personal bias is that grade-skipping should be completed by the end of third grade and not used again until the student is in high school. By the time students enter fourth grade, social and peer considerations are far more important in their lives than academics, and changing peer groups after that time may be counterproductive. When the child reaches high school, acceleration of some kind may again be considered, and the student may complete high school in fewer than four years. Some high schools, such as those in Rochester, New York, are even implementing programs in which students can finish high school in 3, 4, or 5 years. This is great news for gifted students.

At the high-school level, students may be eligible to demonstrate their competency in certain subjects before actually having to take them, and may earn high-school credit for those subjects. Such compacting of the curriculum could enable them to start college early. For students who graduate high school before their classmates and don't wish to go on to college immediately, many urban areas offer a rich variety of community college experiences where gifted students may broaden their horizons and take some classes that might transfer to actual university credits. Some high schools will allow students to postpone their actual graduation so they can participate with their classmates in this milestone event.

If it's clear that a student would benefit from grade-skipping but isn't given the chance, don't be surprised if his motivation and productivity in school are adversely affected. Kids who are rarely challenged in school become less willing to work hard. Furthermore, if the primary reason for keeping him with his age peers is concern about social adjustment, this sends the message that peer relations are more important than academic achievement. This can put pressure on the child to conform to peer attitudes, behaviors, and values.

In the words of Sylvia Rimm, "No one expects an average child to repeat skills after they've demonstrated competence. Why should an intellectually gifted child be punished with such meaningless learning tasks?"*

Completing Two Grades in One Year

Some schools prefer this method to the more usual one of having a student skip an entire grade. Here's an example of how it might work.

Benjamin begins first grade already very mature and sociable and with exceptionally high skills in all subject areas. It soon becomes obvious that he has mastered most of the first-grade curriculum. The teacher recognizes that Benjamin is bored. School personnel determine that it would be fruitless for him to finish first grade, and he completes first grade and second grade in the same calendar year. He does it without missing any significant portion of either year, and without cutting himself off from social contact with age peers from either grade.

It's possible that the second half of first grade will cover some area Benjamin has not already mastered. Some adult, such as the gifted program coordinator or a teacher's aid, should take responsibility for tutoring him in those areas. Benjamin's classmates in both grades should be prepared for the change. They might be told, in very simple terms, that Benjamin has learned all the first-grade content and is ready to learn the second-grade content earlier than most other first-grade students.

Acceleration in One Subject

More frequently, we find students who are precocious in one or two subject areas but average in others. For these students, accelerating the curriculum only in their areas of strength is more appropriate than skipping a grade. For example, a second-grade student working at a fourth-grade

* Rimm, Sylvia. *Tips for Parenting the Gifted Child.* Hauppauge, NY: Barron's Educational Service, 1994, page 80.

level in math would go to thc fourth-grade class for math every day, but return to her regular class for the rest of the day.

It's imperative to consult all of the people who will be affected by this plan. They must agree to work together to make it a success. For some teachers, this will mean facilitating the continuation of the plan into the next grade level and beyond. For some parents, it may mean providing transportation when the student goes to a middle school for math each morning and returns to the elementary school for the rest of the day.

See Questions and Answers, pages 197–198, for more on the topic of acceleration in math.

THE QUALITIES OF TEACHERS

Do teachers have to be gifted themselves in order to teach gifted students? I worried about that the first time I attended a national training program for teachers of gifted students. I was always a competent student who worked very hard in all subjects, but I was never considered gifted by myself or any of my teachers.

I have since learned the answer to my question: No! However, teachers who are successful with gifted kids tend to possess certain qualities that gifted children respond to positively. Those qualities are:

- Enthusiasm about teaching and the joy of lifelong learning.
- Flexible teaching style. Comfort with situations in which some students are doing different activities than others and in which students are flexibly grouped for learning.
- Strong listening skills. Keeps inquiry open.
- Knowledgeable about the unique characteristics and needs of gifted students and willing to accommodate them.
- Able and willing to set up and nurture a learning environment in which risk-taking and mistake-making are expected and encouraged.
- Respectful of students' strengths and weaknesses. Able to encourage students to accept both without embarrassment.
- Willing and eager to expose students to new ideas and provide opportunities for exploring those ideas.
- Well-developed sense of humor about themselves and their students.
- Able and willing to connect the curriculum to students' learning styles, interests, and questions. Good at empowering students to follow their passions.
- Well-organized though not necessarily "neat." Able to do multiple tasks simultaneously with effective time-management skills.
- Comfortable providing a wide range of learning materials, including those that are appropriate for older students.
- Able and willing to locate and organize resources or to steer gifted kids to other people who know how to do this.
- Aware that gifted students need less time with practice and more time with complex and abstract learning tasks.
- Comfortable communicating with students about their individual progress.
- Able and willing to advocate for what gifted students need.
- Able and willing to encourage parents of gifted students to find and take advantage of experiences available for their children through college and community resources.

SECURING EXTENSION MATERIALS

Most teachers are on very tight budgets. They worry about where to find extension materials and how to obtain them without going into bankruptcy. As you've probably noticed, the strategies described in this book don't depend on costly materials. As you consider whether to provide differentiated activities in your classroom, please don't base your decision on the perception that adequate materials are prohibitively expensive or unavailable. Try one or more of these suggestions:

1. Look through what you already have on hand. Check your file drawers, cabinets, and the piles of materials you've purchased or collected over the years. Rediscover resources you've forgotten you own. Wonderful surprises await you.

2. Ask your colleagues to look through their materials. What can you borrow from them? (What can you share with them?)

3. Find and use materials your school has purchased for gifted students in the past.

4. Look through your teachers' manuals. Most include suggestions for extension activities (usually called enrichment activities). Parents, aides, student teachers, or students from higher grades may be able to help you get these activities ready for students to use.

One year, the parents of my gifted students worked at home to create a Math Extensions Lab for my classroom. I gave them an extra copy of the teacher's manual for the math book, in which I had checked the activities I wanted them to produce. I provided simple materials (tagboard, colored markers, etc.) so parents could make activity cards, and they came to school to laminate them. Since their own kids were going to benefit from their work, the parents were happy to help.

5. Check to see if extension or enrichment materials are available from the publisher of your text. Maybe your district has already purchased them.

6. Most educational publishers offer a variety of books with activities suitable for gifted learners. See what's available in your school or personal library. Check your colleagues' libraries.

7. Contact the librarians at your local public library. With a few weeks' advance notice, they are usually delighted to collect the materials you need to support a student's independent study. Often, you may keep the materials for an extended time, if you ask.

8. If you're fortunate enough to have a librarian at your school, ask him or her to be your partner in facilitating your gifted students' independent studies. Let the students work on their projects in the library, where the librarian can help them locate and use software, Web sites, and other support materials.

9. Have students create extension materials. See Strategy: Learning Centers starting on page 132.

If you wish to purchase materials for extension activities, see Appendix B.

PULL-OUT PROGRAMS

During the 1990s, pull-out programs* for gifted students came under attack. Most school districts in the U.S. either scaled back or totally eliminated pull-out programs and attempted to replace them with plans to educate gifted kids only in regular, mixed-abilities classrooms. I fear that the title of this book, first published in 1992, lent credibility to the notion that in-class differentiation was all that was needed. However, anyone who actually read the book understood that my philosophy is not to eliminate programs or services but to find an effective combination of services. The research actually favors full-time, self-contained classes for gifted students in districts that have the political climate to support them. So far, only districts with large populations seem able to arrange for self-contained classes. Other districts must design less comprehensive programs. For more on grouping gifted students, see Chapter 8.

The first eight chapters of this book describe how to accommodate gifted students in mixed-abilities classrooms. This section explains how to successfully design and maintain pull-out programs for gifted kids that can supplement and complement the program in the regular classroom. Please don't form an opinion about whether pull-out programs for gifted kids should continue until you have taught or observed in one. There's no easy way to describe how different gifted kids are when they are surrounded by like-minded peers and can be their wonderfully competitive and love-of-learning selves without fear of censure.

Eight Steps to Successful Pull-Out Programs

"Could all students do this work? Would all students want to?" These questions are key to understanding what a pull-out program is for and what it should comprise. The content and activities gifted students experience in a location away from the regular classroom should be more advanced, sophisticated, and rigorous than their age peers could possibly handle. If everyone could benefit from a particular activity, then everyone should experience it.

Following is a suggested approach based on my own experience with pull-out programs. It can help you start and maintain a program that meets the needs of gifted students. Almost as important in the current climate, it can help you lessen resistance to the program from teachers, parents, and students who are not eligible for participation.

1. Identify the areas of the regular curriculum in which gifted students are being sufficiently challenged. For example, many science programs have

* In some states, these are called resource room programs.

moved from textbook-oriented learning to exciting hands-on experiences. If most kids are being challenged by science in your school, a pull-out program in science is probably not necessary.

2. Identify the areas in which gifted students are not being sufficiently challenged. If your school already has advanced opportunities for gifted kids in math and reading, look hard at social studies and science.

3. Identify students who are exceptionally capable in the areas of learning that the pull-out program will address. Use a combination of standardized tests, state or standards-based tests, and actual performance by applicants on tasks similar to those that will be part of the pull-out program.

One gifted education teacher invited kids to "apply" for each extension unit by completing an application and presenting a product demonstrating their ability and interest in that unit. The units were purposefully designed to appeal to different learning strengths so more students could participate in one or more pull-out opportunities.

4. Once the students have been identified, visit their classrooms. Ask all of the children to identify classmates who are very talented in different areas, such as drawing, building, playing a musical instrument, football, computers, or using the Internet. Point out that everyone has some kind of talent, and say that the pull-out program is designed for kids who are talented in school-type activities.

Demystify the selection process by explaining how it worked. Reassure kids that at some future time, their special interest and talent might allow them to be included in a differentiated unit of study. Say that even if they don't ever get to participate, they all have special abilities or talents that will enable them to shine in some other setting.

Make it very clear that kids who are in the program are in no way "better than" other kids. They are simply more talented in whatever the program content is. Emphasize that students in the program shouldn't brag about it or put down others who aren't in the program. Say that if any student experiences inappropriate attitudes or behaviors from identified kids, you want them to tell you about it.

5. Try to get the identified kids together for a two-hour experience once a week. One long block of time is preferable to several shorter segments.

Remember that one reason for putting gifted kids together is because they enjoy each other's company. Don't let them spend all of their pull-out time on independent study. Offer a variety of activities including academic contests. Focus on the value of struggling to learn, facing challenges, and learning through mistakes.

Never send pull-out students back to the regular classroom with required homework.

NOTE: If the classroom teacher is doing compacting, he or she may allow the pull-out students to work on some of "your" material in the time they buy back. Be prepared to facilitate that situation.

6. Coach classroom teachers on how to capitalize on the time the identified kids are with you. Instead of teaching new concepts, they can reinforce concepts the identified kids have already learned. The rest of the class will benefit from the additional emphasis on concepts they need to know, and the pull-out kids won't have too much make-up work when they return.

If teachers need evidence that pull-out kids have mastered the content they missed, demonstrate the Most Difficult First strategy and encourage teachers to use it. See pages 35–39.

7. Spend 15–20 minutes on a regular basis talking to the pull-out kids about the challenges they face because they are highly capable learners. Coach them on ways to avoid behavior that might cause other kids or teachers to develop negative attitudes about the program. See References and Resources, page 199, for a list of resources you can use to help kids with social-emotional issues.

8. Set aside some of your weekly time to coach teachers on the compacting and differentiation strategies described in this book. Help them locate and use appropriate extension materials. You want them to see you as a resource, not as a threat to their ability to challenge their most capable students. Do whatever you can to make this happen.

★ ★ ★ ★ ★ ★ ★

Possible Pull-Out Program Activities

- Creative Problem Solving (CPS) or Future Problem Solving including writing scenarios for those activities
- Chess
- Spelling bees
- Junior Great Books
- Olympiads (competitions)
- Science fairs
- Destination ImagiNation
- Writing for publication (see pages 123 and 127)
- Debates
- Playing with language—puns, figures of speech, transmogrifications (see Vocabulary Activities starting on page 109)
- Stock market simulations
- Economics issues, including going into business
- Logic puzzles and other higher-level thinking challenges

★ ★ ★ ★ ★ ★ ★

THE CHANGING ROLE OF THE GIFTED EDUCATION SPECIALIST

Gifted education is following the Special Education Model, which has changed the role of the Special Education teacher from a person who provided service to kids in a separate location to a person who co-teaches with and coaches classroom teachers in the regular classroom. Today's gifted education specialists (also called resource teachers) must be willing to take on roles and responsibilities that go far beyond providing direct services to identified gifted students in out-of-class locations. If you're a gifted education specialist, you'll be called on to:

- Monitor that the learning needs of gifted students are being met.
- Monitor that gifted students are experiencing the school's mission statement promises.
- Provide leadership in equitable identification methods and practices for gifted students and those who are twice exceptional.
- Find ways to offer regular learning opportunities to more than just the identified gifted kids. *Example:* Joseph Renzulli's *Schoolwide Enrichment Model.* (See References and Resources at the end of this chapter.) Invite teachers to send students to your class who have not been formally identified but who would clearly benefit from participating in a particular unit or activity.
- Provide ongoing consulting services to classroom teachers about compacting, differentiation, and acceleration of content.
- Invite yourself into other teachers' classrooms to demonstrate compacting and differentiation strategies, coach the teachers in how to use them, and provide extension materials.

NOTE: When the teachers observe how some formerly nonproductive students become active, eager learners, they will be impressed enough to ask for more of your expertise. Be sure you "wean" them from too much dependence on your actual presence by insisting they do some of the work themselves, after they have seen you demonstrate a strategy once or twice.

- Help teachers use alternate methods of assessing the work students do on extensions and projects. Show them how to document whether gifted students are actually making forward progress in learning.
- Invite the principal in to see what's happening with a certain youngster with whom you've been successfully using compacting, independent study, etc. As spring approaches, ask the principal to consider placing this student next year with the teacher who would be most likely to continue the differentiation options. Naturally, this is in the best interests of the principal, who will probably have less trouble with the student and the parents if the student's school experience continues to be positive.
- Provide ongoing opportunities for staff development on issues related to gifted education. *Example:* You might offer to lead a study group of

teachers interested in learning more about compacting and differentiation.*

- Help parents understand their role in seeking out and obtaining appropriate learning opportunities for their children without alienating staff. Offer "How to Parent Gifted Kids" courses following the SENG model by James Webb and Arlene DeVries (see the References and Resources for Chapter 10) or using other information from Chapter 10 of this book.
- Advocate for cluster grouping of gifted students. For a discussion of this topic, see Chapter 8.

HOW TO WIN SUPPORT FROM PARENTS

Some parents are confused by their gifted child's advanced abilities. They become uncomfortable when people call attention to the ways in which their child is different from his age peers. They may actually say something like, "I only want my child to be normal!" The child needs to know that he *is* normal. He is simply behaving in ways that reflect his advanced abilities. Hearing valued adults express distress that he is not okay can't help but cause distress for the child.

Other parents become over-invested in making sure their child is always "the best." Families experiencing these situations might benefit from family therapy, or from reading some of the books listed in the References and Resources sections at the end of this chapter and Chapter 10.

Parents sometimes make the same mistake as educators in assuming that if their child is gifted, consistently high grades will be the norm. Many parents expect their gifted kids to be doing lots of work, all of which should be graded by you! In order for them to support your efforts on behalf of their children, you'll need to reeducate them about what it means to be gifted, and also what it means to provide appropriate school experiences for gifted children. The following guidelines may be helpful as you "teach" the parents of the gifted kids in your classroom.

- Take time to explain your plans regarding compacting and differentiation. Parents need reassurance that you're not just assuming that their children have mastered certain concepts. Explain how you will be carefully assessing what their children know.
- Be aware that parents are concerned about their children's popularity. Most will be happy to learn that their children are part of a gifted cluster, especially if they understand that clustering has positive effects on the social acceptance of gifted children. If you have no cluster, explain to parents that compacting and differentiation opportunities are routinely offered to other students, so their children will not appear so unusual or always be expected to work by themselves.
- Recognize that parents are concerned about their children's grades. You'll need to reassure them—probably more than once—that gifted kids and A's don't always go together. Parents need to understand how your efforts to provide meaningful learning experiences and opportunities for real struggle are more important that perfect report cards.
- Invite parents to share information about their children—anything that will help you to know and understand them better. For example, you'll want to find out about the children's passionate interests, hobbies, and collections as possible topics for resident expert projects. Use the Interest Survey on page 147.
- Be a source of information for parents. Refer them to appropriate articles and books on parenting gifted children. For suggestions, see References and Resources in chapters 9 and 10 and Appendix B.
- Encourage parents to read the final chapter in this book. If you read it, too, you'll have more information in common, which will lead to better communication.

QUESTIONS AND ANSWERS

"Are there any special considerations regarding acceleration in math?"

Fernand Prevost, Implementation Director of the New Hampshire Impact Center at Plymouth State University and former State Director of Mathematics for New Hampshire, suggests that

* I have produced an 80-minute video that demonstrates some of the strategies described in this book being used in actual classrooms. The video package is accompanied by a Discussion Leader's Guide that will coach the discussion leader in how to lead the group's efforts effectively. For ordering information, contact Free Spirit Publishing.

educators and parents be cautious when considering radical acceleration in math for students in grades 5 and 6. Students who have had primarily arithmetic up until then, rather than programs that focus on critical thinking and problem-solving, may not be ready for advanced work when it comes.

Prevost further recommends that you accelerate only those students who seem clearly qualified. Students who are "added on" to make classes of even numbers for all teachers may lose interest and self-confidence when they have to struggle to keep up with more advanced students. Prevost also advises not teaching algebra in grade 8 unless students have had several years of NCTM-based programs.

Not following these guidelines may lead to students at the junior level and above who have "burned out" in math and refuse to take a full four years of math curriculum.

Two comprehensive programs that help kids develop the necessary competencies to be successful in math into high school and college are *Connected Mathematics* (grades 6–8) and *Mathematics in Context* (grades 5–8). You can get in-depth overviews of both programs at the Show-Me Center Web site (www.showmecenter.missouri.edu). Or contact the publishers.

- *Connected Mathematics:* Prentice-Hall Inc., Upper Saddle River, NJ 07458; (800) 848-9500 (www.phschool.com). For detailed queries, the publisher recommends you refer to the CMP Web site at Michigan State University (www.math.msu.edu/cmp).
- *Mathematics in Context:* Encyclopaedia Britannica, Inc., 310 South Michigan Avenue, 8th Floor, Chicago, IL 60604; (800) 554-9862 (www.ebmic.com/ebec).

To contact Dr. Prevost, write or call: NH-IMPACT Center, Plymouth State College, 17 High Street, Plymouth, NH 03264-1595; (603) 535-2985.

"Our school doesn't have a gifted education specialist. Can we still offer a pull-out program?"

Yes, you can, with a little help from parents and other interested parties. For example, at Loos Elementary, an inner-city school in Dayton, Ohio, several teachers have created the "Down the Hall Gang." Parents of gifted kids sign up in advance and take turns teaching lessons prepared by classroom teachers to kids who need differentiation opportunities. The parent teachers leave notes for the classroom teachers after each lesson that gives them valuable feedback. It is understood that the kids who attend this program will experience regular compacting opportunities in their regular classroom. For more information, see References and Resources at the end of this chapter.

I can also see it working to have parents teach something that interests them personally. In my fifth-grade classroom, I had parents who brown-bag-lunched it with kids who chose to attend sessions on calculus, etymology, global warming, being a veterinarian, and other topics.

"How can I deal with concerned or negative reactions from my colleagues?"

Occasionally, you will meet colleagues who criticize your compacting and differentiation practices. They may fear that they will have to carry on what you started when the students reach their class. They may worry that you will allow students to work with materials that should be reserved for a subsequent grade levels. What to do?

My first suggestion is to offer to lead a study group based on this book. If educating them doesn't work, remember this: Every great person credits one teacher with providing the inspiration, confidence, and motivation they needed to realize their potential. Perhaps you are that teacher. Enjoy the contribution you're making in the lives of your own students.

"What can I say to parents who try to convince me that their child is gifted?"

Some parents seem to have inflated views of their child's talents, abilities, and intelligence. However, the sad reality is that many gifted kids hide their giftedness at school because they perceive that it's not welcome by their teachers or classmates. But while the child is working very hard to look normal and average at school, parents see evidence of gifted behaviors at home.

I recommend you respond to parents by saying, "Thank you so much for bringing this information to my attention. I'll be keeping a special eye on your daughter/son." Meanwhile, you might invite them to read Chapter 10 in this book, which includes suggestions for talking with teachers and advocating for what their child needs in school.

SUMMARY

This chapter has touched briefly on several topics related to teaching gifted students. Greatly expanded information is available from many other sources, including those described in the References and Resources section below and in Appendix B. What's really exciting is that the Internet is fast becoming an excellent source of information, research, findings, suggestions, insights, ideas, and more about gifted kids. There are so many wonderful Web sites that didn't previously exist that any teacher or parent who wants information about virtually any topic can access it quite easily.

REFERENCES AND RESOURCES

Programming

Coleman, Mary Ruth. "Appropriate Differentiated Services: Guide For Best Practices in the Education of Gifted Children." *Gifted Child Today* 18:5, 23–33, September–October 1995.

Destination ImagiNation. Creative problem-solving for grades K–college/university. Formerly Odyssey of the Mind. Glassboro, NJ, (856) 881-1603 (www.idodi.org).

Maker, C. June. *Teaching Models in the Education of the Gifted.* Austin, TX: PRO-ED, 1995.
—— and Aleene B. Nielson. *Curriculum Development and Teaching Strategies for Gifted Learners.* Austin, TX: PRO-ED, 1996.
—— and Shirley Schiever, eds. *Programs for Gifted in Regular Classrooms.* Austin, TX: PRO-ED, 1992.

Renzulli, Joseph, and Sally Reis. *The Schoolwide Enrichment Model: A How-to Guide for Educational Excellence.* 2nd ed. Mansfield Center, CT: Creative Learning Press, 1997.

Shore, Bruce, et al. *Recommended Practices in Gifted Education.* New York: TC Press, 1991.

Weiner, D., and B. Woolhiser. "Creative Collaboration." McMinnville, Oregon Schools. Includes information about their version of a Differentiated Education Plan.

Winebrenner, Susan, and Sandra Berger. "Providing Curriculum Alternatives to Motivate Gifted Students." ERIC EC Digest #E574, 1994 (www.eric.ed.gov).

Counseling and Social-Emotional Well-Being

Colangelo, Nicholas, and Gary A. Davis. *Handbook of Gifted Education.* 2nd ed. Needham Heights, MA: Allyn & Bacon, 1996.

Delisle, Jim, and Judy Galbraith. *When Gifted Kids Don't Have All the Answers.* Minneapolis, Free Spirit Publishing, 2002. Helpful information for teachers and counselors on the social and emotional needs of the gifted.

Ellis, Albert, and Robert Harper. *A Guide to Rational Living.* New York: Albert Ellis Institute, 1990.

Silverman, Linda, ed. *Counseling the Gifted and Talented.* Denver, Love Publishing, 1993.

Van Tassel-Baska, Joyce, ed. *A Practical Guide to Counseling the Gifted in a School Setting.* Reston, VA: Council for Exceptional Children, 1990.

Early Entrance and Grade-Skipping

Academic Acceleration: Knowing Your Options. Baltimore, MD: Center for Talented Youth Press, 1995. Contact CTY at Johns Hopkins University, (410) 735-4100 (cty.jhu.edu).

Assouline, Susan, et al. *Iowa Acceleration Scale.* Scottsdale, AZ: Great Potential Press, 1999. The research for this publication was conducted as an IAS Research Project by the Connie Belin and Jacqueline N. Blank International Center for Gifted Education and Talent Development at the University of Iowa in Iowa City, IA, (800) 336-6463.

Feldhusen, John, et al. "Guidelines for Early Entrance into Kindergarten" (1988). Available from the Gifted Education Resource Institute (GERI), Purdue University, West Lafayette, IN, (765) 494-7243 (www.geri.soe.purdue.edu).

Lynch, Sharon J. "Should Gifted Students Be Grade-Advanced?" ERIC EC Digest #E526, 1994 (www.eric.ed.gov).

Pull-Out Programs

"Down the Hall Gang." A pull-out program at Loos Elementary School in Dayton, Ohio. For more information, contact Jacqueline Moore or Cathryn Leedy by email (jmoore5@hotmail.com or Leedycs@aol.com).

Jenkins-Friedman, Reva, et al. "Professional Training for Teachers of the Gifted and Talented." Reston, VA: ERIC Clearinghouse on Disabilities and Gifted Education, ERIC Digest #ED262525, 1984. Read it on the Web (www.eric.ed.gov).

Renzulli, Joseph. "Point-Counterpoint: The Positive Side of Pull-Out Programs." *Journal for the Education of the Gifted* 10, 245–254, 1987.

Winning Support

Dettmer, P. "Gifted Program Advocacy: Overhauling the Bandwagons to Build Support." *Gifted Child Quarterly* 35, 165–171, 1991.

Karnes, Frances, and Joan Lewis. "Public Relations: A Necessary Tool for Advocacy in Gifted Education." ERIC EC Digest #E542, May 1997 (www.eric.ed.gov). How to advocate for what gifted students need.

10

Parenting Gifted Children

In a book for teachers, the final chapter is written to parents. Why? Beyond the obvious reason that many teachers are parents, too, this chapter is here because parents have requested it. I've done a lot of work with parents since the first edition of this book was published. Many teachers have told me that they originally learned about my book from a parent who found it, read it, and passed it on to them. So, parents—this is for you.

Educating gifted students is a responsibility that parents and teachers must share. Everyone needs to work together to make sure that appropriate educational opportunities are in place at school as well as home. It's unrealistic for parents to expect the school to do the entire job, and it's impossible for teachers to provide optimum results without full cooperation from parents.

This chapter considers several issues related to parenting gifted children, offers tips on how to advocate for your child in school, and suggests ways to provide a nurturing environment at any stage of your child's life. Whole books have been written about these topics, and I don't pretend to cover everything or to go into great detail. I hope you'll continue to educate yourself about gifted children. The References and Resources at the end of this chapter can point you toward many possibilities for learning much more.

As you read this chapter, you may discover some things you'll wish you'd known before now. I'll tell you exactly what I say to teachers in the Introduction to this book: Don't waste any time or energy feeling guilty about what you should have done differently in the past. If you had known what to do, you would have done it. Look forward, not back. I've never met a caring parent who didn't want the best for his or her child, and I'm assuming that includes you.

PARENTING ISSUES

Parenting Style

Parenting is quite possibly the most difficult job around. When the child is an exceptionally capable learner, it can be even more challenging. Many of these kids seem to be born ready for work in a courtroom. They love to argue and to bamboozle adults with their highly effective logic. They are tireless, often resurfacing after an apparent defeat, fresh for new battle with their frazzled mom and/or dad. Rest assured that these children need parenting, even though they sound as though they are ready to parent themselves! Being smart is no excuse for inappropriate behavior.

The parenting style that seems most effective with gifted kids is non-authoritarian, while still setting and enforcing reasonable limits. "Because I said so!" almost never works. Gifted kids respond best to adults who are fair, reasonable, respectful, and sensitive to the special needs that arise when a child's mental age exceeds his chronological age by several years.

Power Struggles

Do your best to avoid power struggles with your child. It may appear that you're winning, but victory is almost always temporary. Instead, consider your child's request very carefully before giving any response. Then, when you do share your decision, it will be clear that you've thought it through and feel comfortable with it. You'll find it easier to resist your child's efforts to wear you down or convince you to change your mind.

A related issue is the importance of consistency. If two people are sharing parenting responsibilities, it's essential that they get their act together, out of the child's hearing, before delivering their decisions regarding rights, privileges, and consequences. Gifted kids can gain a lot of power by playing adults against each other.

Listening

It's hard to really listen to a child who seems to talk endlessly. One parent I know met this challenge by scheduling personal "sharing time" with one of her children every week night. Her husband also participated, and each week they would "switch kids." The children were asked to keep notes in a small notebook about things they wanted to discuss with their parents. Each child received a parent's undivided attention for the same amount of time at the same hour each day. Appointment times could not be changed unless both parties agreed.

The tricky part for the parents was really listening to their kids. Really listening means focusing exclusively on your child and responding only to him or her. The basics of really listening are:

- No newspaper, book, dish towel, TV, radio, phone, or computer is allowed. There's nothing in your hands and nothing in your line of sight besides your child.
- Use body language that shows how interested you are in what your child is saying. Lean forward. Maintain eye contact.
- From time to time, nod your head and say, "Mmmmm. Okay. I understand."
- Ask for clarification when you need it.
- Occasionally "reflect" what your child has just said. *Examples:* "He told the teacher you copied his homework." "She said she doesn't like you anymore." "He made you feel angry, and you wanted to get back at him."
- Every so often, comment on your child's feelings. *Examples:* "You must have been really frustrated." "That must have been pretty frightening."
- Try never to deny your child's feelings. If she says, "I was really scared!" don't respond, "Oh, there's nothing to be scared about." And especially don't respond, "That's silly! Big girls don't get scared." Feelings aren't right or wrong, good or bad. Feelings just are. Acknowledge your child's right to have her feelings. Guide her to find her own solution to the problem.

When your child knows that she can have your full attention—when you really listen—her need to talk to you incessantly will diminish. If she mentions something at a time when you're not available to really listen, suggest that she write it down so she won't forget it. Then set a time for talking.

Comparing

Avoid comparing your children to each other. Many parents have been told that some of their kids are gifted while others are not. In fact, research done by Dr. Linda Silverman, a leader in the field of gifted education, indicates that birth-related siblings are usually quite close to each other in intelligence. Apparent discrepancies are more often the result of sibling dynamics than innate smarts.

Help your children understand that individual differences exist, and once they get to college and into the world of work, no one will know or care about their siblings. Notice and praise each child's personal growth and improvement in any area of endeavor. Resist the temptation to label your kids by their strengths—as in "She's a math wiz" or "He's the writer in the family"—as they may perceive this as evidence that being better at something makes one a better person.

You want all of your children to be secure in the knowledge that you love them unconditionally for who they are, not just for their achievements in intellectual or other areas. The key is to discover the areas in which each of your children can excel and support their talents in those areas. Learn about multiple intelligences and learning styles, then take another look at your kids. See References and Resources at the end of this chapter for suggestions.

A few more tips to keep in mind:

- When your children bring home their report cards, don't count the A's. Don't give monetary rewards for top grades. Don't display only perfect report cards (or perfect papers) on the refrigerator or family bulletin board. Don't display "My Child Made the Honor Roll" bumper stickers on your car. Any and all of these actions send the message that you love your kids best when they are perfect students—and that the sibling who brings home the highest grades is better than the others.

- Avoid asking a more capable sibling to help a less capable one with his or her school work. If one of your children is struggling, talk with the teacher or get tutoring help. You're not your child's teacher, and neither are his or her siblings.
- Monitor your own conversations with your partner, other family members, and friends, including your telephone talk. When you discuss your kids' abilities and achievements, avoid making it sound as if you're proudest of how smart they are. Children need ongoing reassurance that they are valued for who they are, not what they can do. They need to know that they won't lose your approval if they earn less than perfect grades.

Perfectionism

Many gifted children are perfectionists. This can seriously interfere with their motivation and productivity in school. Too much praise for products that took little effort leads kids to conclude that they are always expected to get great results without trying very hard. Too much verbal attention paid to their wonderfulness gets kids hooked on adult attention and approval.

Many of these kids conclude that smart means easy. The longer they believe that fallacy, the less likely they are to venture into learning areas that are challenging for them. Challenge becomes terrifying as these children conclude, "If others observe me working hard, they'll think I'm not really very smart!" This can become a vicious cycle: the more praise received, the less effort expended. And then we begin to think the child is lazy, not working up to his potential, or not "applying himself."

This condition is exacerbated when kids feel intense pressure to get into the "right college" or choose the "right career." Giftedness is often accompanied by multiple talents. Career choices should be kept open as long as possible so these kids can explore their many interests.

How can you help your child avoid the perfectionism trap? Try these ideas:

- Constantly reinforce the fact that your child is separate from his accomplishments. We are who we are, not what we do or don't do. Coach him to avoid statements like, "I'm so stupid!" Help him choose statements like, "That was a careless mistake. Next time I try this, I'll make sure I have all the materials I need before I start working."
- Avoid the phrase, "Do your very best." Replace it with, "Make your best effort." This changes the emphasis from the product to the learning process.
- Help your child learn to set realistic, short-term goals and take satisfaction from accomplishing something he planned for today.
- Ease your child into competitive situations by starting him out in those where he is competing only with himself. Gymnastics, self-defense classes, and other non-team sports are sometimes easier for perfectionistic gifted kids to handle, since they are totally in charge of the results for themselves.
- Examine your own life and behaviors for signs of perfectionism. Model setting priorities and letting go of less important tasks.
- Laugh at your own mistakes. Avoid self-criticizing statements that indicate there's something wrong with a person who makes mistakes.
- Talk often about the value of learning from mistakes. Share examples from your own life. Help your child find and read stories and biographies of people who achieved success only after many frustrations and failures. The librarian at your local public library will be happy to assist.
- Let your child do things for himself rather than jumping in to show him the "right way."
- Teach your child to give constructive criticism and receive it gracefully.
- Please don't "help" your child with his homework, especially not when your goal is to make it perfect. You are not your child's school teacher, and when you act like one, you may be sending a message that you expect your child to be perfect all the time and that you value him more highly if his grades are always superior.
- Please don't worry if your child doesn't read aloud fluently. Often, gifted children's eyes and thoughts are far ahead of what their mouth is supposed to say. The only valid test of a child's reading ability is comprehension.

Perfectionism can contribute to the development of eating disorders and other physical and emotional problems. Any efforts you make to alleviate the stresses related to perfectionism can pay off in terms of your child's well-being. For more information about perfectionism, see Chapter 1, pages 13–15.

Praise

Replace praise with encouragement. Encourage your child when you see her working hard and long at a difficult task. Notice and comment positively on her refusal to give up in favor of an easier task. Encourage risk-taking behavior in learning new games and skills. Model ways in which you take risks without knowing that a positive outcome is guaranteed. Teach your child how to ask for help, without embarrassment, when she needs it.

Instead of always saying, "I'm so proud of you!" ask her to describe her own pride in her accomplishments. You want her to please herself, not worry about pleasing you. Constant praise can lead kids to do what they think we want them to do. For more on this topic, see *The Skills of Encouragement* by Don Dinkmeyer and Lewis Losoncy. See References and Resources at the end of this chapter.

Grades

As I train teachers to provide more challenging learning experiences for gifted kids, I hear them worry aloud that parents will react negatively if their children start getting lower grades. The teachers know that many parents share the misperception that high grades mean all is well in school and anything less means something is amiss. I like to suggest that teachers tell parents (and students), "Intelligence does not equal effortlessness." Putting these words on banners and hanging them in the classroom (and wherever the child does homework) would help us all remember what the true goals of learning should be.

You want your child's teacher to provide a challenging environment and expectations. You want your child to learn not to fear hard work. To my knowledge, there is no college application that asks for transcripts from elementary or middle schools. Therefore, grades K–8 are the best, safest times for students to learn to welcome hard work rather than avoid it.

You certainly don't want your child to glide through grades K–12, get high grades with little or no effort, then go off to a highly competitive college with no clue how to study and work hard to learn. This is a recipe for disaster. Everyone in the freshman class came from the top 5 percent of their high school graduating class. Most are accustomed to getting all A's in school. Unfortunately, the college doesn't work that way. Many students will get low grades for the first time in their lives. When that happens, they can become seriously discouraged or even depressed.

It's much better if your child understands that real learning means forward progress from wherever one enters the learning curve of a particular subject. Straight A's mean that your child knows the material. They don't necessarily mean that your child is learning. Maybe he knew it six months ago or a year ago. So instead of marching into school at the first sign of a lower grade, toting all of your child's previously glorious report cards and asking the teacher how she can be the one to ruin your child's perfect record, send flowers and/or candy and count your blessings.

Social Skills

Do whatever you can to help your child find suitable friends. Don't worry if the friends she chooses are older or younger than she is. Children who learn at a level that exceeds their chronological age by 2–3 years may not be comfortable with kids their own age. Think of your friends. Now think of how many are within one year of your own age, and you'll understand the point I'm making. There are some activities your child will want to share with her age peers, and others where age is irrelevant and interest and maturation are much more important.

Help your child develop physical and social interaction skills in line with her precocious abilities in other learning areas. Coach her in areas of physical education or sports where she may feel inferior. This gives her insight into how it feels to work hard to learn something difficult. Teach her how to be tolerant of individual differences, in much the same way she would like others to be tolerant of her exceptional learning abilities.

If your child is having trouble finding friends who understand and appreciate her just the way she is, and with whom she can be her very smart self without worries about having to hide her intelligence, look to groups and opportunities outside of school. For example, if art is her passion, sign her up for art classes at a local museum.

If you can afford it, arrange for your child to attend Saturday classes or summer camps for gifted kids. Those experiences provide priceless validation that "I'm okay just the way I am." They also give children the chance to form lasting friendships with like-minded kids. Thanks to email, it's easier than ever to stay in touch with long-distance friends. Your child will love the chance to be with kids who understand and appreciate her, and you'll be relieved to observe that she does have social skills after all. Contact your state department of education and the education departments of local colleges and universities to find out what opportunities they offer.

If your child is invited to participate in an Academic Talent Search, allow it to happen. Taking the SAT at age 12 is a great experience, because at the very least, it may give your child an edge when she takes it again as a junior in high school. Don't tutor your child to prepare for the test. However, do use the manual the school sends home to help her learn the "tricks" of taking the test. For example, on the SAT, test-takers actually lose points for guessing incorrectly.

The value of the Academic Talent Search lies in identifying students who have already mastered content at a high-school level. For those who score in the top 5 percent of all kids taking the test, extended learning opportunities may be available that will allow your child to interact with other gifted kids in a stimulating learning environment.

Gifted Girls

Believe it or not, many of today's gifted girls still believe they have to choose between being smart and being popular. Gifted girls need lots of interaction with other gifted girls in order to maintain a positive attitude toward high achievement. Some studies show significant benefits for girls who attend same-sex schools in high school and college.

Gifted girls also benefit from affirmation of assertive behaviors, and from interaction with positive female role models. If their mothers work outside the home, gifted girls need consistent feedback that Mom enjoys being in the working world. They also need evidence that Mom doesn't need to be perfect in every aspect of her life. Shortcuts in housework and cooking are okay.

Encourage gifted girls to take as many math and science courses as possible. The U.S. Department of Labor predicts that anyone who finishes high school without four years of high school math and science has effectively closed the door to a significant percentage of 21st-century careers. If you weren't good in math or science, don't let your daughter know. That really has no bearing on her potential.

Gifted Boys

Gifted boys have their own unique problems. They worry about being labeled "nerds" and teased about their giftedness. They feel strong peer pressure to fit in and conform. Especially if they have a very sensitive and artistic nature, they may encounter negative attitudes and bullying because they are perceived as "too feminine." They may find themselves in direct conflict with many of the cultural stereotypes of the way boys are supposed to be—namely strong, athletic, and interested in competitive activities. Finding like-minded friends may be very frustrating for them.

Like gifted girls, boys who experience these pressures may choose to hide their interests and abilities. Rather than do what's best for them, they may try to meet others' expectations. Here are ways to support your gifted boy:*

- Encourage him to feel and express his emotions.
- Invite him to share his hopes, dreams, fears, and insecurities with you. Listen and empathize.
- Talk about how gender stereotyping and expectations limit both boys and girls.
- Help him to find other adults and mentors who accept him as he is.
- Encourage him to follow his own interests and make time to learn about things he wants to know.
- Help him to look for and identify interest-based groups he might want to join. He's likely to find new friends there who can appreciate him and accept him as he is.
- Especially if he's good at many things, watch for signs of stress and overload. Help him to prioritize his activities and commitments. If he decides to drop one or two, support his decision.

---

* Adapted from *The Gifted Kids' Survival Guide: A Teen Handbook* by Judy Galbraith and Jim Delisle. Minneapolis, Free Spirit Publishing, 1996, page 115. Used with permission of the publisher.

Peer Pressure

Peer pressure against students who want to achieve in school is alive and well in urban and suburban schools. In the past decade, I have seen it manifest itself in some of the most affluent communities. Sooner or later, most gifted kids will ask themselves, "Can I still be popular with my peers if I work hard in school and get high grades? Or should I hide my intelligence and keep my friends?" Gifted boys who are also talented in sports seem more able to retain peer approval. Gifted girls don't seem to have the same advantage.

Sylvia Rimm has addressed this issue with refreshing originality. She suggests that you encourage your children to be true to their abilities, even if they lose some friends along the way. She tells gifted kids to remember, "The benefits of conformity end on the night of high-school graduation."

Support your child's access to opportunities that allow him to interact with other gifted kids on a regular basis, even if those contacts come from sources outside the school environment. Role-play with him things he might say to deflect peer ridicule about his work in school, like "Everyone has a right to their own opinion" or "Differences make the world more interesting." Above all, make sure your child knows the difference between real friends and people whose friendship isn't worth seeking.

Role Models

All children need strong, positive role models. Gifted children in particular need proof that being smart, capable, and "different" can lead to interesting options later in life. Look around your family, neighborhood, and community for adults you can point to as good role models. If your child seems interested in occupations that challenge gender stereotypes, make a special effort to locate positive role models in those careers. Work with librarians to find books (fiction, nonfiction, biography, autobiography) that spotlight worthy examples. You might arrange for your child to have a mentor. See References and Resources at the end of this chapter.

Down Time

Make sure that your child has plenty of "down time." Resist her insistence on getting involved in too many activities or lessons. Suggest that she focus each year on one area she wants to excel in, and one in which she feels inadequate and would like to improve. Encourage daydreaming, socializing, and goofing off. Emphasize the importance of a balanced life.

The Future

Many gifted kids suffer from what author and educator Jim Delisle calls "an embarrassment of riches." They have so many strengths that the prospect of choosing just one career is depressing. They can take heart in knowing that most workers in the 21st century will have to change careers at least three times before they retire.

Suggest that your child keep his career options open as long as possible. Don't insist that he plan to go to a certain college. Don't choose his career for him. It's estimated that more than 70 percent of the jobs that will available in 2025 have not yet been invented! Encourage your child to take four years of high school science and math, as that preparation appears essential for many 21st-century jobs.

Getting Help If You Need It

If your child appears to be depressed or in need of professional help for identity and validation issues, arrange for it to happen. Don't assume that all therapists know about the special challenges gifted children face. Dr. Linda Silverman's office in Denver can help put you in touch with therapists who understand gifted persons. See References and Resources at the end of this chapter.

Special Cases

A very small percentage of gifted kids are profoundly gifted. At some point in their school life, they will need grade-level or content acceleration. Please read Chapter 9, starting on page 187, for more on this topic.

Some gifted children are what we call "twice exceptional." They are gifted, but they also have some type of learning disability, attention deficit disorder, or physical or emotional challenge. Please read Chapter 1, pages 18–22, and consult the References and Resources at the end of that chapter for information about national networks.

ADVOCATING FOR YOUR CHILD AT SCHOOL

As a parent, you know your child better than anyone. If you think your child has exceptional abilities, you're probably right. But what if your child's teacher or school hasn't yet recognized what's obvious to you?

Deciding how to approach your child's teachers and ask for some consideration may be one of the most daunting challenges you'll ever face. You may be reluctant to tell anyone that you believe your child is gifted. Parents who do tell are often perceived as bragging and may be labeled "pushy parents" or "squeaky wheels." There's also the concern that going to the teacher may have a negative effect on your child's experience with that teacher.

It helps to know something about the realities of teaching in today's classrooms. Many teachers are not adequately prepared to meet the diverse learning needs of students whose learning abilities span 5–7 years. It's not unusual for a 5th-grade teacher to have some kids who can barely read at all and others who read and comprehend at an 8th-grade level or higher. There's intense pressure from political sources to concentrate teaching efforts on kids who can't meet grade-level standards. Most teachers have never been required to take even one course in how to teach gifted kids. No wonder some teachers assume that kids who do great work and get high grades don't need any special attention.

It's important to realize that educating gifted kids is a team effort. As the parent of a gifted child, you're responsible for her learning outside of the classroom. Contact community resources, investigate extended learning opportunities available through colleges and universities, and find other ways to show her that learning isn't limited to school. Be careful not to go overboard with lessons, commitments, and learning activities.

Never disparage your child's teacher in front of your child. At least, try very hard not to, no matter how frustrated you are. This can make some underachievement problems much worse. Sylvia Rimm's books (see References and Resources at the end of this chapter) will help you understand the implications of this issue.

All this being said, how can you advocate for your child appropriately and effectively? In my experience, these are the techniques that seem to work best.

1. Be careful of what you say and how you say it. Avoid using the words "gifted," "special," "best and brightest," or "bored." Don't immediately describe all the things your child can do at home that exceed grade-level expectations. Try not to use any language that states or implies that your child is better, more important, or more deserving than other children.

Gifted kids are not special. All kids are special. But gifted kids do have serious frustrations with curriculum designed for age-appropriate learners. Those frustrations deserve attention.

> **NOTE:** Please don't ask teachers to give your gifted child more work! Would you like your boss to give you more work to take home just because you always finish ahead of everyone else? Instead, ask for opportunities for your child to work on activities that are personally challenging.

2. Before approaching your child's teacher with a request, send some positive messages ahead. Tell the teacher about activities your child has enjoyed. Offer to help by volunteering in the classroom or working at home on materials the teacher can use in the classroom. Convey the message that you want to work as a partner in your child's education, not as a thorn in the teacher's side.

3. Get a copy of the school's or district's mission statement, which describes the goals set for all children. In each of those statements, there is a sentence that promises something like, "All students will actualize their learning to their highest potential," or "All students will experience a challenging learning environment." Your advocacy efforts should center around the promises made for all students. Ask for evidence that your child is experiencing those promises. Notice that you're not asking for special treatment for your child, nor are you inferring that the teacher should spend a lot of extra time on your child's behalf. You're simply expecting that your child will receive the benefits all children in the school are promised.

In Oregon, for example, the gifted education legislation states that all students should be learning at the rate and level appropriate for them. Parents of all students, including those who are gifted and talented, need only to ask for evidence that the expectations of the legislation are being satisfied.

4. Understand that gifted students are as far removed from "average" in ability and performance as students who qualify for special education services. Your advocacy should be based on the expectation of equal treatment for all atypical learners. If students in special education receive differentiated content, expectations, pacing, teaching methods, and assessment options, then exceptionally capable students should be equally eligible for such differentiation opportunities.

On the other hand, be careful not to misinterpret standardized test scores. If a fourth-grade student gets a GE (Grade Equivalent) score of 6.5 (sixth grade, fifth month), this doesn't mean that she could handle sixth-grade, fifth-month learning material. It only means that , in comparison with other kids her age, she scored in the higher ranges.

5. Familiarize yourself with the latest research on grouping practices. Find out which ones are considered most beneficial for highly capable learners. Read Chapter 8: Grouping Gifted Kids for Learning, especially the section on cluster grouping starting on page 175. Become an advocate for cluster grouping in your school. Suggest that administrators from your school contact me and request my "Cluster Network" list.

6. Unless you feel you have no alternative, don't request specific teachers by name. Instead, request teachers who:

- Have had some training in how to teach gifted kids.
- Regularly allow students to demonstrate what they already know.
- Give students class time to work on alternate activities.
- Allow gifted students to work together on a regular basis.

7. Join and support the efforts of your local and state advocacy groups. Gifted education is strongest in districts and states where parents are vocal and well-organized. Don't be afraid of being a squeaky wheel. Push hard for state certification in gifted education for teachers who will have gifted students in their classes, and for financial support for gifted students. I have seen miracles happen for gifted kids when their parents become politically savvy and courageous. Special education legislation was the result of parent advocacy. And it could be the same for gifted education.

PROVIDING A NURTURING ENVIRONMENT

There are so many excellent resources on parenting that I'm just going to list a few of my favorite tips and suggestions here.

The Preschool Years

1. Keep a journal of your child's learning development. Include the exact ages at which he starts to walk, talk, exhibit intense curiosity, and demonstrate abilities to think creatively and critically. Note other precocious behaviors in music, athletic ability, art, science, and so on.

The act of journaling focuses your attention on specific behaviors. The observations you record may be shared later with teachers as you advocate for your child. And the journal itself becomes a wonderful keepsake your child will treasure as an adult.

2. Notice your child's special interests. Provide him with learning experiences in those areas. Go beyond the usual books and library visits to multimedia materials (videos, CD-ROMs, interactive Web sites) and on-site visits to places that relate directly to his interests (the airport, the zoo, an art museum, a television studio).

3. Expect asynchronous development. This is a fancy way of saying that just because your son talked earlier than other kids doesn't mean he'll be able to tie his shoes any sooner. Gifted kids aren't gifted at everything, and some areas of learning and ability may lag behind others. Don't be alarmed; it's perfectly normal. Stephanie Tolan, coauthor of *Guiding the Gifted Child* (see References and Resources at the end of this chapter), has this to say:*

> Highly gifted children are many ages simultaneously. A 5-year-old may read like a 7-year-old, play chess like a 12-year-old, talk like a 13-year-old, and share toys like a 2-year-old. A child may move with lightning speed from a reasoned discussion of the reasons for taking turns on the playground to a full-scale temper tantrum when not allowed to be first on the swing.

4. Use praise sparingly. Avoid showing off your child's talents in a public way or calling others' attention to his grades, school status, or participation in special programs.

---

* Tolan, Stephanie. "Helping Your Highly Gifted Child." ERIC Digest #E477, 1990.

Refrain from statements like, "You're the smartest kid I've ever known," or "You're going to be a prize-winning scientist when you grow up." Although such praise is well-intentioned, it puts pressure on the child to always excel and creates anxiety that he might lose your approval if he doesn't.

5. Use encouragement generously. Emphasize the process of learning and growing, not the product. One of the most valuable lessons your preschooler can learn from you is that mistakes are for learning. Model this in your own behavior and encourage it in your child.

6. Don't feel you need to answer all of your child's questions. That may lead him to believe that there's one right answer to every question. Instead, ask him, "What do you think?" "Why do you think that?" Help him notice that different sources may have different answers to the same question.

7. As often as possible, give your child two limited options and let him choose between them. *Examples:* "I'm going to make lunch now. Do you want peanut butter or macaroni and cheese?" "It's time for your bedtime story. Would you like me to read *Goodnight Moon* or *Where the Wild Things Are*?" This gives him some control over his life and a safe way to practice choice-making.

8. Strictly limit television, computer programs, and video games until your child is 4 years old. Too much exposure to images that change rapidly can adversely affect attention span.

9. Provide thought-provoking toys, puzzles, and games. Model strategies and self-talk your child can use to endure frustration, lose gracefully, and solve problems while playing.

10. Expect your child to be somewhat impatient and bossy with kids his own age. Understand that those behaviors come from frustration and the need for control. Of course, you'll want to teach and model socially acceptable behaviors. From time to time, arrange for playmates who are your child's intellectual and learning peers. Often, gifted kids' behaviors improve when they play with children who are more like them.

11. If you become convinced that your child is precocious, arrange for an individual IQ test by a trained psychologist, even if you have to pay for it yourself. For more on this topic, see Early Entrance to Kindergarten on page 191. If the test shows that your child is learning at a level that exceeds his age by 2–3 years, consider requesting early entrance to kindergarten or grade-skipping. See Chapter 9, pages 191–192, for more on these topics.

The Elementary School Years

1. Reassure your child that it's okay to be different. Tell her that she'll meet many people in life who will appreciate and value her differences. She may feel intense pressure to conform, and how she reacts may determine her achievement motivation for years to come.

2. Understand her need to spend time with older kids, especially those who share one or more of her passionate interests. If her mental age exceeds her chronological age by 2 or more years, her interests will more closely parallel those of older kids.

3. Try not to expect consistently high grades. Let your child know that even when she's struggling to learn, you still think she's smart. These are the years when your child needs to learn how to learn, not how to get high grades with little or no effort. You want her to welcome hard work, not avoid it. For more on this topic, see page 204.

4. Model lifelong learning. Show by example that learning is something people can and should do throughout their lives, not just in school.

5. Have many books and magazines available in your home. Spend time reading and communicate to your child that reading is important—and enjoyable. Read aloud to your child every day if you can, and don't stop just because she reaches a certain age.

6. Create a home library of reference books. Include a current dictionary, thesaurus, world almanac, book of world records, book of facts, book of quotations, and a one-volume encyclopedia, for starters. Add reference books on topics that interest your child. If you have a home computer, you might purchase an encyclopedia on CD-ROM. If you have an Internet connection, you have access to many online encyclopedias.

7. Make your home a fun-filled and creative place to be. Listen to music. Hang prints and posters on the walls. Put on family skits and plays. Encourage and affirm each other's talents.

8. Support your child's passionate interests. Provide books and magazines on topics that interest her. (Let her have her own library card as soon as she can sign her name.) Look for related Web sites and explore them together. Introduce your child to other people who share her passions.

9. Ask your child about her school experiences. Really listen to what she says. (See page 202.) Stay in touch with your child's teacher, and attend as many parent-teacher conferences and school events as you possibly can. Consider bringing your child to parent-teacher conferences. (Why not, if the conferences are about her?) Check with the teacher first to make sure it's okay.

10. Model the importance of a balanced life. (I know first-hand how hard this is, but do your best.) Avoid overscheduling your child. Make sure she has time to just be a kid.

11. Whenever possible, let your child solve her own problems. Help her brainstorm solutions, but don't insist that she choose the one you think is best. You'll avoid power struggles and build self-reliance and responsibility in your child.

Adolescence

1. This is a high-pressure time for conformity, especially for gifted girls. Adolescents struggle to find a balance between the need to be accepted and the need to be themselves. Give your child all of the support, encouragement, love, and understanding you possibly can. Sometimes that means just listening.

2. Your child may need help organizing his busy life and meeting his many commitments, including school, sports, service projects, other outside activities, and maybe a part-time job. Teach him how to prioritize, schedule, follow through—and let go.

3. Watch for signs of the "imposter syndrome." Especially during adolescence, a time of intense self-awareness and self-criticism, many gifted kids wonder, "Am I really that smart?" They may deny or bury their talents because they're afraid of being "found out" and they're desperate to fit in.

Think of the many things you like and admire about your child, then tell him. Reinforce his self-esteem with sincere and specific comments.

4. Is it true that gifted kids are more prone to suicide than other kids? It really doesn't matter. If you observe signs of depression in your child—such as changes in behavior, sleeping, or eating habits, falling grades, withdrawal from normal activities, or giving away personal belongings—seek professional help immediately. Also stay alert for signs of eating disorders, which may be more common in gifted children and are not limited to girls.

5. Your child isn't really a child any longer, so don't treat him like one. You can avoid many power struggles by letting him make many of his own choices. Tell him that if he wants your opinion or advice, he can ask for it. It's amazing how often children will ask if we give them that option instead of a lecture.

6. During the summer before your child starts high school, help him obtain college catalogs from schools he might want to attend. Ask him to pay special attention to the entrance requirements and keep them in mind as he plans his high-school experience.

7. Help your child discover the possibilities offered by your school or state for completing high school in less than the required time. Don't worry about sending him away to college at a very young age; perhaps he can take several semesters worth of introductory courses at local community colleges and postpone entrance to a university program until he is a bit older. He can also wait to formally graduate with his friends and go to college when they do.

SUMMARY

In an article written for the Gifted Development Center in Denver, Colorado, which she directs, Dr. Linda Silverman offers parents comfort and reassurance. With her permission, I'll end with her wise words.*

> Gifted children are expensive and time-consuming. They usually need less sleep than you do, ask more questions than you can answer, want 100 percent of your attention 24 hours a day, have obsessive hobbies, are unstimulated by the school curriculum, react intensely to everything, endlessly long for a best friend who understands them completely, hold perfectionistic standards for themselves and you, want to know the meaning of life when other children only want to know how to tie their shoes, and keep their bedrooms in a condition you can never show company. If you have three or more of them and there's only one or two of you, you're outnumbered. In order to be the perfect parent, you need unlimited funds, unlimited patience, an encyclopedic mind, and someone to sleep for you.
>
> But don't despair. Gifted children grow up even better with imperfect parents than with perfect ones. Eminent adults rarely came from peaceful homes

* Used with permission of Linda Silverman, Ph.D.

where all their needs were met; they came from families that exploded and made up often; that shared their interests; that stimulated their thinking; that recognized and encouraged their abilities; that loved them a whole lot; and that had faith in them. If you find yourself exhausted, remember that some day your-daughter-the-doctor or your-son-the-artist will have you to thank. No matter what schools you put them in, it is their home life that determines what they do with their lives. Trust your intuitive judgment abut their needs; no one knows them better than you do. Gifted children really enrich your family life. They have a great sense of humor and their development is so remarkable that they're exciting to watch grow. They grow up fast, so enjoy their childhood while you can.

REFERENCES AND RESOURCES

See also the References and Resources for Chapter 1, especially under Giftedness.

Parenting

Alvino, James. "Considerations and Strategies for Parenting the Gifted Child." Storrs, CT: NRC/GT, 1995. Practical suggestions for interacting with gifted children at home.
—— *Parents' Guide to Raising a Gifted Child* (Boston: Little, Brown and Company, 1996) and *Parents' Guide to Raising a Gifted Toddler* (Boston: Little, Brown and Company, 1989). General information on parenting gifted kids.

Armstrong, Thomas. *Awakening Your Child's Natural Genius.* Los Angeles: J. P. Tarcher, 1991. Through practical suggestions and activities, the author shows how parents can play a pivotal role in helping children develop their gifts and describes how to encourage the child's school to provide the kinds of experiences all children need.

Barkley, Russell A., and Christine M. Benton. *Your Defiant Child: 8 Steps to Better Behavior.* New York: Guilford Press, 1998. Although there is a difference between the gifted highly verbal youngster and defiant behaviors, tips in this book may be helpful in dealing with this issue.

Betts, George, and Maureen Neihart. "Profiles of the Gifted and Talented." *Gifted Child Quarterly* 32:2, 248–53, 1988. Six profiles of theoretical types of gifted and talented children are offered including (1) the successful gifted, (2) the divergently gifted, (3) the "underground" gifted (who want to hide their giftedness), (4) the dropouts, (5) the double-labeled (with physical or emotional handicaps) gifted student, and (6) the autonomous learner.

Birely, Marlene. *Crossover Children: A Sourcebook for Helping the Learning Disabled/Gifted Child.* Reston, VA: Council for Exceptional Children, 1995. Addresses the educational needs of students who are gifted and have learning disabilities.

Bloom, Benjamin, ed. *Developing Talent in Young People.* New York: Ballantine Books, 1985. Describes the influences talented people have in common.

Campbell, J.R. *Raising Your Child to Be Gifted: Successful Parents Speak!* Cambridge, MA: Brookline Books, 1995. Specific, concrete strategies for nurturing giftedness distilled from interviews with more than 10,000 parents of gifted children in the U.S. and other countries.

Carroll, James. *Helping Gifted Children Succeed at Home and at School: A Comprehensive Resource for Parents and Teachers.* Manassas, VA: Gifted Education Press, 1997.

Celebrating Gifts and Talents. A 9-minute video that explains various services available for gifted students and some of the frustrations gifted kids face as students. From the National Association for Gifted Children (NAGC), Washington, DC, (202) 785-4268 (www.nagc.org).

Channing L. Bete Co., Inc. (800) 477-4776 (www.channing-bete.com). Publications for parents on numerous topics.

Clark, Barbara. *Growing Up Gifted: Developing the Talent and Potential of Children at Home and at School.* 5th ed. Paramus, NJ: Charles E. Merrill, 1997. The definitive textbook in gifted education.

Cline, Foster, and Jim Fay. *Parenting with Love and Logic.* Colorado Springs, CO: Pinon Press, 1990. Excellent, practical, easy-to-use parenting tips. For more information, visit the Web site (www.loveandlogic.com).

Cohen, Lenora M., and E. Frydenberg. *Coping for Capable Kids: Strategies for Parents, Teachers, and Students and Strategies for Students.* Waco, TX: Prufrock Press, 1996. Designed to help gifted children, their parents, and teachers consider a variety of coping strategies for dealing with their concerns. It is uniquely formatted into two inverse parts. One part is written for teachers and parents, and the other part is specifically designed for adolescents and preadolescents.

Davis, Gary A., and Sylvia B. Rimm. *Education of the Gifted and Talented.* 4th ed. Needham Heights, MA: Allyn & Bacon, 1997. A standard introductory textbook in gifted education.

Dinkmeyer, Don Sr., Gary D. McKay, and Don Dinkmeyer Jr. *The Parent's Handbook: Systematic Training for Effective Parenting (STEP).* Circle Pines, MN: American Guidance Service, 1997. Dinkmeyer Sr. invented STEP, and it is used by many parents. Active listening is described here.

Dinkmeyer, Don, and Lewis Losoncy. *The Skills of Encouragement: Bringing Out the Best in Yourself and Others.* New York: St. Lucia Press, 1995. Learn how to replace praise, which reinforces perfectionism, with encouragement, which facilitates risk-taking.

Ellis, Albert. *How to Raise an Emotionally Healthy, Happy Child.* North Hollywood, CA: Wilshire Book Company, 1985. Contact the Albert Ellis Institute at (212) 535-0822 (www.rebt.org) for more materials on how to teach yourself and your children to think and behave in a rational manner, which means you no longer blame other people or events for what happens to you.

Faber, Adele, and Elaine Mazlish. *How to Talk So Kids Will Listen and Listen So Kids Will Talk.* 20th ed. New York: Avon, 1999. Popular for more than 20 years, this book teaches adults how to communicate more effectively with their children.

Feldman, David Henry, and Lynn T. Goldsmith. *Nature's Gambit: Child Prodigies and the Development of Human Potential.* New York: Teachers College Press, 1991. Reports on a 10-year study of six child prodigies whose talents are manifested in writing, music, and mathematics.

Galbraith, Judy. *You Know Your Child Is Gifted When . . . A Beginner's Guide to Life on the Bright Side.* Minneapolis, Free Spirit Publishing, 2000. Information, advice, and good humor for parents of young gifted children. A quick and easy read.

Greenspan, Stanley I., and Jacqueline Salmon. *The Challenging Child: Understanding, Raising, and Enjoying the Five "Difficult" Types of Children.* Reading, MA: Addison-Wesley Longman Inc., 1995. Ways to deal effectively with children who seem to always need to be in control.

Halsted, Judith Wynn. *Some of My Best Friends Are Books: Guiding Gifted Readers from Pre-School to High School.* Rev. ed. Scottsdale, AZ: Gifted Psychology Press, 1994. This guide proposes that by reading and discussing books with children, parents and teachers can meet two needs in one pleasurable activity. Books can provide a focus for nonthreatening discussions and improve children's self-awareness. Indexes to the annotated bibliography include author, title, and category. *Examples:* identity, relationships with others, perfectionism.

Knopper, D. *Parent Education: Parents as Partners.* Boulder, CO: Open Space Communications, 1994. A slender book, written especially for parents, that provides information on raising gifted children.

Miller, Alice. *The Drama of the Gifted Child: The Search for the True Self.* Rev. ed. New York: Basic Books, 1996. A poignant look at the super-sensitive world of gifted children.

National Parent Information Network (NPIN) (http://npin.org). A project of the ERIC system, which is administered by the National Library of Education in the U.S. Department of Education. Learn from the information in the Virtual Library; try out the Parents AskERIC question-answering service. Type *gifted* in one of the Search windows for a lengthy list of articles about parenting gifted children.

Parenting for High Potential. Quarterly magazine published by the National Association for Gifted Children (NAGC), Washington, DC, (202) 785-4268 (www.nagc.org).

Piirto, Jane. *Talented Children and Adults: Their Development and Education.* New York: MacMillan/Merrill, 1994. This comprehensive introduction to the characteristics and education of the gifted and talented takes a lifespan approach, focusing on factors that encourage talent from birth through adulthood.

—— *Understanding Those Who Create.* 2nd ed. Scottsdale, AZ: Great Potential Press, 1998. A unique perspective on the study of creativity, with chapters on the biography of talented individuals.

Rein, RaeLynne, and Rachel Rein. *How to Develop Your Child's Gifts and Talents During the Elementary Years.* Rev. 2nd ed. Los Angeles: Lowell House, 1994. Tips for parents of kids ages 6–12.

Rimm, Sylvia. *Keys to Parenting the Gifted Child.* Hauppauge, NY: Barrons Educational Series, 1994. How to work with schools, manage problems, and advocate for your child.

——*Why Bright Kids Get Poor Grades and What You Can Do About It.* New York: Crown Publishing, 1995. Describes how family interactions can create and maintain underachievement patterns in school. Touches somewhat on school-based issues.

Saunders, Jacqueline, and Pamela Espeland. *Bringing Out the Best: A Resource Guide for Parents of Young Gifted Children.* Minneapolis, Free Spirit Publishing, 1991. Information and suggestions for coming to terms with giftedness, parenting a gifted child, and coping with the schools.

Smutny, Joan, Kathryn Veenker, and Stephen Veenker. *Your Gifted Child: How to Recognize and Develop the Special Talents in Your Child from Birth to Age Seven.* New York: Ballantine Books, 1991. Another great resource for parenting very young children with an emphasis on maintaining their creative behaviors.

Smutny, Joan Franklin, ed. *The Young Gifted Child: Potential and Promise, an Anthology.* Cresskill, NJ: Hampton Press, 1998. An outstanding collection of articles by experts on young gifted children.

Stone, Nancy. *Gifted Is Not a Dirty Word: Thoughts About Being Bright in an Average World.* Irvine, CA: Technicom, 1989. Tips on how to have positive attitudes about being exceptionally capable.

Strip, Carol, and Gretchen Hirsch. *Helping Gifted Children Soar: A Practical Guide for Parents and Teachers.* Scottsdale, AZ: Gifted Psychology Press, 2000. A book for parents and teachers who know very little about the field of gifted education. Also available in Spanish under the title *Ayudando a Niños Dotados Volar.*

Sullo, Robert A. *Teach Them to Be Happy.* Rev. ed. Chapel Hill, NC: New View Publications, 1993. Based on the work of Dr William Glasser, this book helps readers understand and apply the principles of Reality Therapy.

Tolan, Stephanie. "Helping Your Highly Gifted Child." ERIC EC Digest #E477, 1990 (www.eric.ed.gov).

Understanding Our Gifted. A journal published by Open Space Communications, Boulder, CO, (800) 494-6178 (www.our-gifted.com).

Walker, Sally. *The Survival Guide for Parents of Gifted Kids.* Minneapolis, Free Spirit Publishing, 1991. Information about giftedness, gifted education, problems, personality traits, and more from an educator of gifted kids and their parents.

Warren, Sandra. *Advocating for Your Gifted Child.* A 40-minute video helps you and other parents of gifted youngsters understand parenting and advocacy issues. Available at: www.arliebooks.com.

—— *Being Gifted: The Gift.* A 13-minute video that presents basic information about what it's like to be a gifted child.

Webb, James. *Parenting Successful Children.* A 52-minute video of tips on raising children in our high-speed society. Scottsdale, AZ: Great Potential Press.

Webb, James, Stephanie Tolan, and Elizabeth Meckstroth. *Guiding the Gifted Child: A Practical Source for Parents and Teachers.* Scottsdale, AZ: Great Potential Press 1996. Tips on dealing with the various issues that accompany the challenges of parenting gifted children.

Winebrenner, Susan. *Advocating for Your Gifted Child* (40 minutes) and *Parenting Gifted Children* (60 minutes). Two videos to use on your own or at meetings of parent advocacy groups. The first is a dramatization of how parents can advocate for what their gifted children need at school; the second is a video of a talk I gave to parents. (517) 592-8857 (www.susanwinebrenner.com).

Books to Share with Gifted Kids

Adderholdt, Miriam, and Jan Goldberg. *Perfectionism: What's Bad About Being Too Good?* Rev. ed. Minneapolis, Free Spirit Publishing, 1999. For all parents of kids, and the kids themselves, who believe that being less than perfect is intolerable.

Bottner, Barbara. *The World's Greatest Expert on Absolutely Everything...Is Crying.* New York: Dell Publishers, 1984.

Cosgrove, Stephen. *Persnickety.* New York: Price, Stern, Sloan, 1988.

Flanigan, Beverly. *Forgiving Yourself: A Step-by-Step Guide to Making Peace with Your Mistakes and Getting on with Your Life.* New York: Macmillan, 1997.

Foltz-Jones, Charlotte. *Mistakes That Worked: 40 Familiar Inventions and How They Came to Be.* Upland, PA: DIANE Publishing Co., 1998.

Galbraith, Judy. *The Gifted Kids' Survival Guide For Ages 10 & Under.* 3rd rev. ed. Minneapolis, Free Spirit Publishing, 2009. Written to and for gifted kids, invaluable for their parents and teachers.

—— and Jim Delisle. *The Gifted Kids' Survival Guide: A Teen Handbook.* Rev. ed. Minneapolis, Free Spirit Publishing, 1996. Also essential for parents as well as gifted teens themselves.

Goldberg, M. Hirsh. *The Blunder Book: Colossal Errors, Minor Mistakes and Surprising Slip-ups That Have Changed the Course of History.* New York: HarperTrade, 1988.

Grier, Roosevelt. *Rosey Grier's All American Heroes: Today's Multicultural Success Stories.* New York: MasterMedia Publishing Co., 1993.

Hermes, Patricia. *I Hate Being Gifted.* New York: Pocket Books, 1992.

Pringle, Laurence. *The Earth Is Flat and Other Great Mistakes.* New York: Morrow/Avon, 1995.

Schultz, Robert A., and James R. Delisle. *Smart Talk* and *More Than a Test Score.* Minneapolis, Free Spirit Publishing, 2006, 2007. How gifted children and teens think and feel about school, friends, their families, and the future—in their own words.

Learning Styles and Learning Challenges

A.D.D. WareHouse, Plantation, FL, (800) 233-9273 (www.addwarehouse.com). Request their catalog of materials for parenting and teaching kids with learning challenges.

Armstrong, Thomas. *In Their Own Way: Discovering and Encouraging Your Child's Personal Learning Style.* New York: Putnam/J. P. Tarcher, 1987.

Axline, Virginia M. *Dibs in Search of Self.* Reissued. New York: Ballantine Books, 1990. The psychiatrist who invented play therapy helps readers understand the importance of accepting children as they are, rather than with conditions about how we want them to be. Based on a true story.

CHADD (Children and Adults with Attention-Deficit/Hyperactivity Disorder). Contact the national headquarters for information about a chapter near you. (800) 233-4050 (www.chadd.org).

Coil, Carolyn. *Encouraging Achievement.* Marion, IL: Pieces of Learning, 1999.

Dixon, John Philo. *The Spatial Child.* Springfield, IL: Charles C. Thomas, 1983.

Dunn, Rita, Kenneth Dunn, and Donald Treffinger. *Bringing Out the Giftedness in Your Child: Unlocking Your Child's Unique Talents, Strengths, and Potential.* New York: John Wiley and Sons, 1992.

Fadely, Jack L., and Virginia N. Hosler. *Attentional Deficit Disorder in Children and Adolescents.* Springfield, IL: Charles C. Thomas, 1992.

Fisher, Gary, and Rhoda Cummings. *When Your Child Has LD (Learning Differences): A Survival Guide for Parents.* Minneapolis, Free Spirit Publishing, 1995.

Fowler, Mary. *Maybe You Know My Kid: A Parent's Guide to Identifying, Understanding, and Helping Your Child with Attention Deficit Hyperactivity Disorder.* Rev. ed. Secaucus, NJ: Carol/Birch Lane Press, 1999.

Freed, Jeffrey, and Laurie Parsons. *Right-Brained Children in a Left-Brained World: Unlocking the Potential of Your ADD Child.* New York: Simon and Schuster, 1998. If you feel you must help your kids with learning challenges with their homework, read this book so the time you spend with them can focus on compensation strategies rather than content.

Heacox, Diane. *Up from Underachievement: How Teachers, Students, and Parents Can Work Together to Promote Student Success.* Minneapolis, Free Spirit Publishing, 1991.

Irlen Clinic for Perceptual and Learning Development, Long Beach, CA, (800) 554-7536. Ask for referrals to people in your area who can screen children for scotopic sensitivity, which causes some readers to perceive that letters are moving on the printed page.

Khatena, Joe. *Enhancing the Creativity of Gifted Children: A Guide for Parents and Teachers.* Cresskill, NJ: Hampton Press, Inc., 1999.

Koplewicz, Harold S. *It's Nobody's Fault: New Hope and Help for Difficult Children and Their Parents.* New York: Times

Books/Random House, 1996. Discusses situations likely to lead to parental guilt, including ADD, anxiety problems, eating disorders, and school phobia.

Landfried, Steven E. "Educational Enabling: When Protecting Children Fosters Dependence." *PTA Today,* 18–20, May, 1991. Are you "over-helping" your child and making him or her ever more dependent on that help? Landfried helps you break that cycle.

Lavoie, Richard. *How Difficult Can This Be? The F.A.T. City Workshop, Last One Picked...First One Picked On,* and *When the Chips Are Down.* Dr. Richard Lavoie, a specialist in teaching kids with LD, helps you finally understand what learning difficulties are all about and provides concrete suggestions for helping kids develop and use appropriate compensation strategies. These are truly remarkable resources for parents of kids with LD. Available from PBS Video, (800) 531-4727 (www.shoppbs.org).

Lazear, David. *Pathways of Learning: Teaching Students and Parents About Multiple Intelligences.* 2nd ed. Tucson, AZ: Zephyr Press, 2000. Explains the theory of multiple intelligences for parents.

Lee, Christopher, and Shirley Jackson. *Faking It: A Look into the Mind of a Creative Learner.* Portsmouth, NH: Heinemann, 1992. This book, written by a young man with serious learning difficulties, helps people without LD understand what it's like to experience it.

Osman, Betty. *Learning Disabilities and ADHD: A Family Guide to Living and Learning Together.* New York: John Wiley and Sons, 1997.
—— *No One to Play With.* Novato, CA: Academic Therapy Publications, 1996.

Vail, Priscilla L. *Smart Kids with School Problems: Things to Know and Ways to Help.* New York: Dutton/Plume, 1989.

Winebrenner, Susan. *Teaching Kids with Learning Difficulties in the Regular Classroom.* Minneapolis, Free Spirit Publishing, 2005.

Gifted Girls and Gifted Boys

Ellis, Julie, and John Willinsky. *Girls, Women and Giftedness.* Unionville, NY: Trillium Press, 1990.

Hebert, T.P. "Using Biography to Counsel Gifted Young Men." *Journal of Secondary Gifted Education* 6:3, 208–19, 1995. Biographies can help gifted young men deal with issues including underachievement, self-inflicted pressure in athletics, cultural alienation, and father-son relationships. The author suggests biographical works and strategies for using this approach, with case examples.

Kerr, Barbara. *Smart Girls: A New Psychology of Girls, Women, and Giftedness.* Rev. ed. Scottsdale, AZ: Great Potential Press, 1997.
—— and Sanford Cohn. *Smart Boys: Talent, Masculinity, and the Search for Meaning.* Scottsdale, AZ: Great Potential Press, 2000.

New Moon: The Magazine for Girls and Their Dreams, Duluth, MN, (800) 381-4743 (www.newmoon.com).

Pipher, Mary. *Reviving Ophelia: Saving the Selves of Adolescent Girls.* New York: Ballantine Press, 1999.

Program for the Exceptionally Gifted, Mary Baldwin College, Staunton, VA, (540) 887-7039 (www.mbc.edu/peg). There is evidence that gifted girls who attend all-girls schools are more likely to actualize their learning potential.

Reis, Sally Morgan. *Work Left Undone: Choices and Compromises of Talented Females.* Mansfield Center, CT: Creative Learning Press, 1998.

Rimm, Sylvia, Sara Rimm-Kaufman, and Ilonna Rimm. *See Jane Win: The Rimm Report on How 1000 Girls Became Successful Women.* NewYork: Crown Publishing Group, 1999.

Smutny, Joan. *Gifted Girls.* Bloomington, IN: Phi Delta Kappa Educational Foundation, 1998.

Subotnik, Rena, et al. *Remarkable Women: Perspectives on Female Talent Development.* Creskill, NJ: Hampton Press, 1996.

Education and Advocacy

Berger, Sandra L. *College Planning for Gifted Students.* Rev. ed. Reston, VA: Council for Exceptional Children, 1998. Presents a six-year plan to guide gifted students to making the best possible college selection.
—— "Supporting Gifted Education Through Advocacy." ERIC EC Digest #E494, 1990 (www.eric.ed.gov).

"Charting a New Course in Gifted Education." A special double issue of the *Peabody Journal of Education* (72: 3&4). Philadelphia, PA: Lawrence Erlbaum Associates, 1997. (800) 354-1420.

Durden, William, and Arne E. Tangherlini. *Smart Kids: How Academic Talents are Developed and Nurtured in America.* Kirkland, WA: Hogrefe and Huber Publishers, 1994.

Educational Opportunity Guide: A Directory of Programs for the Gifted. Durham, NC: Duke University Talent Identification Program (TIP). Updated annually; look in your library for the most recent version. For information about TIP's various programs and publications, visit the Web site (www.tip.duke.edu).

International Reading Association, Newark, DE, (800) 336-READ (www.reading.org). Provides lists of books for various ages and interests.

Karnes, Frances A., and R.G. Marquardt. *Gifted Children and the Law: Mediation, Due Process, and Court Cases.* Dayton, OH: Ohio Psychology Press, 1991. Compiles, analyzes, and synthesizes legal actions related to identifying and providing services for gifted and talented youth.
—— *Gifted Children and Legal Issues in Education: Parents' Stories of Hope.* Dayton, OH: Ohio Psychology Press, 1991. A report on the trials and tribulations of parents who have faced problems obtaining an appropriate education for their gifted children.

Scheiber, Barbara, and Jeanne Talpers. *Unlocking Potential: College and Other Choices for LD People: A Step-by-Step Guide.* Bethesda, MD: Adler and Adler, 1987.

Schroeder-Davis, Stephen. *Coercive Egalitarianism: A Study of Discrimination Against Gifted Children.* Manassas, VA: Gifted Education Press, 1993. Describes how gifted kids are forced to settle for mediocrity.

Singal, Daniel J. "The Other Crisis in American Education." *Atlantic Monthly* 268:5, 59–74 (November, 1991). A moving article that documents how daily learning for gifted students is compromised in the interests of helping students who struggle to learn. Because it was published in a consumer magazine (as opposed to an education journal), it has more credibility with policymakers.

Smutny, Joan Franklin. *Stand Up for Your Gifted Child: How to Make the Most of Kids' Strengths at School and at Home.* Minneapolis, Free Spirit Publishing, 2000.
—— Sally Yahnke Walker, and Elizabeth A. Meckstroth. *Teaching Young Gifted Children in the Regular Classroom: Identifying, Nurturing, and Challenging Ages 4–9.* Minneapolis, Free Spirit Publishing, 1997.

U.S. Department of Education, Office of Educational Research and Improvement. *National Excellence: The Case for Developing America's Talent.* Washington, DC: 1993. A conclusive, easy-to-understand report on gifted children's educational needs. Call (877) 4-ED-PUBS to request a copy, or read it on the Web (www.ed.gov/pubs/DevTalent/toc.html).

Warren, Sandra. *Parents' Guide to Teachers of the Gifted—Teachers' Guide to Parents of the Gifted.* Rev. ed. Unionville, NY: Royal Fireworks Press, 1999. Helps parents select teachers who know how to nurture gifted students. (845) 726-4444.

Support, Counseling, and Other Resources

American Mensa, Arlington, TX, (817) 607-0060 (www.us.mensa.org). Support, resources, and local groups for those who score in the top 2 percent of the population on a standardized intelligence test.

Colangelo, Nicholas, and Gary A. Davis. *Handbook of Gifted Education.* 2nd ed. Needham Heights, MA: Allyn & Bacon, 1996.

Delisle, Jim, and Judy Galbraith. *When Gifted Kids Don't Have All the Answers: How to Meet Their Social and Emotional Needs.* Minneapolis, Free Spirit Publishing, 2002.

Education Consulting Service (susanwinebrenner.com). Please visit my Web site for updated information.

Milgram, Roberta, ed. *Counseling Gifted and Talented Children: A Guide for Teachers, Counselors, and Parents.* Westport, CT: Ablex Publishing, 1991.

Silverman, Linda. *Counseling the Gifted and Talented.* Denver, Love Publishing, 1993. Linda Silverman is director of the Gifted Development Center in Denver, CO, which provides testing and counseling services, as well as referrals to counselors who can work with gifted kids in other parts of the country. (303) 837-8378 (www.gifteddevelopment.com).

Webb, James T., and Arlene DeVries. *The SENG Model: Gifted Parent Groups.* Poughquag, NY: Great Potential Press, 1998. Contact SENG for information on training parents of gifted children to conduct support groups for each other. (845) 797-5054 (www.sengifted.org).

Organizations

See Appendix B: Additional Resources.

Web Sites

See Appendix B: Additional Resources.

CONCLUSION

The Introduction to this book begins with this question: "Of all the students you are teaching in a given class, which group do you think will probably learn the least this year?" You may remember the answer: "It may surprise you to find that in a class that has a range of abilities (and which class doesn't?), it is the *most* able, rather than the least able, who will learn less new material than any other group."

I feel confident that won't be the case in your class. If you have read this book, tried some of the strategies and techniques, checked out some of the references and resources, talked with your colleagues, and rolled up your sleeves, you're ready to:

- Challenge all of your students.
- Give your students opportunities to demonstrate that they already know what you're about to teach, or can learn it in much less time than you have allotted.
- Use compacting.
- Create instructional groups that are flexible and change their composition depending on the content.
- Allow students whose ability exceeds grade-level expectations in any area of learning to be grouped together for work on appropriately differentiated activities.
- Offer meaningful choices whenever possible.
- Focus on open-ended tasks.
- Encourage independent research based on topics in which students are passionately interested.
- Understand and apply differentiated assessment and grading options.
- Be sensitive to what gifted kids need in cooperative learning situations.
- Understand and support cluster grouping.
- Take advantage of opportunities to learn more about gifted kids and their exceptional learning needs.

Gifted students whose teachers make opportunities available for compacting and differentiation in all subject areas are generally happy, productive students. They enjoy school and learning. They don't suffer from the Jesse James syndrome.

I hope you are as excited about using these strategies as I am about sharing them with you. Writing this revised edition of *Teaching Gifted Kids in the Regular Classroom* has been much less stressful than writing the first edition. I now have ample evidence that these strategies are being used by thousands of teachers to benefit tens of thousands of students.

In the years since this book was originally published, I have traveled to more than 40 states, Canada, Puerto Rico, and Australia. I have seen first-hand how teachers everywhere are reaching and helping countless kids. I can't thank you enough for taking the necessary risks to give your gifted students what they need.

I would love to hear from you. Please send me your feedback about this book and your experiences with the strategies presented here. You can reach me in care of my publisher:

Free Spirit Publishing
217 Fifth Avenue North, Suite 200
Minneapolis, MN 55401-1299
help4kids@freespirit.com
www.freespirit.com

Appendix A
Language Arts Activities

CATEGORIES CHALLENGE

All students enjoy this competitive activity, so I'm including two versions: one for the entire class and one for gifted students.

Directions for the Entire Class

1. Create a chart for students to use. (See the sample chart on page 220.) Write letters in the left column and categories across the top. Choose categories that represent topics and materials with which the students are already familiar. The letters will be the first letters of their responses. *Examples:* For the Birds category, responses might include Mallard, Starling, Rooster, Tern, and Parrot.

2. Divide the class into teams of 4–5 students. Tell them to work together to complete as many boxes on the chart as designated time allows (usually 15–20 minutes).

3. At the end of the designated time, collect the charts. Tell the class that the team with the most correct responses is the winner—and they get to decide which team that is. Don't give them the correct answers. Instead, read the answers aloud and have the students decide if they're correct. Since all teams must rely on each other's fairness in this step, students are usually generous in their judgments.

Directions for Gifted Students

1. Create a chart for students to use. (See the sample chart on page 220). Write letters in the left column and categories across the top. Choose categories that represent topics and materials with which the students are generally *not* familiar. The letters will be the first letters of their responses. *Examples:* For the Poets' Last Names category, responses might include Marvell (Andrew), Paz (Octavio), Dickinson (Emily), Eliot (T. S.), and Frost (Robert).

2. Divide the students into teams of 4. Explain that on each team, every student should pick one of the 4 categories, then work alone to complete as many boxes in that column as designated time allows (usually 20–30 minutes). Students will probably need to use reference materials or the Internet to complete their categories.

3. When everyone is finished, the students work as a team to complete the remaining (fifth) category—the one no one chose to work on alone, probably because it's the one they know least about.

4. Use the same scoring method as described above for the entire class.

Variation: You might want to designate one category or letter on the chart Student Choice.

ACADEMIC BOWL

An enjoyable game for your Great Friday Afternoon Event (see page 123) or any regularly scheduled time for celebrating the week's achievements.

Preparing for Play

1. Prepare two sets of questions.

- Entry questions are worth 5 points each and may represent previously learned material the class is reviewing. Or you may choose to use easier trivia

★ CATEGORIES CHALLENGE: FOR THE ENTIRE CLASS ★

	Birds	Book Titles	Mammals	U. S. States	Teachers
M					
S					
R					
T					
P					

★ CATEGORIES CHALLENGE: FOR GIFTED STUDENTS ★

	U. S. Presidents	World Rivers	Poets' Last Names	Precious Stones	Inventors
M					
P					
D					
E					
F					

questions, such as those found in many popular games.

- Bonus questions are worth 10 points each and may represent material the class is still trying to master. Or you may select more difficult trivia questions from popular games.

Many students enjoy opportunities to create questions and answers for this game during time they buy back from regular classroom activities.

2. Divide the class into heterogeneous teams of 4–6 students. Each team should have one or two high-ability students and one student who has difficulty learning, with the balance drawn from those considered to be more average learners.

Teams stay together for 4–6 weeks, until everyone has had the chance to be captain. The role of captain rotates each week.

3. Set and describe the conditions for play.

- You, the teacher, ask all of the questions and keep track of each team's score privately. You won't display the scores for all to see until the game has ended. (This gives you some flexibility in calling on teams to keep the outcome somewhat even.)
- The team that answers an entry question correctly earns the right to attempt the more difficult bonus questions and earn additional points.
- No points are lost for incorrect answers. The only way students can lose points is by making uncomplimentary remarks or gestures to other students, or by talking with teammates at times other than when they are supposed to confer.

Playing the Game

1. Start by asking an entry question. Students raise their hands individually and you call on someone. He or she has 5 seconds to give an answer without any help from other students. If the student answers correctly, award 5 points to that team. If the student answers incorrectly, call on someone from another team. No points are lost for incorrect answers.

2. When a student answers an entry question correctly, give that team the opportunity to answer a bonus question. The team may confer quietly for 15 seconds, and the answer may be stated only by the team captain. (Because the role of team captain rotates, even shy students can eventually become part of the action.)

3. If the captain answers correctly, award 10 points to that team. If the captain answers incorrectly, call on students from other teams until someone gives the right answer. Award 5 points to that team. Again, no points are lost for incorrect answers.

4. At the end of the designated time (usually 30 minutes), announce the points earned by each team. The team with the most points wins.

ALPHABET SOUP

Kids who like playing with words will happily spend time figuring out these challenging alphabet puzzles.

Give students copies of the Alphabet Soup handout on page 222. Allow them to work on these puzzles for several days, perhaps during spare moments or times they buy back for choice activities. Tell them that if there are any puzzles they simply can't solve, they may come to you for clues. Say that students who finish early may create their own puzzles, and you'll consider adding them to the next Alphabet Soup handout.

Following are clues and solutions, numbered to correspond to the handout.

1. CLUE: a book
   SOLUTION: *500 Hats of Bartholomew Cubbins* (by Dr. Seuss)
2. CLUE: a nursery rhyme
   SOLUTION: 3 Little Kittens
3. CLUE: a superstition
   SOLUTION: 7 years of bad luck for breaking a mirror
4. CLUE: a measurement
   SOLUTION: 2000 pounds in a ton
5. CLUE: a musical
   SOLUTION: 76 trombones led the big parade
6. CLUE: communication
   SOLUTION: 10 digits in a telephone number (including the area code)
7. CLUE: politics
   SOLUTION: 50 senators in the United States Senate
8. CLUE: ancient history
   SOLUTION: 3 parts into which ancient Gaul was divided
9. CLUE: transportation
   SOLUTION: 5 tires on a car (including the spare in the trunk)
10. CLUE: a saying
    SOLUTION: 1 rotten apple in every barrel

★ ALPHABET SOUP ★

Directions: Solve the following alphabet puzzles. You may take several days to work on them. If there are any you can't figure out, ask the teacher for clues.

Example: 20 = Q. (A. V. or M.)
CLUE: a game
SOLUTION: 20 Questions (Animal, Vegetable, or Mineral)

1. 500 = H. of B. C. (by D. S.)
2. 3 = L. K.
3. 7 = Y. of B. L. for B. a M.
4. 2000 = P. in a T.
5. 76 = T. L. the B. P.
6. 10 = D. in a T. N. (including the A. C.)
7. 100 = S. in the U. S. S.
8. 3 = P. into which A. G. was D.
9. 5 = T. on a C. (including the S. in the T.)
10. 1 = R. A. in E. B.
11. 3 = S. Y. O. at the O. B. G.
12. 9 = S. in T. T. T.
13. 15 = M. on a D. M. C.
14. 7 = D. with S. W.
15. 9 = J. of the U. S. S. C.
16. 6 = P. on a P. T.
17. 4 = S. on a V.
18. 20 = C. in a P.
19. 66 = B. of the B. (in the K. J. V.)
20. 88 = P. K.

11. CLUE: a sport
SOLUTION: 3 strikes you're out at the old ball game

12. CLUE: a game
SOLUTION: 9 squares in Tic-Tac-Toe

13. CLUE: a song or chant
SOLUTION: 15 men on a dead man's chest

14. CLUE: a fairy tale
SOLUTION: 7 dwarves with Snow White

15. CLUE: government
SOLUTION: 9 justices of the United States Supreme Court

16. CLUE: a sport
SOLUTION: 6 players on a polo team

17. CLUE: music
SOLUTION: 4 strings on a violin (or viola)

18. CLUE: a bad habit
SOLUTION: 20 cigarettes in a package

19. CLUE: religions
SOLUTION: 66 books of the Bible (in the King James Version)

20. CLUE: music
SOLUTION: 88 piano keys

TRANSMOGRIFICATIONS

This intriguing activity can be done in two ways. Either students can use a thesaurus to translate simple sayings into complex language, or they can use a dictionary to translate complex versions of sayings (created by you or other students) into their simple original language. Following are several examples of complex versions.

For the Primary Grades

All of the following are based on the first lines of well-known nursery rhymes.

1. Scintillate, scintillate, asteroid minific. (Twinkle, twinkle, little star.)

2. Bleat, bleat, ebony ewe. (Baa, baa, black sheep.)

3. Petite lad cerulean, approach and huff your trumpet. (Little Boy Blue, come blow your horn.)

4. Croon a ditty of six coins. (Sing a song of sixpence.)

5. A petite swine traveled to the retail stores. (This little piggy went to market.)

6. John and Gillian ascended the mound. (Jack and Jill went up the hill.)

7. The capital of England's metal structure is collapsing. (London Bridge is falling down.)

8. John S. could ingest no gristle; his mate could ingest no gaunt. (Jack Spratt could eat no fat; his wife could eat no lean.)

9. Loop circularly the roseate, a cloth holder brimming with blossoms. (Ring around the rosy, a pocket full of posies.)

10. Sway-a-bye infant child, on the loftiest conifer. (Rocky-a-bye baby, on the tree top.)

For the Upper Grades

All of the following are based on well-known sayings or adages.

1. Unpunctuality is preferable to failure to arrive. (Better late than never.)

2. An excess of forward motion results in careless squandering. (Haste makes waste.)

3. Consistent dedication to one's career-related pursuit without interludes of disportment establishes John as a doltish shaveling. (All work and no play makes Jack a dull boy.)

4. Immaculateness is proximate to rectitude. (Cleanliness is next to godliness.)

5. Benevolent deeds commence in one's domicile. (Charity begins at home.)

6. The stylus is more potent than the bayonet. (The pen is mightier than the sword.)

7. Male cadavers are incapable of relating any testimony. (Dead men tell no tales.)

8. Neophytes' serendipity. (Beginners' luck.)

9. The vegetation perpetually has a deeper hue when situated across a style. (The grass is always greener on the other side of the fence.)

10. A pair of skulls is more valuable than half of two. (Two heads are better than one.)

SILLY NILLIES

In this challenging activity, students make up two-word definitions for phrases provided. In their definitions, the words must rhyme and have the same number of syllables.

Give students copies of the Silly Nillies handout on page 225. Don't reveal any solutions until everyone has finished. Following is a list of possible solutions. Be sure to allow for other solutions the students can justify.

Invite students to create their own Silly Nillies for future lists.

1. better sweater
2. wild child
3. wrong song
4. wee key
5. fat cat
6. sassy lassie
7. sky pie
8. dragon wagon
9. thinner dinner
10. funny money
11. flower power
12. rational national
13. faster plaster
14. precise device
15. fission mission
16. scare pair
17. fight knight
18. pop top
19. hobby lobby
20. long songs

★ SILLY NILLIES ★

Directions: Make up two-word definitions for these phrases. The words must rhyme and have the same number of syllables. *Examples:* An escaped gander is a *loose goose.* Chocolate bars with nuts and caramel are *dandy candy.*

1. An improved wool pullover is a____________________

2. An undisciplined youngster is a ____________________

3. An out-of-tune chorus sings a ____________________

4. A minuscule tool for unlocking things is a____________________

5. An overweight feline is a____________________

6. A girl who talks back to her parents is a____________________

7. Pizza served on an airplane is ____________________

8. A cart to carry a fire-breathing monster is a____________________

9. A meal for someone who is on a serious diet is ____________________

10. Coinage used to purchase items that can't be bought with regular currency is __________

11. A tall, strong rose on a very thick stem has ____________________

12. A citizen who thinks very clearly on politics is a ____________________

13. A worker who finishes walls speedily uses ____________________

14. An instrument that is used only for one specialized task is a____________________

15. Someone who's determined to build an atomic device is on a ____________________

16. Two very ugly monsters make a ____________________

17. A brave soldier on a white horse who saves a town from a dragon is a ____________________

18. A jar lid that comes off with very little effort is a____________________

19. A display of people's handiwork in the registration area of a hotel is a ____________________

20. An opera contains a series of____________________

Appendix B
Additional Resources

Publishers

A.D.D. WareHouse, (800) 233-9273 (www.addwarehouse.com). Materials for teaching and parenting kids with learning challenges.

Albert Ellis Institute (formerly the Institute for Rational-Emotive Therapy), (212) 535-0822 (www.rebt.org). Rational Thinking resources.

Alternative Learning Publications (ALPS), (800) 345-ALPS (www.alpspublishing.com). Many resources for facilitating independent projects and teaching kids to do in-depth research.

Association for Supervision and Curriculum Development (ASCD), (800) 933-ASCD (www.ascd.org). Publishes *Educational Leadership, The Journal of Curriculum and Supervision, Education Update,* newsletters, books, and audio- and videotapes.

Center for Creative Learning (formerly DOK), (941) 342-9928 (www.creativelearning.com). Donald Treffinger and colleagues help teachers use Creative Problem Solving in the classroom.

Center for Gifted Education, The College of William and Mary, (757) 221-2362 (cfge.wm.edu). Publishes curriculum units for gifted students in language arts and science.

Classroom Connect, (800) 825-4420 (corporate.classroom.com). Develops original Web-based curriculum products and professional development programs for K–12 educators.

Council for Exceptional Children (CEC), (888) CDC-SPED (www.cec.sped.org). Source for information about gifted kids with learning difficulties.

Creative Education Foundation, (508) 960-0000 (www.cef-cpsi.org). Home of the Creative Problem-Solving Process for business people and educators. Ask for their Creativity Catalog.

Creative Learning Press, (888) 518-8004 (www.creativelearningpress.com). Unique collection of materials to facilitate Type III research activities.

Creative Publications, (800) 648-2970 (www.wrightgroup.com). Part of the Wright Group, this imprint offers math and critical thinking extensions.

Critical Thinking Books and Software (formerly Midwest Publications), (800) 458-4849 (www.criticalthinking.com). Source for many activities in critical thinking for all ages.

The Curriculum Project, (800) 867-9067 (www.curriculumproject.com). John Samara's Product Guides and Curry/Samara Model (CSM) unit planning.

Discovery Toys, (800) 341-8697 (www.discoverytoysinc.com). Think-It-Through tray activities and other learning toys.

Educational Assessment Service, (800) 795-7466, (www.sylviarimm.com). Sylvia Rimm's materials.

Engine-Uity, Ltd., (800) 877-8718 (www.engine-uity.com). Fabulous array of differentiated units in all subject areas.

Enslow Publishers, Inc., (800) 398-2504 (www.enslow.com). Science projects, social studies, biography, etc.

ETA/Cuisenaire, (800) 445-5985 (www.etacuisenaire.com). Source for Versa-Tiles, cuisenaire, and other hands-on materials for math, science, and reading/language arts.

Free Spirit Publishing, (800) 735-7323 (www.freespirit.com). Books and materials for lifeskills learning, with special emphasis on gifted.

Great Books Foundation, (800) 222-5870 (www.greatbooks.org). Home of Junior Great Books.

Great Potential Press, (877) 954-4200 (www.greatpotentialpress.com). Books for parents, teachers, counselors, and educators of gifted and talented children

Greenhaven Press, (800) 877-4253 (www.galegroup.com/greenhaven). Debate materials.

Interact, (800) 421-4246 (www.interact-simulations.com). Materials for classroom simulations.

Learning to Learn, (616) 249-3983. Learning projects designed by Phil Schlemmer.

Learning Quest, Inc., (760) 431-2232 (www.learning-quest.com). Educational software and instructional materials.

Learning Styles Network, (718) 990-6335 (www.learningstyles.net). Ken and Rita Dunn's resources about learning styles. Ask for CAPS—Contract Activity Packages designed to challenge high-ability learners but which may be modified for other students as well.

Lesson Lab, (800) 348-4474 (www.k12pearson.com). Thinking, problem-based learning, cooperative learning.

LinguiSystems, (800) 776-4332 (www.linguisystems.com). Source for materials about autism, Nonverbal Learning Disorders, Dyslexia and Dysgraphia, and interventions for all kinds of learning difficulties.

Magination Press, (800) 374-2721 (www.maginationpress.com). Books that help children deal with their problems. Magination is an imprint of the Educational Publishing Foundation, a publishing unit of the American Psychological Association (www.apa.org).

Mindware, (800) 999-0398 (www.mindwareonline.com). Creative enrichments.

NewsCurrents, (800) 356-2303 (www.thekustore.com). Weekly current events background and discussion program with filmstrips and teacher's guides. Gifted kids can use this to present news programs to the class.

A.W. Peller and Associates, Inc., (800) 451-7450 (www.awpeller.com). Their Bright Ideas for the Gifted and Talented catalog is a comprehensive collection of materials for gifted and talented students.

Peytral Publication, Inc., (952) 949-8707 (www.peytral.com). Twice-exceptional resources.

Philosophy for Children, (973) 655-4278 (http://cehs.montclair.edu/academic/iapc). Novels and teachers' manuals to teach philosophy to children of all ages.

Pieces of Learning, (800) 729-5137 (www.piecesoflearning.com). Books by Nancy Johnson and others.

PRO-ED, Inc., (800) 897-3202 (www.proedinc.com). Materials for all categories of special education and gifted education.

Professional Associates, (866) 335-1460 (www.kingore.com). Bertie Kingore's company.

Prufrock Press, (800) 998-2208 (www.prufrock.com). Home of periodicals in gifted education including the *Journal of Secondary Gifted Education.* Also distributes many materials for gifted education, including several identification instruments.

Recording for the Blind and Dyslexic, (866) 732-3585 (www.rfbd.org). For gifted kids and others with reading problems.

Royal Fireworks Press, (845) 726-4444. Michael C. Thompson's work; creativity; Bloom's Taxonomy.

Social Studies School Service, (800) 421-4246 (www.socialstudies.com). Multiple catalogs to support social studies learning.

Sunburst Software, (888) 492-8817 (www.sunburst.com). Best collection of educational software.

Teacher Created Materials, (888) 343-4335 (www.teachercreated.com). Materials for all areas of the curriculum.

Zephyr Press, (800) 232-2187 (www.zephyrpress.com). Multiple intelligences and brain games.

Magazines and Journals

Gifted Education Press Quarterly. Newsletter of unique articles by authors often not found in the larger journals. Gifted Education Press, (703) 369-5017 (www.giftedpress.com).

From the National Association for Gifted Children, (202) 785-4268 (www.nagc.org):

- *Gifted Child Quarterly.* Research and practice in gifted education.
- *Parenting for High Potential.* Tips for parenting gifted children.

From Prufrock Press, (800) 998-2208 (www.prufrock.com):

- *Creative Kids.* By and for gifted kids.
- *Gifted Child Today.* For teachers and parents of gifted kids.
- *Journal for the Education of the Gifted.* Analysis and communication of knowledge and research on the gifted and talented. The official publication of the Association for the Gifted (TAG), a division of the Council for Exceptional Children (CEC), published through a cooperative partnership with Prufrock Press.
- *Journal of Secondary Gifted Education.* For teachers and parents of gifted adolescents.

Our Gifted Children. Unique, in-depth essays regarding many aspects of gifted education. Royal Fireworks Press, (845) 726-4444.

Roeper Review. Quarterly thematic issues on topics of interest to gifted children, their teachers, and families. Published by the Roeper School in Bloomfield, Hills, MI, (248) 203-7300 (www.roeper.org/roeperinstitute/roeperreview).

Understanding Our Gifted. Quarterly journal for parents and teachers of gifted children. Open Space Communications, (800) 494-6178 (www.our-gifted.com).

Videos

Celebrating Gifts and Talents. A 9-minute video that explains various services available for gifted students and some of the frustrations gifted kids face as students. From the National Association for Gifted Children (NAGC), Washington, DC, (202) 785-4268 (www.nagc.org).

Challenging the Gifted in the Regular Classroom and *Differentiating Instruction for Mixed Ability Classrooms.* Two videos help teachers provide differentiated learning for gifted students. Available from ASCD, Alexandria, VA, (800) 933-ASCD (www.ascd.org).

Warren, Sandra. www.arliebooks.com. *Advocating for Your Gifted Child.* A 40-minute video helps you and other parents of gifted youngsters understand parenting and advocacy issues.
—— *Being Gifted: The Gift.* A 13-minute video that presents basic information about what it's like to be a gifted child.

Webb, James. *Parenting Successful Children.* A 52-minute video of tips on raising children in our high-speed society. From Great Potential Press, (877) 954-4200 (www.greatpotentialpress.com).

Winebrenner, Susan. (517) 592-8857 (www.susanwinebrenner.com). *Teaching Gifted Kids in the Regular Classroom.* Designed to support a school-based study group of educators who meet together to provide peer support as they learn and apply compacting and differentiation strategies. An 80-minute video demonstrates many of the compacting and differentiation strategies in actual classrooms. A *Discussion Leader's Guide,* assists the person who leads the group.
—— *Advocating for Your Gifted Child* (40 minutes) and *Parenting Gifted Children* (60 minutes).Two videos to use on your own or at meetings of parent advocacy groups. The first is a dramatization of how parents can advocate for what their gifted children need at school; the second is a video of a talk I gave to parents.

Organizations

American Association for Gifted Children at Duke University, Durham, NC, (919) 783-6152 (www.aagc.org). The nation's oldest advocacy organization for gifted children.

The Association for the Gifted (TAG), The Council for Exceptional Children (CEC), Reston, VA, (888) CEC-SPED (www.cec.sped.org). Provides information to professionals and parents about gifted and talented children and their needs. TAG is a division of CEC, and you must be a CEC member to participate.

Center for Gifted at National-Louis University, Glenview, IL, (847) 901-0173 extension 2150 (www.centerforgifted.org). Summer and weekend programs for gifted kids.

Center for Gifted Education, The College of William and Mary, Williamsburg, VA, (757) 221-2362 (cfge.wm.edu). Contact the Center for information about summer institutes, talent searches, conferences, the GiftedNet listserv, and more. Publishes curriculum units and *Gifted and Talented International.*

Center for Talent Development, Northwestern University, Evanston, IL, (847) 491-3782 (www.ctd.northwestern.edu). Talent searches, programs for gifted students during the school year (Saturday Enrichment Program, Letter-Links correspondence courses), summer programs, conferences, and more.

The Connie Belin and Jacqueline N. Blank International Center for Gifted Education and Talent Development, University of Iowa, Iowa City, IA, (800) 336-6463, (www.education.uiowa.edu/belinblank). Talent searches, summer programs, scholarships, assessment, and workshops. Directed by Nicholas Colangelo.

The Council for Exceptional Children (CEC), Reston, VA, (888) CEC-SPED (www.cec.sped.org). The largest international professional organization dedicated to improving educational outcomes for individuals with exceptionalities, students with disabilities, and/or the gifted.

Duke University Talent Identification Program (TIP), Durham, NC, (919) 668-9100, (www.tip.duke.edu). Model programs and services for academically talented students.

Education Program for Gifted Youth (EPGY), Stanford University, (800) 372-3749 (www-epgy.stanford.edu). Offers advanced online courses for students in elementary, middle, and high school in math, physics, English, and computer science.

Future Problem Solving Program, Melbourne, FL, (800) 256-1499 (www.fpsp.org). Center for information about the national Future Problem Solving competition.

Gifted Development Center, Denver, CO, (888) GIFTED1 (www.gifteddevelopment.com). Provides comprehensive testing, referrals to testers in other states, and referrals to counselors who have experience in working with gifted kids and their families.

The Hollingworth Center for Highly Gifted Children, Dover, NH, (www.hollingworth.org). A national volunteer resource and support network for highly gifted children, their families, schools, and communities.

International Baccalaureate Organisation (IBO) (www.ibo.org). A nonprofit educational foundation based in Switzerland. Curriculum and assessment development, teacher training and information seminars, electronic networking, and other educational services for 1,000 participating schools in 100 countries around the world. Emphasis on critical and compassionate thinking.

Jacob K. Javits Gifted and Talented Students Education Program, U.S. Department of Education, Office of Educational Research and Improvement, Washington, DC, (800) 872-5327 (www.ed.gov/programs/javits). Created by an Act of Congress in 1994, the Javits program funds grants, provides leadership, and sponsors NRC/GT.

Johns Hopkins Center for Talented Youth, Baltimore, MD, (410) 735-4100 (www.jhu.edu/~gifted). Conducts national and international talent searches; provides challenging and innovative learning opportunities in mathematics, science, and the humanities through summer programs, distance education programs, and conferences; publishes *Imagine,* a magazine for middle and high school students.

Mensa International (mensa.org). The international association for children and adults with high IQs. In the U.S., contact American Mensa, Arlington, TX, (817) 607-0060 (www.us.mensa.org).

National Association for Gifted Children (NAGC), Washington, DC, (202) 785-4268 (www.nagc.org). A national advocacy group of parents, educators, and affiliate groups united in support of gifted education. Join to receive the quarterly magazine *Parenting for High Potential,* discounts on selected NAGC publications, and more. NAGC has affiliates in every state.

National Conference of Governors' Schools (www.ncogs.org). Summer programs for gifted and talented high-school students.

National Research Center on the Gifted and Talented (NRC/GT), University of Connecticut, Storrs, CT, (860) 486-4826 (www.gifted.uconn.edu/nrcgt.html). A collaborative effort of several universities, state and territorial departments of education, public and private schools, content area consultants, and stakeholders representing professional organizations, parent groups, and businesses. Funded by the U.S. Department of Education, NRC/GT investigates characteristics, development, and educational services for gifted and talented students.

National Research Center on the Gifted and Talented, University of Virginia, Charlottesville, VA, (434) 982-2849 (curry.edschool.virginia.edu/overview-gifted-277).

Rocky Mountain Talent Search, University of Denver, (303) 428-2634 (www.centerforbrightkids.org). One of a network of places in the U.S. through which gifted kids in grades 6–7 can take the high-school-level SAT and possibly qualify for special learning opportunities.

Summer Institute for the Gifted, Stamford, CT, (866) 303-4744 (www.cgp-sig.com). Information about U.S. summer programs for gifted kids.

Supporting the Emotional Needs of the Gifted (SENG), Poughquag, NY, (845) 797-5054 (www.sengifted.org). Helps parents identify giftedness in their children; helps children understand and accept their unique talents. Provides a forum for parents and educators to communicate.

World Council for Gifted and Talented Children, (204) 789-1421 (www.worldgifted.ca). An international organization that seeks to focus world attention on gifted and talented children and ensure the realization of their potential.

Web Sites

A to Z Home's Cool Homeschooling Web Site (www.gomilpitas.com/homeschooling). A comprehensive collection of articles, links, and resources.

Education Consulting Service (www.susanwinebrenner.com). My Web site. Stop in and see what's new.

The Gifted Child Society (www.gifted.org). This nonprofit organization provides educational enrichment and support services for gifted children, assistance to parents, and training for educators. Since 1957, the Society has served over 50,000 children and their families. In 1975, the U.S. Department of Education named it a national demonstration model.

Gifted Children (www.gifted-children.com). *Gifted Children Monthly,* an award-winning newsletter "for the parents of children of great promise," has ceased publication and returned as Gifted-Children.com, a networking and information site. Members have access to news, articles, archives, resources, downloadable files, chats, and more.

GT World (www.gtworld.org). An online support community for parents of gifted and talented children. Look for articles, links, testing information, definitions, three mailing lists, and a MOO where members can talk to each other in real time.

Hoagies' Gifted Education Page (www.hoagiesgifted.org). Much more than a "page," this is a wide and respected variety of resources for parents and educators of gifted youth, from research to everyday success stories, personal support groups, and links.

The Homeschooling SIG of American Mensa (groups.yahoo.com/group/homeschoolingmensans). A SIG is a special interest group. The Homeschooling SIG is a support group for parents who are homeschooling their gifted children.

LD OnLine (www.ldonline.org). Clearinghouse for information on children with learning difficulties. A wonderful Web site full of information about learning disabilities and related conditions.

National Excellence: A Case for Developing America's Talent (www.ed.gov/pubs/DevTalent/toc.html). The complete text of *National Excellence: The Case for Developing America's Talent.* U.S. Department of Education, Office of Educational Research and Improvement, Washington, DC: 1993.

National Foundation for Gifted and Creative Children, Warwick, RI, (401) 738-0937 (www.nfgcc.org). Information for parents.

Northwest Regional Educational Laboratory, Portland, OR, (503) 275-9500 (educationnorthwest.org). Provides research and development assistance in delivering equitable, high-quality educational programs. Ask about other centers throughout the U.S.

Parents' Resources (www.ri.net/gifted_talented/parents.html). Lots of links to information about gifted children, parenting, homeschooling, and more.

Prisoners of Time (www.ed.gov/pubs/PrisonersOfTime). The complete text of Prisoners of Time: Report of the National Education Commission on Time and Learning, Washington, DC.

Programs for Gifted Kids (www.ri.net/gifted_talented/programs.html). Descriptions, links, and contact information.

TAG: Families of the Gifted and Talented (www.tagfam.org). An Internet-based support community for talented and gifted individuals and their families. Read the articles and join one or more of the mailing lists.

Index

C

D

E

F

G

H

I

J

K

L

M

N

O

P

Q

R

S

T

U

V

W

ABOUT THE AUTHOR

Susan Winebrenner has an M.S. in curriculum and instruction and a B.S. in education. She has been a classroom teacher, a program coordinator and teacher in gifted education, and a consultant in staff development. A leader in the field of gifted education, she also is the coauthor of *The Cluster Grouping Handbook* and the author of *Teaching Kids with Learning Difficulties in the Regular Classroom* and the *Differentiating Content for Gifted Learners in Grades 6–12* CD-ROM. Through her consulting and workshop business, Education Consulting Service, she presents workshops and seminars nationally and internationally, helping educators translate education research into classroom practice. Susan lives in San Diego.

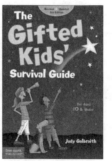

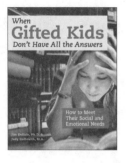

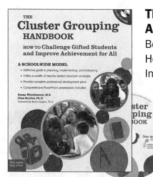

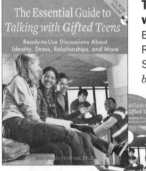

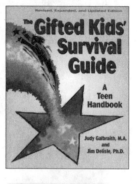

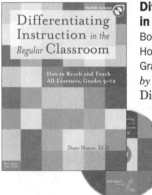

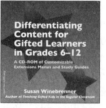